KU-429-199

73/2

(a)

305406494Z

Subjecting
and Objecting

Max Deutscher

Subjecting
and Objecting
An Essay in Objectivity

Basil Blackwell

© University of Queensland Press, St Lucia,
Queensland 1983.

First published in Great Britain 1983
Basil Blackwell Publisher Limited
108 Cowley Road, Oxford OX4 1JF, England

British Library Cataloguing in Publication Data

Deutscher, Max
    Subjecting and objecting.
    1. Objectivity
    I. Title
    121'.4   BD220

    ISBN 0-631-13404-2

Printed in Great Britain
by Billing and Sons Ltd, Worcester.

Contents

Introduction

The reader will quickly realize that philosophers and their views are mentioned very briefly just to locate, by contrast or agreement, the theme or point of view of this philosophical work. (The only exception to be discovered is the discussion of Descartes' "scepticism" and Berkeley's "idealism" in the tenth chapter, and even there the primary aim is to identify by contrast the direction taken in this enquiry.) Sometimes I venture a virtually one line dismissal of some aspects of a philosopher's ideas. (Feyerabend, Foucault, and Popper sometimes suffer this treatment.) In a different work directly addressed to their claims and arguments, I would gladly acknowledge that their writings sustain extended criticism. Yet, even my one line jabs are meant to get directly to the nub of a central weakness.

The outlook of this enquiry is located beside or against the work of other philosophers, but also against general movements of thought; religion and Marxism are the most typical. The problem here is to identify their general character swiftly. They are now vast historical clusters of ideas and happenings and deeds and alleged glories and definite horrors. Criticism of and reply to such amorphous but powerful winds of ideas can easily turn into endless verbal distraction from the main issue. One has to sniff it out. I do not hesitate to follow my nose when I smell a rat. Physicalism, my other *bête noir,* does exist more as an intellectual, or perhaps just academic, phenomenon. But it shares with Marxism and religion the emotional and intellectual character of totalitarianisms and I attempt to characterize and analyse it as such.

My most positive debts for opinion, method, style and for choosing the level of language appropriate to what I want to say, to expose and to explore are due in about equal weight to Gilbert Ryle and Jean-Paul Sartre, and in a different way to my first two teachers in philosophy, J.J.C. Smart and C.B. Martin. The lesser, though still strong influences, are from Maurice Merleau-Ponty and Wittgenstein, and the John Austin of *Philosophical Papers*. The rest are too numerous to mention: Hegel, Nietzsche, Husserl, Heidegger; Descartes, Locke, Berkeley, Hume and so on. I would also acknowledge inspiration for style, approach and topic from the various essays, philosophically spirited and informed, by Susan Sontag (*Styles of Radical Will, Against Interpretation* and *On Photography*). I have gained continual encouragement, ideas, observations and criticism from my family and friends.

And finally, on that note of "observations": the experiences and observations which lie behind the direct assertions and affirmations (and every work of finite length must contain them — it is not a conceded fault) all those gained in about equal measure from private and from public involvements. The experiences, actions, passions and observations whose employment makes us want to write a philosophical book and not just a textbook or research project, arise from our closest relationships — with those we like or love, but also with some we detest.

So far as public involvements go, I learned most from working in the "Moratorium" opposing conscription and Australia's "involvement" (what do we ca'l it, "fighting"? "killing and maiming"? "contribution to the horror"? "callous (supposed) self-interest"?) in the war in Vietnam. Apart from the debates about the war itself, there were the debates and fights about the proper role of intellectuals and academics themselves: whether the objectivity which they were supposed to provide to the public who paid them was negated by their involvement on one side or the other, or whether, rather, any serious objectivity required such involvement. All the old shibboleths about objectivity were trotted out and so the first part of the book attempts to expose and undercut them. But once the stereotypes are shattered, we have to find and even recreate what we need in a concept of objectivity, if we are to reconstruct our emotional and intellectual cities.

Every detachment is another kind of involvement — the idea of complete objectivity as complete detachment is a complete fraud — so runs one main theme of this book. Yet though the myth of detachment is a distortion, it is a distortion of real needs. What we may become prepared to call a kind of objectivity is a style of coping with and within our involvements: in positive terms, the book attempts to outline, to recall to our attention and to suggest some new forms of these styles and ways of coping. Some people would suggest that no exploration or recreation is needed. We can simply identify the objective attitude with using the "scientific" method. But what is the scientific attitude? The phrase means "the attitude which enables us to come to know". And what is this attitude? It is not confined to the special sciences. We need it in all our enquiries and dealings. My aim is to present a broad account of the possible forms of what we might call "objectivity", within which we can find the scientific attitude, in the narrower sense of what is practised by specialists in special areas of enquiry. What I say is not (except from time to time by way of example of a particular issue) about "science" in the new conventional sense of physics, chemistry, etc. But I am claiming this much about science, that this story about the possibility and conditions for kinds of objectivity applies to one's work in those sciences as much as to anything else.

The rest of this introduction will take the form of a synopsis. This will indicate ahead the shape and strategy of the investigation, and the aims and intentions of the author.

The first chapter describes how we begin to wonder how we can be "objective"; we find that we think, perceive and act from a point of view different from those to whom we relate. We fall back upon measurements and "facts", but we have to evaluate the importance of these to some issue, we have to argue and show and explain what the issue itself is and why it matters. We have to understand that these facts and issues are seen from points of view other than our own. On the one hand, we cannot avoid "subjectivity" in our desire to be objective; if we are to be right about anything we must take a position, we must have beliefs. Yet, in our beliefs we involve ourselves and our culture. Similarly, unless we sense and observe, we must be ignorant and out of touch, yet we cannot but sense and observe from where we happen to be. We need the involvement intrinsic to perception and belief in order to get close enough to things and people in order to understand them. On the other hand, we need an imaginative displacement from our own position of thought and experience, if we are to take account of that "position" (literal and metaphorical) when we think and perceive.

The second chapter begins to expose the myths and distortions in the conventional wisdom about objectivity — that it consists in being cool, detached, uninvolved, unemotional and so on. This distortion is called "objectivism", in contrast with the more elastic and live sense of objectivity which a close and sensitive knowledge of things and people requires. Our tendency (in religion, morality and politics) to turn ideas and feelings, legitimate enough in themselves, into absolutes and "-isms", is criticized. Such absolutist tendencies, even about the value of human life itself, debase our sense of value, rather than offering the intended secure basis.

Objectivity requires us to understand our own beliefs, attitudes and experience; in turn this requires us to understand and to be understood by others. If this is to be possible, we have to treat people on a level: by elevating instead of describing people in the categories of priest, judge, professor, doctor etc., or by debasing them in our minds into a lower group — criminals, the insane, layabouts, hippies etc. — we debar ourselves from understanding them or ourselves. There are some brief references to writers who have treated these themes: the satirist, Swift, and more recently Nietzsche and, in this century, Sartre. There is description and criticism of the tendency of some recent writers, in their desire to secure an "objective" standpoint, to "de-centre" or even completely dismiss the person as "subject". The emphasis, though, is on the issues they raise; for instance, the relation of a person to the book he or she reads, and to the person who wrote it.

In the third chapter, the move is away from the static abstract nouns "objectivity" and "subjectivity" towards the sense of process in "objecting" and "subjecting". Being objective is not a static condition, but a way of carrying out our thinking, perceiving and acting. The relevance of emotion to being objective is explained and defended, and with it the idea that, within our own motives, feelings and self-interests, we can develop "pure" interests. These pure interests, though real, are evanescent and another "-ism", purism or puritanism, results from the vain attempt to avoid this instability. The chapter ends by initiating a discussion about the place of being detached and disinterested. It is argued that affection, love or any concern for something, requires a capacity for disinterest while, at the same time, this partial displacement of oneself from one's own interests is of limited value and that, if made a permanent or exclusive style of approach, destroys its own ends.

The fourth chapter concerns the tension between, on the one hand, the need for tolerance, literality, generosity, in one's dealings with opinions and lives contrary or different to one's own and, on the other hand, the need to be consistent with one's own ideas, and not to give up one's own line whenever one has to choose between one's own judgement and that of others. Having given some support to the idea of liberality, attention is then paid to the need for being partial, even though one thus sees only a "part" of any thing or issue. This emphasis connects back again with the theme of emotion and objectivity. Being partial, we cannot always be cool; sometimes coolness is maintained, not by objectivity, but by ignoring disturbing facts. This then leads to a discussion of control, of the need for a free and flexible control of one's thought and feeling and action, rather than a rigid or brittle calm. We need control as well as spontaneity, for we need steadiness for the reflectiveness which is necessary in order to maintain our objectivity; yet a forced steadiness is a too conservative solution, leading to a number of totalitarianisms. The common examples mentioned are Marxism, Christianity and physicalism.

So, the path has been traced from the initial ordinary defence of liberality to an understanding of the consciousness within which one totalitarianism or another seems overwhelmingly to present the only truth.

In Chapter Five, the critical analysis of dogmatism and associated phenomena is counterbalanced by a favourable stress on confidence. Certainly, we do not know everything, and we do not know how we will be regarded in future times, but this cannot be used as reason for present doubt. If the future will correct us, we must wait for that; it is no use being nervous now. The speculative/experimental character of the theoretical sciences, it is argued, exhibits a direct and confident sense of the possibility of being able to explain what is observed to occur; it is this confidence which allows our scientific mind not to be too disturbed by, to easily accept, the always open possibility that later experience may upset even what seems most certain. In this connection, there is then given a brief account of the seventeenth century French philosopher Descartes' general scepticism about the senses. The self-refuting character of such scepticism is exposed, from which is drawn an account of the reasonable confidence we can and need to maintain in order to persist with an objectivity of attitude.

This emphasis on confidence, of being confident, is then counterbalanced by a discussion of the importance of not being too confident. In overconfidence we lose sight of ourselves and think that we have the "facts themselves" entirely divorced from our manner of approach to them. Various forms of the desire to lose oneself are distinguished. Paradoxically, romanticism becomes virtually indistinguishable from objectivism, as one pushes those positions to their limits. In a section, "Privacy and confidences; autonomy and subjectivity", it is argued that the need for confidence, while escaping dogmatism, is paralleled by the need for privacy (of various kinds) while yet escaping the trap of a purely self-centred consciousness, untouched by the kind of objectivity which can only come from sociability. In this way, quite domestic or everyday points are brought into relation with general themes in the problems of knowledge and mind — even in our sociability, our continued confidence and that of others in us, requires "confidences" — the keeping of something from some others; on the other side of the balance, even in our privacy, we require the imagination of sociability, and the arts and modes of expression learned socially, if we are to maintain, alone, the rounded picture of things, and sense of perspective, required by any objectivity.

This chapter closes the first part of the book, with a section on the need for consistency, which is a requirement of any truth in thought and perception; a consistency which still must be distinguished from a rigid belief in everything that follows from what we already hold. In Part II, the enquiry is opened afresh, with a definition of being objective. A connection is then made between being objective, and suspect notions such as "objective truth", "objective facts" and so on. It is argued that it is we who can be objective (or not), not the things or facts we know.

In Chapter Seven begins the main investigation of this section of the book: of those traits of character and action conventionally held to be destructive of one's objectivity — being vain, narcissistic, envious, jealous, arrogant and proud. These conventions are challenged to the extent that these so-called vices are explained as malign forms of virtues. It is argued that in any objectivity worth the name, we must run the risk of sliding towards these faults. Without the traits which in excess and without control are vanity, we lack the interest in ourselves and our appearance which is necessary for an understanding of how others relate to us, and the effect we have on them. Similarly, without the self-love which can degenerate into narcissism, we lack the immediate concern with human wellbeing without which we are detached and abstracted. Nevertheless, being vain is criticized, and it is argued that much of arrogance is the aggression in which we engage to defend our vain conception of things. Furthermore, when one's vanity collapses in its internal contradictions, we may readily attempt to salvage what we want in being vain, by attempting to be envied. This desire to be envied requires explanation after all, for why would we wish to be the butt of the malice intrinsic to envy? A respect for the achievements and qualities of others, and even a desire to be like them, are distinguished from envy.

Being envious is also distinguished from being jealous. Each is closely tied, nevertheless, with desires and interests essential to any objectivity. Envy is tied closely to the intense interest in the life, consciousness and possessions or achievements of others, without which we would be narrow, ignorant or parochial. Jealousy is an extreme and uncontrolled form of the necessary realization that what we love has its own dimension apart from the way in which we know it. In personal jealousy we realize what another may be for someone else, and thus see a different side to them. The chapter concludes with a section on intimacy and self-intimacy. (This parallels a discussion of privacy and sociability, in Chapter Five.) The need for intimacy with others and ourselves in developing and maintaining our objectivity with respect to ourselves and others is defended. It is argued that we are not automatically intimate with our thoughts and feelings just by having them. We learn such an intimacy, or the possibility of it, by learning arts and modes of creative expression, much as we learn to be intimate with others. Being intimate is not a matter of the destruction of inhibition, but of artfully exploiting it.

This need for intimacy with others in order to maintain one's own objectivity, and so that they can measure themselves against you, makes the risk of envy and jealousy unavoidable. To attempt an objectivity not threatened by envy and jealousy would be to attempt such a distance in one's relationships that one would lose the objectivity one hoped to protect. Thus the theme of the need for only a limited and occasional detachment within involvement is picked up and developed.

In Chapter Eight, there is a continuation of the theme that the traditional vices are really malign forms of virtues, which are necessary to objectivity. The arrogant person rightly recognizes that he needs more than himself and what he has; he is attracted by the values of what another has. But he cannot recognize what is his own and what is another's, and he cannot recognize what it takes to make something genuinely his own. Some of the moral complexities of arrogantly judging the attitudes and actions of people in other countries are pursued. Arrogance is distinguished from pride. Pride is described largely in favourable terms, though the tendency of someone who perceives and thinks and acts principally out of pride to tie everything too much to himself is noted. Pride acts first to extend our objectivity. It makes us genuinely and deeply interested in things and people other than ourselves, but still, too much to things and people only as they reflect credit on ourselves. The religious rejection of pride is undermined, and the moral schizophrenia of Christianity and Judaism analysed.

In the ninth chapter, the need for pride is linked with the need for momentum and the requirement to persist in our interests and involvements, if we are to achieve and to maintain a serious or revealing objectivity. This dual need for the "virtues" (momentum and persistence) is paralleled against by two "vices" (compulsions and obsessions). Persistence and momentum are described as allowing change of priority and direction, and as allowing free perception. One can modify and change without losing everything one had. Thus, the contrast is set up with the criticized obsessions and compulsions. Various political, moral and religious ideas — futurism, fascism, as obvious examples, and various current philosophical obsessions about science (such as physicalism), issues raised in Chapter Four — are discussed again within this changed framework.

The importance of momentum and persistence for a loving interest, and that in turn for one's objectivity, is described and analysed. Further, the tendency of the commitment needed to sustain love to lapse into formality or duty is paralleled by the tendency of the need for persistence to turn it into obsessiveness. Descriptions of various concepts — forcing, allowing, being wilful, etc. — find their place at this point.

Chapter Ten begins with another consideration of Descartes' doubts; this time from the point of view that every form of thinking and perceiving is itself a way of living or "being" something, and also that our perceiving forms part of other things we are more overtly or publicly "doing" or "being". Thus the traditional philosophical categories of "acting", "being" and "perceiving" find their place. For this reason, there is, for the first time, this more extended treatment of and connection made with the opinions and arguments of philosophers; Descartes has already been chosen, and attention is to be paid to Berkeley's idealism. The views about the connections between what we are, what we are doing and what we are perceiving, are traced in examples of what is involved in living in a city, in being a tourist, in being involved in business or simply in travelling on a train. The view of one who sees a city as a "natural" place is contrasted with the eye of someone from the country, or perhaps a geologist, who sees it as placed on and cutting across previously existed terrain, bush and grass.

The themes of the need for the acculturation of perception, and also for the imaginative escape or transcendence from the immediate or total effect of culture, are traced out and developed. The issues of certainty, and the acceptance of the disturbing variety of views which by themselves seem ultimate or exclusive of what others see and know, are taken up. It is argued that we must accept various relativities of perception: in how we find and see and feel things in relation to what we are already, and what we are already doing. Yet, it is shown, this acceptance of a variety of relativities is not a lapse towards idealism. To make this clear, Berkeley's idealism is outlined and criticized. It is maintained, also, that scepticism and idealism are not merely abstract philosophical theories, but express distinctive perceptual and emotional outlooks on the things we sense. Philosophies of the nature of the world, though they seem extreme and strange, are articulations of quite common accentuations and concentrations of thought and perception. By this juxtaposition, it is intended to achieve a greater understanding of the tradition of philosophy, from reflections upon everyday life and, in turn, a new remark on the character of everyday life from the metaphysical expression and description of it.

The theme of idealism is also linked with the earlier topic of jealousy, as idealism is characterized as a sort of "metaphysical jealousy". The idealist's description of what we perceive is an expression of our wish to make things our own just by looking at, hearing or touching them. These reflections on perception and possession are brought to an end in a consideration of one's personal identity: what are the limits of oneself, and where do one's possessions begin?

Chapter Eleven, the concluding chapter, resolves these themes within the categories of "resolving", "working" and "resting". The interplay of these activities is described and evoked. There is a philosophical elaboration of the nature and importance of all kinds of work; this is distinguished from labour. The necessity to relax and rest in order to keep one's objectivity, and not to work stupidly, is argued. From this point of view, there is fresh criticism of the puritan work ethic.

Calm, rest and repose are described and distinguished, and each is placed to show its distinct importance, in its appropriate moment, to objectivity and understanding. The conservatism of recent British and Australian philosophy in the face of a different culture and new trends from Europe, and its reluctance to co-ordinate the experience of everyday life as material for serious metaphysics, are diagnosed as part of a compulsion about what constitutes philosophical "work". That conservatism is a refusal to let new ideas have time to re-solve. The time for resolving is mistaken as giving up serious "work". Part of this chapter, like the previous, is directly about philosophical writing, but the focus then reverts to direct or original philosophical reflection to bring the book to its end of exploration. The themes of work and rest are paralleled by those of determination (by itself too wilful) and resolve (with its more relaxed overtones of letting things settle and sort themselves out). The limits of avoiding the shocks of objectivity by even the best philosophical understanding of it are stressed. To understand objectivity is rather to be prepared for the shocks of change of view, focus, information and feeling, rather than to avoid them altogether.

In resolving new ideas and feelings and issues, we keep our desires, or form new ones, rather than lapsing into having blind wants or lacks. These desires keep our imagination quick and, in turn, this aids in maintaining an unfractured sense of objectivity — of the distinct otherness of other people and things, on the one hand, and of their comprehensible and sympathetic likeness to us on the other.

The issues of calm, of movement and of free spontaneity, of the unreasonable character of the demand for total "reasonableness" are interwoven with a brief discussion of how a free objectivity can allow us to move from past to future, neither disclaiming our past, nor living in it.

The final page is an anecdote in which is portrayed the themes of the book — of our conception of alternative lives while living our own, of the need for privacy while accepting the need for the cultural density of the city — the shifts of perspective in which each new perspective seems at last to reveal "reality", and finally the humorousness of the constant slight non-understanding by each person of the other's preoccupations, values and perceptions which is involved in the most ordinary interchange. The reader is intended to be left with a sense of a continual resolving of thought about objectivity, rather than a fixed or final solution.

PART I

Chapter One

Involvement, Judging and Detachment

Self-maiming denials that objectivity is possible

Truth, evidence, probability, perception, judgement, rationality, facts and theories — all of these are much discussed, but objectivity and subjectivity are ignored. In aesthetics one argues about whether beauty is an objective property, in morals one argues about the objectivity of goodness. But what objectivity is, that is left alone. Among historians and social scientists there is discussion about the possibility or impossibility, desirability or undesirability of objectivity, but precious little enlightenment on its nature.

The whole history of the philosophy of knowledge might be regarded as an account of the search for the conditions of objectivity. However, that is not the way it has been seen, and, furthermore, to clarify the character of objectivity and its relation to subjectivity is not simply to examine at greater length the areas already investigated. To make a parallel: the history of the philosophy of knowledge might be regarded as the history of the search for truth, but that leaves room for a separate study of the concept of truth. Equally there is room for a separate study of objectivity.

We can kill "Objectivity is impossible" quickly. Is the speaker being objective about what he or she says, in which case what is said is false? Or does the speaker mean merely "Subjectively speaking, objectivity is impossible" which is dull? (It is no denial of the possibility of objectivity.) We can get nowhere with these debates until we clarify our concepts of objectivity and subjectivity and what we mean to be when we aim at objectivity, or what we allow ourselves to be when we concede our "inevitable subjectivity". There are useless uses of the terms. Otherwise intelligent people still ask whether there are objective moral, aesthetic, political, etc. facts. But "objective" must here be merely a pleonasm. To say that something is a fact is to stress that it is so. To speak of objective facts is an apoplexy of stress. And to suppose that if moral, aesthetic, etc. matters are not matters of objective fact, then they must be subjective facts would only spread more verbal rubbish. To say that something is a fact is to stress that it is so; to say that something is merely subjective is to say, though with too little clarity about the exact lack, that someone has not properly established it as a fact, or that someone has failed to take an objective view of the matter. In "subjective fact" (or "objective fact") "subjective" (or "objective") is a displaced epithet, like "healthy" in "healthy food".

Not realizing that we cannot take ourselves very seriously, we sometimes do think that objectivity is impossible, and we think this unserious thought fervently because we are freshly impressed by some new version of the old facts that the ways we take and see things, and the opinions we form when we confront situations, are so much influenced by our own unique combination of previously formed opinions, habits, knowledge, perceptions, desires, aversions, fears, hopes and dispositions. And these creatures of our own minds, so essential to any perception and judgement, are owned by us as creatures of a culture. Were we from another century or another tribe, we should take very differently what is now presented to us. So we act anthropologist to our own psychologist, never asking, of course, from what point of view we make these so modest sounding covertly cosmically oriented judgements of general relativity. We are now close to the central paradox, that it is only in the so-called subjectivity of our point of view that objectivity can arise. If there is any genuine judgement that how we judge things is dependent on our class, culture, personality or whatever else, then it is made from some particular describable standpoint. As soon as we have described where we are, we can see that we might have been at some other place.

Anyone who regards things seriously and coherently does so from a point of view. That a person may have different points of view at different times, and different points of view at the one time on different matters is a complication of, not an objection to, this claim. In the use of the senses, this point of view (or touch, hearing and so on) includes most obviously the physical position of the observer, his angle of vision (hearing, etc.) Further, because we must interpret what we sense, we must take it in some way or other, our point of view includes our perceptual skills, what we know, think, expect, fear, desire and the rest. All of these may be thought of, according to the stress of the moment by the person or somebody else considering what he makes of the situation, as our personal concern, or as what we have as members of a culture.

A difference of point of view need not arise from a difference of culture or of opinion. When someone speaks to an audience, the point of view of the speaker is, in one sense, fundamentally different from that of the audience, even if they already agree mainly in their opinions and attitudes. His interest in what he says may be the interest of whether he will be well regarded, will gain power or applause, whether he will be understood, whether he will afford the audience the enjoyment he has had from the ideas he presents. She may speak from a love of the sound of her own voice. She may speak because she is paid to speak, and is interested in nothing but continuing long enough and interestingly enough so that the audience does not walk out and she can collect her fee. The audience may understand this point of view well enough, may heckle or tolerate, be moved or annoyed as they happen to construe it. The speaker must work to hold attention. The audience must work to pay attention. The speaker is one looking at many. Each member of the audience, though only one himself or herself, is one of many looking at one.

A parent is, proverbially, supposed to understand the child's point of view. That is the first requirement of parental care. But he or she is equally required not to share it, though he or she may well play games of pretending to share it, partly just for fun and partly to aid the imaginative displacement necessary for understanding what one cannot share. These differences are rooted in differences of size, experience, understanding, presumptions and, not least, perhaps most, power. So we could quickly include the ineluctable differences between the one who goes shopping and the one who works behind the counter, the one who works in a factory, the one who runs it, and the one or ones who own or invest in it. Or, in socialism, the ones who work in it and the ones (who at most include them) whose special community interest it is. I have stressed differences of point of view which centrally involve differences of power and status because they are vivid and undeniable and show that crucial differences of point of view are not restricted to differences of opinion, theory or general culture. But there is more. Ineluctable differences also arise between those who are equal in power, experience and status.

That we see things from where we are, and that things would look different if we were elsewhere; that we find things according to what we desire, need, expect or fear, and would find different things, or the same things differently, were we to have a different constellation of these needs and so on, that things and of course people, oneself no less than others, are seen and felt with positive or negative sexual interest, and that at most this can be altered, not escaped — all of this may be felt as and referred to as "man's inevitable subjective predicament". I would be the last to attempt to diminish the sense of the reality of it. But this subjectivity is the foundation of objectivity, not its antithesis. These facts are exploited, distorted or misunderstood by those who would argue from such undeniable "subjectivity" in our knowledge to our necessary lack of objectivity. And, probably in the same breath and for similar reasons, they have a distorted "objectivist" notion of objectivity which arises from the propagandist use of "objective" to assault one's opponent with the inescapable presence of his subjectivity in an effort to show that his view is not serious, not to be trusted, is emotionally biased and the like. There are uses, harmless in their place, but ready made for confusion or exploitation, as when doctors and psychologists speak of a patient's "subjective" reports of his condition. They might go on in the same vein to say, "When the patient makes his subjective reports of certain feelings, we can ascertain certain objective physiological conditions in his body". They may go on to deplore the way people still hanker after their subjective outlook when the advances of scientific observation and language are available to them or, if more romantic, they may marvel at the rich wonders of subjectivity in contrast with the desiccated account of things we find in the systematic sciences. But the distinction, thus developed, is propagandist. The only clear licence for talk of "subjective" reports, in the first place, was that they were the subject's. But the patient was a "subject" only because others assuming wider knowledge and perspective were observing him. When the doctor, psychologist or physiologist observes and speaks, his or her statements are no less "subject's" reports. They are attempts to say how things are, in the midst and in the necessity of their own sensitivity. The distinction implied between the "subjective" expression or description of feelings and the "objective" account of physiological conditions is itself unobjective, since it is biased. What is sauce for the goose is sauce for the gander.

When one complains that all that should be meant in these contexts by "subjective" is "subject's", the speaker may well retort, "Who suggested I meant anything else?". This is dishonest. What was insinuated was that the "subjective" reports were inferior, unreliable, not to be taken seriously as a guide to how things really are. But then, viewed without prejudice, the "subject" really feels happy, cross, in pain, a dread and so on, and the observing subjects really experience their actions and perceptions in determining the physiological conditions. Also, if they adopt an interacting personal point of view with respect to the subject they are equally really smiling or frowning, smiling or frowning at him, speaking to and with him, and so on. But now we rush headlong into a major question whether there are some specially privileged "objective" standpoints. That is a theme to be picked up and dealt with at many times in many different ways.

Although people often speak as if there were an absolute distinction of objective and subjective, one can never criticize them for any implications of this, since they will be wise enough to back off when confronted with the embarrassing implications of the position. No-one wants to have truck with absolutes these days. Still we should explore the incoherency of the idea of absolute objectivity. Supposing that one's subjectivity as such tainted one's objectivity, then a subject would have to be entirely out of the picture when he or she . . . what? Observed something? Inferred something? Measured something with a glance, a microscope, a micrometer? One would have to put oneself entirely out of the way. Suicide as perfect objectivity. "Well," one might mutter, "of course it must be a matter of degree, but matters of degree are real enough!" But degrees of what? Degrees of involvement? This won't do. When someone is wholly involved in solving a mathematical problem he or she may be more objective about the matter than when only half-thinking about it. No, if there is an objectivity such that to say someone is objective is to give praise, and to say that someone is approaching something subjectively is to give criticism, then objectivity must be a kind of involvement, not an absence of it and this is necessarily an involvement of oneself, even if it is not "self-involvement" in the idiomatic sense.

There is a tendency to think and speak as if the objectivity of something were simply the thing itself, in contrast to our subjective way of taking it. Thus, in the uncritical use I attack, people may

say, "Objectively, lines A and B are the same length, whereas, subjectively they differ". To attack this uncritical use is not to slur the

fact that the lines are the same length, but appear to be different,
but one uses one's eyes (or hand) in both cases. The unaided eye is
in error in this example. And so we aid the eye. And every aided use
of the eye involves a new unaided use of the eye. (As when we make
"objective" checks on our merely "subjective" memories.) This is
obvious. Yet it needs to be put as a reminder against the objectivist
talk of objectivity which half-promises a way of simply having the
facts by a short cut which bypasses some person's way of appre-
ciating them. It is really the failure to be conscious of the absurdity
of perceiving and knowing without being affected and without
having to judge from some point of view, which allows the
misperception called "man's inevitable subjectivity".

In a primary meaning of the term, to say that someone is being
objective is to give a kind of praise (though one may imply another
kind of criticism) and to say that someone is being subjective is to
give a kind of criticism. Since, as we have seen, no matter how he or
she twists and turns the subject is still there, what can we make of
this? Consider a parallel problem: undoubtedly, in a general sense
in all our actions and passions we are all subject to causes. Within
that general fact, we draw distinctions of acting freely, under
duress, not really being able to act at all and so on. Yet, in some
moods and circumstances, the very general fact of causality, or a
particular view of it, makes us feel that really freedom is impossible. In a similar way, in some moods and circumstances, the very
general facts of our "inevitable subjectivity" make us feel that objectivity is impossible; that all the distinctions we draw are illusory,
or that if they are to be drawn, it must be on some new absolute
basis.

Facing the need to judge

Not being inclined to perpetual and, apparently, pointless self-
criticism, a person in that mood is liable to make the best of a bad
job, and to praise what amounts to subjectivism as the real human
feeling thing after all. They give up all aims at ideals of objectivity

because they are at last struck by the involvement of themselves in any process of judging, perceiving, inferring, remembering or calculating: they use their subjectivity as an excuse for the equality or non-comparability of intellectual, perceptual and emotional practices. "Oh dear," they say, "from what standpoint are we to judge these things? Everyone operates from personal and cultural prejudices. Everyone has an equal right to their opinions. Who am I to say what is right or wrong, good or bad, true or false, well or ill founded?" This is self-refuting. If it were true, the person uttering it would be in no position to say that it was true. Who am I to say that it's not for the likes of little me to pronounce upon the facts of this big world? To dismiss all objectivity because of our inevitable subjective involvement is like declaring null and void the culinary arts, the sharing of food around a table, and the use of bowls, chopsticks, knives and forks because without hunger and the need for food there would be no sense in any cultivated practices of preparing, sharing and eating food. Objectivity is an intelligent learned use of our subjectivity, not an escape from it, as the culinary and social arts are a deployment of our need for food, and obviously no escape from it.

To maintain our objectivity while recognizing what we are subject to we must be prepared to make clear judgement of all kinds. This makes us involved and committed on these issues. Yet, according to a stereotyped and repugnant idea, to be objective is to be detached, unaffected, uncommitted and neutral. There is a natural coherence to this nasty cluster, since to aim at objectivity in this sense, is to flee the necessity of judgement. Those who model themselves upon this ideal, speak disparagingly of value-judgements, as merely "value-judgments", as merely "subjective" concerns, to be separated from the "objective" matter of ascertaining facts; for convenience they forget that only those who can and will judge the value of reason, the goodness of evidence, the honesty of people, the character of the motives of those who enquire, can "ascertain facts". Forgetting that the value, the appropriateness and the aptness for its ends of a method of measurement must be judged, they will talk of escaping from "subjective estimates" into the objectivity of "precise numerical measurement". In saying this, they exploit the agreement of any reasonable person that measuring instruments and mathematics can enable us to discover a great deal which would remain hidden or vague to our unaided senses and wrongly identify the attitude of objectivity with just one use of it. And that use is one which must be judged apt in particular contexts. Degrees of precision inappropriate to an enquiry are a betrayal or distraction from objectivity, not its pinnacle of achievement.

To be objective, we must evaluate; in being objective we become involved in making judgements about the general or specific value of things, enterprises, people and actions. We can be basically unobjective though we are being precise, accurate and specific. Imagine a group of people set adrift in a lifeboat: they need to create a makeshift sail, ration water and decide on the most probable direction for land. One begins to make a most precise count of the number of brown shoelaces, another to measure and calculate the number of running feet of timber used in making the boat, and yet another sets out to state in the most highly specific detail the character of the flora and fauna of Kangaroo Island. They are in a state of extreme subjectivity. Overwhelmed, they waste their energies in preserving an appearance, however idiotic, of intellectual business.

It is dangerous to laud being vague, imprecise and general. Nevertheless, where we can as yet be only vague, imprecise and general, we can begin to make an objective approach only by working from that stage. Our budding objectivity then requires our strength of mind and moral force or, perhaps, sarcasm and biting wit, if we are to resist the conventional pressures towards more provably correct, though irrelevant and useless achievements. "If someone can be precise, accurate and specific about the pressing issues at hand, then surely that person is the more objective the more precisely he or she judges and states those judgements?" Broadly that is correct. But not precisely or quite generally. People can bear only so much reality. It is a less than fully objective understanding of one's recognitions, which insists on an expression of them with a precision, accuracy and specificity which drives oneself or others near mad with anxiety, fury, guilt, depression, swollen headedness or humiliation. It is scarcely a fully objective state of mind which would express itself in ways which destroy its own conditions of existence. In these, and in many other ways which will be described, our personal objectivity requires a permanent and accurate sense of one's limitations as a subject in dealing with the object in hand.

Fraudulent and valid forms of detachment

Those who would abstain from or derogate "value-judgements"

and 'keep to what is exactly measurable only' may be forced to confess to the reality of their own ways of handling things, and admit to their need for that larger life. Yet they are liable to retreat from that confession into bogus professionalism, claiming the right to give up objectivity when they go home from work; or worse, they carry objectivism home and don't live anywhere. This dead fish objectivity breeds, in decay, a desire for another spurious objectivity, the desire to transcend oneself; it is the desire to be, at the one moment, in one consciousness, actor and spectator, performer and critic, viewer and viewed. This is because the dead fish, in keeping to the ideals of detachment, uninvolvement, unemotionally, lack of commitment and so on, does not make him or herself real for others, nor can he or she realize for him or herself what he or she is. The dead fish, not being real for others, cannot enjoy their independent criticism, praise, appraisal, for he or she cannot have their understanding. Yet more unhappily, the same excess of restraint and detachment which prevents him or her from being real for others makes him unreal for himself. The excessive interiority of mind which is a central quality of continued detachment of attitude, has no test, no measure, of the seriousness of its thoughts. However materialist the content of belief of the objectivist, his or her attitude has no escape from being the intellectual attitude of idealism. Reality is the reality of its inner thought, the self-convincingness of its own propositions.

Self-protectively, but to keep a semblance of the critical spirit, he or she maintains an active imagination of him or herself as more than one person in one. Father, Son (or Mother, Daughter) and Holy Ghost, one might say. Superior objective, objecting critic, subjected subjective creature, and transcendent detached spirit escaping from both outlooks. As an occasional controlled dramatism this self-splitting has its place in the intellectual life. But for the most part we must give at least our own moments their due. I may be the very one who criticizes what I write. But, for the most part, I must find wholeheartedly write, and then wholeheartedly criticize, even though I know that by suspending criticism while I am involved in writing, illusions and mistakes will appear as assuring truth. Without that temporary involvement, there will be no distinctive realization of one's thought for criticism to operate upon.

To imagine that objectivity can be attained or maintained by even permanent and thorough self-criticism is to "imagine a vain thing". The nature of experience is not to be something in itself, nor merely "of" something: to experience is to be directed towards something. Thus experience is in one important way like opinion or belief: in each case we take things correctly or incorrectly. Unquestionably, the appeal to experience cannot be to something which is in itself an unquestionable basis, since to experience is to direct ourselves towards gaining a basis for belief. Yet, though belief and experience launch us willy nilly into a world beyond themselves and largely beyond ourselves, we have some control in our hurtling flight. We are like parachutists, rather than like suicides leaping from a great height, whose initial act is their last controllable one. We tug at the strings and affect the rate and direction of our fall. In coming to realize that we have a belief, we may discern that the belief is erroneous; we realize in the one dawn that we are in error. A partial ironic detachment is possible . . . so much must be conceded to transcendentalism. I might say, "Almighty Husserl save me! This is a belief I hold . . . what an error!" I am busily detaching myself from my belief in the very recognition that I hold it. But I cannot in good faith represent my belief as a foreign body lodged in me like an arrow from someone else's bow. It is close to me, rather, as breath. As I am under necessity to breathe, but not therefore to take this breath now, so I must believe, but am free not to believe this matter, now. Let me reject my beliefs if I will. This breath, this foul air (Nietzsche) . . . I don't want it. But I must *breathe* it out; I use the breath to speak my disavowal. I must believe my avowal of disbelief, or the avowal is empty. Further, I cannot declare, and speak truly the words, "Yes, alas, I *have this belief, but I am not in error myself,* for *I* see that 'my belief' is mistaken". This is self-deception, not detachment. I am no less the one who believes than the one who disavows the errors contained in the belief. How can I say, "I am not that belief which lies there". My believing self is as real, insofar as that belief lies there, as the disavowing self, which lies if it recognizes the belief as lying there.

There are similar possibilities and limits to our detachment from perceptual experience. Certainly, I can practise an active detachment as I judge, "It is as if I am perceiving that brown bears are in the garden, but I cannot be, since they don't come this far down from the mountains". Yet I come up against the limit of detachment when I make the appraisal, "It is as if I am perceiving that brown bears are in the garden". I cannot detach self and experience so far as to say, with truth or even significance . . . how should one even attempt to put it . . . "There is this brown-bear-in-the-garden-seeming-experience (the perceptual arrow lodged in my eye) . . .

what has it to do with me? . . . It doesn't seem to *me* that there are brown bears in the garden." Striving for detachment at this point is striving only towards nonsense. The perceptual arrow, though shot from another bow, is irrevocably mine once it is lodged. I must take responsibility for it.

There is a difference between belief and experience in respect of the limits of one's detachment: belief involves a commitment of mind — one has at least some power to believe or not, whereas one does not have that power to experience or not. One can decide to put oneself in the way of experience or not, but that is a different matter. Actually, our limited power to believe or not is akin to our power to give ourselves over to our experience or not; either to fully realize, to accept, to live our experience, or else to regard it as an alien intrusion which has nothing to do with us. So someone might see and hear someone choking to death, but refuse to experience it. For her, it remains a visual and auditory datum; interpretation and meaning is withheld. Someone we love or hate dies, but we refuse to experience what is given by our senses. It "matters nothing", it "happens to all", we feel as if we were watching a movie instead of participating in loss . . . This total loss of objectivity in which we feel "quite objective", this treatment of reality as fantasy, is an irony. For it is the diverted energy involved in the ruthless control necessary to keep up a facade of control or normality, which makes it possible to do the nominally impossible — not to experience what we experience. The activities of this self-deception are sufficiently consuming of time, attention and energy to leave what is happening to us at the periphery of apparent importance at the very same time as the importance is being continually attested to by the wilful engagement in distraction.

The value and limited value of detachment

All in all, even this limited capacity we have to detach from our own desires, beliefs, even our own experiences, is highly ambiguous and ambivalent in respect of our capacity for objectivity. Carried on in some ways, with certain purposes and understanding, detachment and concurrent self-criticism constitute at least a condition for developing our objectivity. But considered as the principal device of objectivity, it can only be destructive. This will be a central thesis about objectivity: although there are many important conditions intimately connected with it, the unqualified and unchecked use of any of them is destructive of objectivity. Also, the various conditions for objectivity are in conceptual and practical tension with each other. The development of one changes the character of the others, and inhibits their development. If this analysis can be shown to be correct, then we can see both why objectivity is a practically and intellectually important idea and ideal, but that the impossibility of a perfect objectivity is not the unattainability of one ideal too high for us, or a consequence of our human subjectivity (as if a non-human or superhuman subject might do the trick) nor even a simple consequence of the necessity of subjectivity for objectivity. For, to take the last point, once we see that subjectivity as our feeling, sensing, appraising, involving involved, detached and detached life is a condition for our objectivity, rather than its antithesis, we might suppose that objectivity were as attainable as the measurement of the length of a line; we could admit cheerfully enough that we can only get closer and closer approximations, but understand it as a limit to which we might approach. But objectivity is not such a simple single limit and if, as will be argued, to approach one kind of objectivity is to forgo or forestall movement towards other kinds with equally good claims to approval, then we shall see that there is a serious, though confused and poorly understood sense in which objectivity, even as a limit to be approached, is not a coherent ideal. Yet we shall understand this in such a way that the general sense of the importance of objectivity and our various movements towards it will still be vindicated.

All of this must be shown, gradually, in due course. To take the example we now have: detachment, as the self-imposed distancing from one's own involvements in belief, desire, experience and so on, fails as a single unchecked ideal of objectivity because the person in his or her detachment is not freely showing and expressing his or her beliefs, desires, experience and so on. On this account he or she cannot be properly or directly criticized, praised or appraised. To maintain some activity and semblance of critical objectivity, the detached person must then conduct the drama of his mental theatre as if there were a number of people contending. At its simplest and easily recognized, one conducts a debate with oneself. This is not the place to pay due respect to this process; at least it can enliven the mind, bring consequences of positions to light, and it can keep one in the frame of mind that expects criticism. But the Opposition can raise only a Shadow Ministry. Berkeley's *Dialogues* are a mere rhetorical device. The whole argument is contained within his point of view. It is within Berkeley's terms, premises and outlook that both Hylas and Philonus can speak. The dialogues are brilliant, beautiful and instructive, not to say often sharply logical. But they refute only Berkeley's inner voice of materialism. Think of an everyday example. One is headed for a conflict with someone. Wisely, perhaps, one debates with oneself, in two senses. One might debate, within onself, within the terms of one's own interests, whether or not to undergo or to avoid the conflict. Even in this sense, the debate is liable to be, in part, a debate between oneself and what one imagines another would say. But in another sense, one debates as a rehearsal of the debate which will occur with another person. Debating with oneself, one can feel detached and cool, "seeing both sides of the question" so clearly. (Though, of course, seeing equally clearly which side must finally be seen as true, and as winning.) Debating with another, one must do all one can for one coherent position; this is not unfairness or bias, it is the condition of pressing hard into the truth of the matter. That both parties should equally "see both sides" is a luxury which truth cannot afford. It is collusion, mutual back scratching, not objectivity. In contrast, both with full blooded debate and its anaemic collusive cousin, when a person currently criticizes, praises or appraises his current self, he cannot choose but to be only half hearted and part minded. Thus unsatisfactory self-criticism and self-praise may be worse than none.

Deliberate personal fragmentation, done by someone who knows its dangers and fundamental limitation can, by its division, open up something new in awareness at the interface. Though current self-criticism can only be a feeble rival to criticism by others, even when it is agony and a person tears at himself, it cannot have a fraction of the effect of the separate observing character of a criticism by another; so long as the word is right and timed, it can affect deeply though spoken neutrally or kindly without even the intention to change or upbraid the person criticized; the very neutrality of the intention just to state accurately robs its victim of the self-deception of blustering "I am being unfairly and harshly attacked!". Nevertheless, the internal dramatization necessary for self-appraisal can help to introduce or give pulse to the imagination of a doubt, a gap between one's rapt "massif" self whose sense is given by its own understanding and stories about its intentions and directions, and the whirls of motives and cross-purposes which are revealed to an objective scrutiny.

Though even the best diagnostician will go to another doctor when he is ill, and someone who wishes to study anatomy does not cut up his own body, yet alone and stranded a person might have to risk removing his own appendix. He may well kill himself but if he does not take the risk he knows that certainly he will die. Exclusively or predominantly self-appraisal is a second rate affair which a person might defend as what he was forced into by circumstance, and particularly when we can recollect vividly the integral incisive praise and criticism of those we have known, self-appraisal may enlighten a person more than the actual and independent, but lesser and confused observation and language which might now happen to be available. But all such talk is most liable to be special pleading. It is only another person who can have another independent consciousness; someone whose mind is really not just one's own beating itself at chess and witty repartee. The "ruthless honesty" of exclusively or predominantly self-appraisal chosen against available sources of outside criticism . . . "Don't tell me, I know that in doing that I have been . . . am being . . . wonderful, a rat, witty, stupid . . ." just works as a self-protective device to blunt the invading sharp remark and to muffle the other independent voice.

I have given much less than due value to the activities and passivities of self-scrutiny, self-appraisal, reflectiveness and, in general, inwardness of thought and feeling. Certainly it deserves credit. Without an inner life we cannot maintain our autonomy, and without our autonomy we cannot properly use the appraisals of others, nor make objective and fair observations and remarks to others. All of that must find its place a little later. What I have meant to focus on for exposure and ridicule is an idealization as objectivity, of a fall or retreat from others' appraisals into a detached, unexpressive state in which we maintain a kind of stiffened or even frozen composure by simply not responding or reacting; it is really a refusal to let one's mind work lest it come to conclusions other than those one has already determined to maintain. Again, the real values of calm and composure are not to be underrated. But nor must the costs, particularly of keeping an appearance of calm and rationality. Bad faith enters here at all levels. Partly people are driven into a false appearance of calm and reason because somewhere in their minds they know that the recognition of the facts would be agitating, angering or euphoria inducing. Also they hear that those who do not want the facts recognized will be able to dismiss them as emotional and irrational if they are freely expressive. And people will inhibit themselves out of (often legitimate) desire for self-protection and privacy. Furthermore, it is as likely that the person doing the recognizing will be as loath to admit the full force of what he or she is coming upon, as that others will wish to care for convention, traditional or protocol.

The desire for spurious objectivity stems from the desire to escape one's condition and point of view. You are not committed to the fact of being where you are. You are not prepared to work within and from your outlook. You want at once to be there to have the advantages of point of view. Without it you cannot see. And yet you want at the same time to be away from its limitations so as to escape missing what might never be seen from within it. There are true and there are false ways of coping with this desire. The only true way of coping with it involves the recognition of the unsatisfiability of the desire. You enlarge your knowledge. You broaden your field of vision and extend your skills of thought and perception; you work within your point of view so as to change it. By design you can increase its scope and the number of ways in which something can be seen and thought of and unpredictably you may, by working from within a framework of ideas, come to discover ways in which you must revise or recant. Still, to be in a broader place is no closer to being everywhere than when you were most parochial; one can no more approach "everywhere" and "everything" than one can approach the end of an infinite series. You possess more at the end of this learning than you had at the beginning; you are farther from your point of origin; yet in this advance you are not one inch closer to understanding your present position from a point outside it: on the other hand a detachment is possible. In live and informed imagination, we can "see" and "hear" and make ourselves objects of our own thought from many points of time and place, culture, sex and class other than our own. It is the value and limits of such detachments which are part of a possible objectivity.

Chapter Two

Objectivism and Subjectivism

Conventional clusters, and debasement by elevation

Cool, detached, uninvolved, unemotional, dispassionate, disinterested, unaffected, uncommitted, impartial, neutral, an inactive onlooker — entrancement with this cluster is belief in the myth of objectivism. Warm, connected, involved, emotional, passionate, affected, committed, partial, positioned, active and initiating — we are liable to be branded as subjective by these labels, but we cannot guarantee our objectivity by earning the cool epithets. However, not only is it a prejudice that being characterized according to the second cluster puts us outside the intellectual and objective pale, but also it is a too romantic subjectivist immersion which would justify itself by appeal to the impossibility of objectivity as the objectivist would conceive of it.

Objectivism is a distorted and damaging degradation of objectivity and springs from the feeble wish to have the advantage of a position or view, a way of knowing or an involvement without taking the position or using the view; employing the way of knowing, and not standing up to and for the risks and embarrassments of the involvement. Those objectivists who fancy or pretend that they can regard without regard, may then conveniently hold in contempt as "subjective" those who make no secret of holding their view, of taking their position, of practising their way of knowing, of being present in their involvements.

One might well scrap the concept of objectivity altogether. Overused and stinking of propaganda, it might be better buried to rot. But the memory lingers on; weeds grow from the decay, and we shall do better to expose the idea to the air and light, dress it in new words, and introduce it to a wide circle of conceptual relations. The objectivist makes a thing of being cool, detached and uninvolved. The subjectivist makes a thing of being warm, connected and involved. Objectivism is the view that would have us forget that it is a view; the objectivist is a subject who would forget and have others forget that he is a subject. There is only what is viewed; the viewing of it is passed over. There is a distance from the object; that one must take a position if this distance is to be accomplished is neglected. The objectivist, in his fantasy of pure realism, would carry on as if he could possess the advantages of his having eyes without being a person who looked with them in a certain direction and from a certain position; without being a person who chose between a sharp focus but a narrow field of vision, and less distinctness but more scope and perspective; who chose between a fixed stare and scanning, between a sharp questioning look and a relaxed absorbing regard.

To understand the error in objectivism and in subjectivism, we must see that, in general, for every attitude, there is a debased form of it described as an "ism". For liberality, liberalism; for intellectuality, intellectualism; for authority, authoritarianism; for communality, communism; and so, for objectivity, objectivism and for subjectivity, subjectivism. A distortion is derived from the value it debases, by singling it out and elevating it to be high, or by pressing it down deep to be fundamental. For instance, when we elevate the ordinary value and values of human life into the "sanctity of human life" we debase our values in the attempt to put them beyond question, to put them beyond the cynical reach of those who hold life cheap. At the very moment when we form the notion of life as "sacred" and thus its value becomes beyond question, it becomes impossible to explain what is valuable about it. To hold life sacred is to destroy or obscure our perception of it, in the same way that the well known phenomenon of biblical fundamentalism destroys the value of observations, injunctions, warnings and encouragements of the people who figure in the books. For if the words have to be true, if the "voice" of God through the prophet has to be wise, then we cannot know what they mean. We may seem to know what they mean, but if what we thought was meant turns out not to be so wise, not to accord with our own experience, to be inconsistent with some other voicing of God's voice, then what we thought to have been meant cannot have been what was meant.

And this is to say that whatever is given to us as "God's voice" is, taken in that guise, useless to us. But if we take the voice as human, granting ourselves the freedom to criticize, rebuke and to scoff at it, we gain, in this same act, the freedom to be moved, to be enlightened, to admire and to be reassured. If someone says to another who is in despair, "If God is with us, who can be against us?", the one in despair, if he already accepts such language, may be moved to tears of relief, or a keen eye of hope. This is because a human being has spoken to him these words of confidence and support. If he does not accept that language, he will be irritated. Why won't the other person express his own hope and support without such alienating artifice? Just as in taking the "word of God" as priceless, the fundamentalists make it worthless, the attempt to make human life something "priceless" is to make it of no account. If human life is priceless, it is elevated beyond all other values. But what is its value then? It cannot be said. It would be dangerous to say it, lest questions, debate, conflict and complication set in. One man's meat is another man's poison; one man's ceiling is another man's floor. Does the "pricelessness" of human life mean that any person's staying alive is of more value than anything else? Then what of the situation where one person's staying alive is at the cost of another dying? If any human life is priceless, then just so long as I am alive is my life of inestimable value, no matter what I do? So the moral danger lies in these posturings expressed as "Life is sacred", "Life is priceless" though their rejection sounds cynical to those taken in by the imposture. Shall we say that life is of some value to oneself and to others just to the extent that one lives well? Perhaps this is to go too far in the other direction from sacredness. To say such things seems to be part and parcel of attitudes within which we think that alcoholics in tattered clothes, sleeping in gutters, waking to get their next bottle of port, might as well be left to die. Or put out of their misery. And that dangerous criminals should be given the death sentence. For, of what value are their lives? Part of the answer is: they are of some value to themselves, or they would let themselves die, or kill themselves. Just to breathe, to eat, to see what happens, to think, even if merely maliciously or stupidly, is, for most of us, better than not to be at all. Further, there are more alternatives to holding life to be an ultimate value than to hold it cheap, or to put a precise cost price on it, too. True, the actual valuing of life, and of the things we do, is frightening in its shiftingness, its lack of form, its openness to abuse by the unscrupulous who would rationalize their callousness, who would "philosophize disgrace" (Bob Dylan). Still, there is no use in an absolute value which is, by definition beyond description and explanation, and which can offer no word when values and lives diverge, compete and collide, or are incomprehensible to each other.

This flight from objectivity involved in elevating and in fundamentalist thinking, including the fundamentalist attitude to physics or the physical sciences, will be later considered more generally under the heading of compulsions (that is to say, greeds) and obsessions (evasive and surrogate interests). In general, values are debased to the degree to which they are treated as absolutes. Something or someone is debased when it or he or she loses its base. Any value has its base in the variety of values and forms of life and interests which surround it. Within this context, it is just "one among many". Therefore, no matter how valuable, from time to time it must give way to other values, in part or in whole. Elevated above the rest, or made to be the foundation for all the rest, equally, it is debased. No account can be given of its value. To treat something as an absolute, is to absolve it of the ordinary everyday demands of experience and reason. It is to protect it from the normal spontaneous and deliberate demands for credentials, origins and locus.

Treating people or ideas as absolutes is to be understood by contrast with the lively practice of treating them on a level basis. To treat things on a level basis is not to assume or to pretend that they are all the same in quality, achievement or credibility. (There are logical and practical paradoxes in such an approach. These will be discussed under the defence and praise of liberality, and the attack on liberalism.) When a person or idea is admitted to a group, on a level basis, if he is treated as a person among people, he shows his credentials, whether formal or informal; he shows what he can do; he shows in what he can be relied upon; that when he speaks confidently or authoritatively, he knows what he is talking about; that when he is hesistant or speculative, he is not being merely insecure — there is something which rightly causes him real wonder or perplexity; insofar as his credentials are formal, he shows that he knows their meaning by his ability to assess those who assessed him, and to explain the point and force of the judgements, and their basis and criteria to those who are supposed to accept his formal accreditation. To treat a person on the level involves, also, requiring from him an account of his origins; if he is to be accepted on the level as an intellectual, then an account of the sources of his interests, and how and why they are valuable to him. Without that understanding, which some would dismiss as merely historical, another person cannot evaluate the person's values. He is left either being impressed by them, or being indifferent, or being repulsed. The person must say what he is, in terms relevant to the matters about which he would be taken seriously. That is to say, without being rigidly exclusive he must set his priorities. What is he? In Heidegger's term, what is his being? He is "being" a racing driver, though he may do some mechanical repairs; he is being a painter, though he may practise accountancy for a living; she is being a teacher of philosophy though she may attempt to philosophize from time to time in order to enliven her teaching; or, perhaps, she is being a philosopher, though she may teach from time to time out of a sense of the value of philosophy and that it should be spread, to earn a living; he is a detective; though he may play the violin very well; he plays it to relax or to help him to concentrate.

There are two separate points here. One is that a person will be in contact with something only to the extent that he is committed to it. That is, he will have some objectivity about something only to the extent that he is serious or committed, and following from this, to treat someone on the level requires the knowledge and understanding of the level at which they are serious. To know at what level they are serious requires the knowledge of what they are committed to, in some order and degree of priority of value. To be treated on an even level, as a person among people, a person states or shows his purposes and values, defends and explains them, and shows that he understands how they relate to the different or even to the incompatible values and purposes, beliefs and claims of the others by whom he would be taken "on the level". In turn, of course, he makes these same requirements of the others, that they make of him. The person locates his values, beliefs, attitudes and styles in the context of those current and prevailing. Expecting this much of a person, and expecting him to expect it of oneself, is what is meant by taking a person seriously in what they do or say.

Treating a person seriously, or on a level, in this sense, does not mean, exclusively a quiet sobriety. In order to keep the contact with the person necessary for objectivity, and the contact of ourselves, or the other person with the work, we engage all the devices of mockery, irony, sarcasm, deliberate exaggeration, gibe and insult, as much as slow and steady discussion, consideration and structured argument. If someone's argument deserves mockery or ribald comment, then to meet it with a show of solemn discussion is not to treat the person on the level. It is to engage in condescension. Though solemn discussion may pass as the more civilized "reasonable" response, it is an arrogance to pretend respect; one is beginning to regard the other as a fool to be manipulated. Marcuse has aptly entitled it, in the political context, "repressive tolerance". Because one stifles one's real, rejecting response, the other person never gets an open and fair chance of meeting it.

The conventionalized treatment of someone as a judge, a priest, a doctor or a professor, may seem like treating them with a superseriousness. That they have said something becomes a reason for taking it seriously: everything has become reversed. If ever they rightly gained their designations of respect, it was because what they said was impressive, interesting, proven to be true, a good explanation of hitherto mystifying or scattered facts. Since no person can be good at everything, each must use knowledge, explanations and understanding not originally his own. Yet, though for the most part he cannot know or understand what he receives from another as well as the one from whom he receives it (or he would not need to use other people) still there is a world of difference between the cap-doffing, forelock tugging, genuflecting attitude to those who may know more than oneself about something, and the socially level, critical and curious, self-possessed and appraising attitude.

Even a child, particularly a child, will recognize vagueness, condenscension, evasiveness, pomposity and weightiness of manner and speech; a person who has a genuine knowledge and understanding will not normally adopt such manners and speech; if he does, typically, out of laziness of habituation to the way of those who wish to "set him up", he has, for that time, when behaving in that way, lost his credibility. Sharpminded people, even if ignorant of the "expert" area, will withhold acceptance and trust. To set a person above ordinary criticism and beyond level answerability, though it appears to grant them a greater status, and to treat them with a superseriousness, is to be rid of them, just as surely as one is rid of others who are placed beneath us, as say criminals or hippies (to catch up the always recurring Dionysian mood and way of life in a term of the 1960s.) When someone has something to say which moves us, rocks us, shocks us, clarifies and sharpens us, it is not easy to remain on the level with them. To do so is to be available to their influence, and to have to make our response, to find our way between rejecting and trivializing what they say, being overwhelmed by it so losing our own sense of judgement and perspective without which, paradoxically, their influence is without its own distinctive effect, and elevating their ideas to the range of non-comprehending awe.

And, just as to elevate the great is to debase them, to lower people by category is itself to hold them in a kind of awe. This is more easily overlooked. But consider. If we lower people by category, we do not comprehend and respond to them in ways we mean and can realize; as uncomprehended, un-understood, they swim in the imagination into an atmosphere with the great. Criminals and hippies challenge our imagination and our reasons for what we do, and why we regard ourselves and others with the care and concern that is apparent. A criminal is not deterred by the gross damage he causes others. He is prepared to gamble on the risk of great damage to himself. Anyone understands, or can understand this mentality if he will be open to himself about his own feelings. To talk or to think of the criminal as someone far distant, incomprehensible to us, is to confuse oneself. Anyone, in having the fantasies common to us all of violent and radical disregard of the feelings, rights and lives of others, and who openly allows his sense of the flow of those fantasies from his feelings of frustration, envy, jealousy, or even from his simple lacks, wants and hungers, cannot pretend that he "really can't understand" how anyone could "do such atrocious things".

Similarly those who rejected outright and uncomprehendingly the hippie's life and mentality must have pretended not to feel the weights of responsibility, conceptual problems, economies of energy and of the imponderable questions of relative value involved in maintaining a persisting commitment to a defined and limited number and kinds of people, ideas, aims and customs. These problems are clear and considerable. In order not to become arid, dogmatic and unwondering, unpondering and unquestioning, we allow ideas, feelings, other people's moods and ways to flow in upon us; from time to time we allow them to take effect without being able to predict the outcome. Without this openness and fluidity, we can have no sense of a future. Everything becomes a Nietzschean endlessly repeated cycle of the same. Nevertheless to allow this openness, even from time to time, is to risk breaking or losing the capacity or desire to maintain the very commitments in virtue of which we remain open to change. The hippie's outlook simplifies this predicament. The notion of a life which is at once that of dropping out and letting go which is at the same time one of full feeling and sensibility is attractive but spurious, since without an initiating, sustained and directed line of activity there is no continuous return of feeling and information from others or from one's own "essays" in realizing one's interests and curiosities.

There is a distortion involved in considering the previous phenomena under the heading of "hippie". There is a double parochialism, of time, that it refers originally to a development of culture in the sixties. (Was Gauguin a hippie when he left the culture of Paris for the supposedly more original life free from overlay — in search of the pure impression, one might say?) And there is a more serious distortion also when we use the term in the context of the tensed, apparently opposing claims of spontaneity and controlled form: the stereotypical business person in a sharp suit, keeping fixed hours and carefully planning investments for maximum profit and equally the professional philosopher, a business person no less than a corporation executive, maintaining by written investments and as his or her commitments a family, house and car, are contrasted with those who live without commitments: someone with long hair, colourful, loose clothing, living from place to place and with people for just so long as they get along. But the people who keep to this latter kind of life and appearance must do so against pressures to join the business-like and the planners. They are not simply doing whatever they feel. In resisting the social pressures to conform, they are like the business-like who resist the pressures to drop their timing and planning. It takes an active resistance to avoid getting involved in what the hippie repudiated, and it is that resistance which is an essential, though not sufficient ingredient in the character and value of that recognizable way of life. This is why Sartre speaks of negating and nihilating as essential to consciousness in its role of making meaning and value. And it is the same theme, in his very different style and idiom, which is treated by Ryle in "Negative Actions", in which he argues that understanding the consciousness of someone, oneself or other, essentially and equally involves knowing and understanding what the person is not doing, as knowing and understanding what he is doing.

Nietzsche anchors in classical mythology the contrast I have wished to bring to attention: Apollo, the god of form, abstraction and control, but also, by implication, though with surface paradox, of dreams, versus Dionysus, god of dissolving, flowing, dance and frenzy. Abstraction and theory, taken to extreme, lead us to a merely dreamlike consciousness of things — we are too well insulated from the rough flux. It is this connection which Swift satirizes in Gulliver's adventure with the Laputans. The excess of the Apollinian spirit leads to the perfect stoical indifference to all events which, from its original desire to equably take in anything which reality has to show, must become an indifference to whether one lives. Thus Socrates, in stoically accepting his death, far from showing a worthy heroism or devotion to principle, shows the bankruptcy of the pure intellectualism of the philosophy of Forms and Ideals. But on the other hand, the Dionysian desire to loose all bonds and to lose all bounds involves, deliberately or implicitly, the desire to lose the sense of difference between oneself and the rest of reality; this leads to the despairing and hysterical lack of desire to live. The Apollinian sits prim and safe, his ego neatly separated and sustained in his "crafted boat of theory" on the watery sea; as in Quine's dream, theory is a buffer zone between himself and sensory shock. The Dionysian has one wild delight of ontologically diving overboard, and spends the rest of his life in the sense of drowning; like a Heideggerian person, he has the consciousness with a vengeance, of being "thrown" into reality; he is a Sartrean person, abandoned in the world, a nothingness left when even the vanishing point of the Husserlian transcendental ego vanished. He attempts desperately and futilely to create a finite permanent space, a defined, rather than a permanently fluid self. He attempts this by negating and nihilating both the marauding, uncaring in-itself and the shocking incommensurable Others-for-themselves, which disrupt and destroy the personal images he builds as surrogates for the impossible ideal of a real enduring substantial self.

This is the theme: what we put beyond ourselves or embrace so close that we cannot see it (which we use a tasteless clichéd jargon like "hippie") is viewed unobjectively in that we divorce it from our own subjectivity and attempt to see it as a "thing" in "other" people.

Ideas, and the people who have them

Ideas can be treated, whether with veneration, adulation, contempt or steady appraisal only in that they are held in one fashion or another by people. We can't set people aside and just deal with "the ideas themselves" as if ideas were realities quite apart from people in their manner of holding, explaining and defending what they think. It is typical of objectivism to denigrate or to ignore this fact. Karl Popper would have us believe in a "world" of concepts, propositions and theories separate from the merely "subjective" world of those who think, feel and sense. Louis Althusser and, in a different way, Michel Foucault, would have us think of knowledge, and language, as "subjectless". For all that ideas are intrinsically what people form in their minds, and writings are traces of people's verbal actions, we draw vital distinctions between taking an attitude to someone's ideas or writings, and taking an attitude to the person who thinks and writes. As one reads a book, one need to know or even think of the author; one need not think of there being an author, though one must, if sane, know there is one. One takes up an attitude simply to what one reads. The distinction in one's attitude to the writing and the person who wrote is commonly misrepresented in the crude thought that one deals with a matter "more objectively" by "ignoring all personal elements". What can this injunction mean? Certainly one must ignore irrelevant personal elements. This is a banality. Certainly I can put out of mind who it was who wrote what I consider; at some moment I may be conscious of no more than that this is said and conscious of what I think of it. But those attitudes are simply what I would have to a person for writing or thinking what I read; it is the attitude I would have to myself for thinking the things I see set down. And there is a danger of a bad sort of subjectivism when one tries to be totally "objective" and to forget the person of the author altogether. To forget completely the authorship as one considers the ideas themselves (as if to consider the ideas objectively in themselves) is to think as if I am the author. With the disappearance of the author, who is left but the reader? And who is that? *C'est moi.* The contempt I have for the ideas is then the contempt I would have for myself for believing them; the admiration, a pride in myself for holding them. As a deliberate, dramatic pretence this may involve me more vividly, but the distinction itself between dramatic pretence and active illusion requires my ability to disengage my mind from the writing, and this in turn requires that I think of a real author as writing what I read. And if this thought is to lead on any true path from the bare correct point that I am not the author, then I must know something about the writer: why and for whom he wrote; what he took for granted as common knowledge, perhaps something of the customary style and manners of his time. Most obviously, this knowledge can save the reader from crass misinterpretation and at the same time sets up the sense of difference, even of a barrier between writer and reader, so that the reader must remember the writer. To remember the real author is to remember that someone else may be able to defend the ideas I as reader reject or even despise; it is to be encouraged by the sense of another source of live intellect and feeling when I praise and admire what I read. Also, to remember the author is to be ready to make the necessary adjustments of meaning, to keep to the question, "What did the author mean in saying that?", to distinguish it from, "What do I mean if I say that?". To understand a writer one must ask and attempt to answer both of these questions. Not to ask the first is to be arrogant concerning the writings of another. It is to overlook the sense in which a book cannot be bought, either with money or intellectual effort. I buy a copy of Descartes' *Meditations*. I study his writings and "make his thought my own". Suppose that I freshly understand and fully agree, I do not merely mouth or mimic that, ". . . (if) there is some deceiver, supremely powerful, supremely intelligent, who purposely always deceives me . . . then again I undoubtedly exist"; and that I proclaim with all of Descartes' confidence "let him deceive me as much as he may, he will never bring it about that, at the time of thinking that I am something, I am in fact nothing", still I cannot thus reoriginate a new starting point and direction for philosophy. Descartes can say to himself, "Where do I go from here?", whereas I must ask, "What can I make of this? What did Descartes mean? What would I mean if I said this?"

So, to maintain one's objectivity about ideas, to keep them in the common market place is to keep one's objectivity towards those, including oneself, who entertain, assert, defend and speculate in terms of those ideas.

Objectivism and Objectivity

The attitude that one ought to attempt a complete divorce between one's attitude to ideas and one's attitude to a person in holding those ideas is an example of what I wish to locate as a general phenomenon of spurious objectivity. Such objectivism is the attitude which wants the advantage of objectivity without any of the costs. It consists in a complex tissue of confusions and evasions which it will take some time to expose. But, most directly and positively, I mean to lay out in useful and recognizable form the general structure of the well known facts which keep any theory or outlook in its place. This structure is that of our subordinating and being subordinate to ideas and feelings, subordinating and being subordinate to others, subordinating and being subordinate to what we find in other animals, and inanimate nature. Heidegger would have us give ourselves over to the world; we should be still and let Being speak. Popper would have us always approach things, people included we must guess, with a ready made hypothesis to be tested. He will not have it that it is a vital part of reason that our hypotheses should arise within a sensitive absorption in the things about which we then form theories. Similarly, to maintain our objectivity, we must be in a coordinating process of informing people and being informed by them. Only in this way do we keep our realization that it is spurious to dichotomize our "mere personal subjective thoughts" against "public objective information". The latter is no more than widespread cross-checked opinions of what, when we vainly seek for pure objectivity, is reassuringly anonymous opinion and feeling. In remembering what it is like when one informs another, one keeps a due and salutory imagination of oneself being informed by another subject — another complex of motives, illusions, fears and manipulativeness, as well as intelligence and probity.

Of course one cannot inform a non-human animal, nor be informed, as one can with other humans. But a person who is objective about and with their pets is equally open to the conduct and expression which the animal brings to them, accidently or deliberately, as they are "informing" their pets into animals who can thus communicate, by the humanizing use of the voice, stroking, regular feeding, and the teaching of obedience and tricks. We should mean by an objective attitude, one which pays due regard to its object. Naturally, an objective attitude to a dog will include a clinical style of examination of its ears for ticks, but to romp, dog-like, with the animal when it is playful, or to go running with it when one sees it is bored equally evinces an objective attitude. Indeed it is when one is "subjectively" (in the pejorative sense) wrapped up in one's own world than one fails to perceive what the animal wants or needs to do. Yet, again, in merely giving ourselves over to the apparent life of another person or other animal, we do not pay due regard to its separate character nor, more particularly, to our own. A child may be inclined to treat an adult cat as a baby because of the relativity of size; the cat's dignity may be outraged by this, though a kitten's would not. It is by reflection and instruction that a child learns to modify its natural responses and initiatives so as to see the cat as adult to a kitten, and not itself as adult to the cat. And, to give conventional "objectivist" objectivity its due, it is only through some at least rough approximation to the "objectivity" of arithmetic that one learns to see that after twelve years the kitten of what was our baby has become like in time to the child's grandparents, not to the nominally equally-aged child himself.

It would be a presumption, not rigour, to begin with exact definitions of objectivity and subjectivity. This would be to take prior control of the phenomena, and not to allow what is found in the exploration to shape one's ideas. Further, exact definition is a refinement, and as the metaphor of mining engineering suggests, we need the valuable ore first. The point and worth of refinement can be known only after the substance is collected and its character known in a general way. Nevertheless, even if we shouldn't take Being by the throat and torture it to say what we have already decided it must confess, Being won't speak unless spoken to — without a little stimulus — and if we haven't asked even a provisional question, we shan't know what it is talking about. Further, since every response of "Being", that is, to whatever is, is received by us in terms of our own subjectivity, some preliminary definition helps us to take account of ourselves as the receivers, and thus to keep a sense of being different from, and to some extent of how different we are in our conceptions from the things we think of. So a preliminary definition: To put it as broadly as possible, objectivity, considered as an intellectual, moral, emotional and sensual virtue, is the capacity and preparedness to draw one's ideas and attitudes, and to gain one's emotions and feelings from their own objects. It is to enjoy or suffer one's sensual responses, as responses to their causes and objects. This, at any rate, is the first stage. It is the stage of encouraging, inducing, the maximum impingement of the "object" which is possible without being swamped. It means taking the risk of being swamped, and of having to surface, find bearings and to try again.

Similarly I mean to work from a broad and rough account of subjectivity. "Subjectivity" has a conventional meaning as an opposite of "objectivity". It is this conventional understanding which I wish to attack. However, I hope to show the natural source of the conventional error, to show in terms of a new understanding how the error arose from a taking, though a mistaking of the phenomena of objectivity and subjectivity. To say, pejoratively, that a person is being "subjective" is to speak dimly of facts such as his/her being immersed in their own sensations, instead of responding towards the objects of those sensations. So a person is "subjective" in love who becomes in love with, or otherwise primarily involved with, his state of loving, rather than the one or thing he or she began by loving. And a person is subjective in his or her seeing who is absorbed in the seeing, rather than in what he or she can see. (These remarks are too simple to be quite accurate. A person can consider, objectively, his or her feelings of love, or manner of perceiving; these become new chosen objects of attention. The now classical treatment of this is in Husserl's phenomenological writings. In contrast, the empiricists, Locke, Berkeley and Hume are subjectivist in being launched upon the confusion between the truth that to perceive we must act or allow and be affected, and the falsity that therefore doings and occurrences "in our mind" are the real objects "of the mind", the real objects of our attention. Taken literally, out of their jargon of "mind" and "ideas", this is the absurdity which Ryle lampoons, that we hear our hearing, taste our tasting and see our seeing. If not taken literally, what is meant hangs obscurely between an unsubjectivist recognition of our subjectivity — that in all perception we act and enjoy or suffer, and the subjectivist error that it is our subjectivity rather than its objects which we can attend to, and learn about.)

"Subjectivity" is also linked conventionally with "idiosyncrasy". A person is thoughtlessly described as "subjective" in his or her tastes, opinions, responses of feeling, when those affections seem especially unusual or distinctive to him or her. "Thoughtlessly described", because in thus calling the person "subjective" one passes without thought to the conclusion that the person is in error or out of touch with things, from the observation that they are unusual in their perceptions and judgements. As meaning "idiosyncratic", "subjective" does not stand in logical opposition to the favoured sense of "objective" as meaning "carefully and truly in touch with the object". When one eliminates the confusions underlying the pejorative sense of "subjective", it is possible to see that objectivity is a form, a style, an employment of our subjectivity, and not its antithesis. That one is not always objective in one's subjectivity is no proof that they are separate things, any more than the fact that only some of a batsman's shots are stylish and well placed means that there are two things — his shots, and the style and placement of them.

A person's subjectivity, in the descriptive, unabusive sense which I favour, is the tissue of his or her knowledge, opinions, emotions, feelings and tastes, which yields the flavour, the style, the personalness of his or her approach to things. A person's subjectivity may be largely commonplace, and thus scarcely noticeable except to someone of another culture. Nevertheless, one's subjectivity is one's spiritual complexion and one's own possession, as surely as is one's physical complexion, however ordinary that may be. One might call one's subjectivity one's "taste" for things, following the way literary critics often use the visual metaphor of a writer's "vision". Those like Popper, Feyerabend and Quine, who think that the philosophy of knowledge and perception must have a study of the character of the systematized sciences at its centre, like to speak of all perception and opinion, however common and unadventurous, as "theory laden". Although this metaphor correctly calls attention to the impossibility of one's being "open to the things themselves" in perfect innocence or neutrality, it is misleading in suggesting that one's main and leading ways of approaching and dealing with things are already spoken, articulated, before or as we employ them. With some banality, but little prejudice, we can speak of a "point of view" and say that objectivity is possible only within a point of view and is thus a quality of one's subjectivity.

Objectivity is commonly held up as an ideal, though some would deride that attitude as a vain search for an idealistic impossibility, while others would condemn it as a cold removal of oneself from the stage of "real life". And while the second condemnation presupposes that objectivity is an attitude which really may be attained, still it is typically allied with the suspicion that the gains of objectivity are, in any sense, only imaginary: the suspicion, supportable by at least some fact, is that the cool detached removed observer does not really know what is going on. Why is objectivity supposed to be a worthy ideal? Because it is supposed to make it more likely that a person will be correct in his opinions, fair in his or her judgements, balanced in his emotions, being responsible for, rather than victim of his or her feelings, and sensitive and reliable in his or her tastes. Of course, to put the matter so broadly is to trail one's coat in the face of the already enraged disputants. Those for whom objectivity is the fetish which makes those who would make a virtue of subjectivism condemn objectivity as a cold withdrawal, will tie objectivity solely to "Truth", and contrast as an excluded opposite, the detached search for objective truth, with being subject to one's feelings — they will contrast as exclusive opposites, matters of objective truth, and matters of feeling and taste. So we have those worn and fruitless debates about whether there can be an objective morality, an objective aesthetics, an objective politics. As we begin to describe the qualities of mind and character which make a person objective in establishing and holding statements as true, we shall see that it is these same qualities of mind and character which are required for fair political conduct and opinion, for discerning aesthetic perception and appraisal, and for accurate and discriminating taste. It is not truth which is objective, any more than "aesthetics", whether aesthetic object or aesthetic theory. We are the ones who may lay claim to being objective. It is a thoroughly "subjectivist" projection upon the things we attempt to deal with objectively to give them the praise or blame, and to call them objective or subjective.

"Objectivity" is a misleading word. It suggests either or both of two attitudes. The first is that we should deal only with lifeless, non-conscious objects, or at any rate treat everything, so far as possible, as if it were a lifeless, non-conscious object. (Behaviourism in psychology — the view that if there is to be scientific "objective" study of motives, learning, perception and so on, then it must be of behaviour interpreted without any presupposition, assumption or inference of consciousness.) The second suggestion of the word is the mirror image, reverse direction of the first: to try to make oneself an object in relation to the things which inevitably do surprise us with their independent forces, chemistry, and inner and outer autonomous lives. It is as if the requirements of objectivity required one to admonish oneself: be fixed, therefore hard, rigid, unmoving, so that you're not the thing which changes, being still you can measure movement. Naturally, as in all the illusions of objectivism, there is some truth behind this. Illusions are illusions of reality. When emotionally upset or overwrought, one must find means to calm down before one can think or perceive properly. Furthermore, some persistence of vision, some commitment to a line of thought or investigation is needed, partly to turn up the facts, and equally to have some point and some standard by which to describe and measure them. (The difference between persistence and dogmatism, its obviously threatening surrogate, is a topic to be treated.) These, and other similar facts are the legitimate source of the myth of objectivity according to which the more like an unpassioned, universal, unchanging thing one can make oneself, the more objective one will be. (The classical extended mythology for this illusion is, of course, theology. Certainly, in this sense, Jews, Christians, Muslims and Buddhists all "worship the one God". Total and perfect knowledge is to be had only in the ideal of an unmoving unchanging thing which is no way subject to the world it knows. The difference with Buddhism is that this ideal is supposed to be found within one's own consciousness; it is not something "objectively apart" from the believer.)

The first attitude, that objectivity primarily is to be concerned with objects, or with things as they are objects, is either a formal truth which puts no limits on the range of "object" — an object is simply anything we can pay attention to and learn about — or it is a falsehood limiting the range of things we may be objective about to objects in the idiomatic material sense, and things like enough to them. In truth, the range of objects for the attitude of objectivity is as wide as the day is long. Music in general, and particular compositions and particular resonant renditions of them; painting and paintings; people and their actions both as general kinds (such as murder, sarcasm, encouragement, adultery and fidelity) and as individual deeds as committed in the morning shortly after breakfast; motor cars, the principles according to which they work and are repaired; the economic conditions and costs of production and the political character of the forces which effect such ubiquity of those machines; scientific theories about any or all of these things and matters and issues and about the cosmos cosmically considered; dogs and their relationships to people: the relationships of people to other people and to cats; there is no end to it.

Chapter Three

Subjecting and Objecting

Being "subject"; making our "objections"

The meaning of the abstract nouns "objectivity" and "subjectivity" quickly lose the substance of the issue; the real return to a sense of substance is through process and act; through the spirit we have expressed in active verbs. A person "subjects" himself to an Arctic climate in order to study the life of polar bears. Madame Curie "subjects" herself to the risks of radiation in studying, *avant garde,* the properties of radium. Embarrassed, angry and astounded, still a person has the objectivity to subject himself to the force of an argument. Impatient, curious or sceptical, still a person subjects himself or herself to the whole of someone's story in explanation of events. Philosophers subject themselves to the strangeness of the conceptual worlds they create in their efforts to find a standpoint from which to comprehend everything. "Philosophy is properly homesickness; the wish to be everywhere at home" (Novalis). When we find ourselves too subject, or too long the subject, we object. If we do not, we lose our objectivity. To object, we must detach ourselves from the involvement in which we are subject, we must be prepared to break a commitment, we must resist an emotional tie. Here, in the active life, are some of the sources of the myth of objectivism, of the uninvolved unemotional dispassionate onlooker. We can sense the disparagement of the objecting, the "objectionable" person who will not be agreeing and reassuring; he will not be one of us. "Objectionable!", we cry. "Objective", he insists. And we can sense equally the excessive retreat made by the objector in dismay or disgust. The objecting requires passion, even if coolly delivered. The seriousness needed to break an old commitment is, or contains the directions of new commitments; the detachment is a new involvement. But the objector becomes trapped in his own conceit, aided and abetted, unwittingly, by the slanderous stereotyping of those who want loyalty from him. His objectivity is not necessarily a matter of coolness, though it may well need to contain some of that quality. His objecting required some warmth. What is commonly called a complete detachment is a complete involvement in one's inner life. Anyone who pleads the necessity of a detachment is involved in a sense of the need for the detachment. This is no criticism of his plea. It is only a brake upon the car which would roll out of the river of time to leave us high and dry on the desert shores of pure detachment, of a complete disinterest; a non-involvement whose diffidence becomes indifference, whose dispassion becomes a passion for no passion. We would be completely committed to neutrality, utterly partial to impartiality, strictly positioned on having no position, and very hot about being cool.

Objectivity as drawing one's ideas, feelings, tastes as closely as possible from their proper objects, objectivity as thus aiding rather than opposing impingement of the object is possible only as we will become fully absorbed in the object, forgetting ourselves and other things, giving a single minded concentration, the deep attention of a fully resolved mind. This is what in realistic terms is known as a pure interest. So much tribute to the facts behind the myth of subjectivism, but without a counterbalance one will not distinguish objectivity sharply from a romanticist image — an unabashed subjectivism in which the object must be wholly trusted to give us our understanding of it; the self is nothing (Hume and Sartre) with consciousness everything (Hume) or a pure intentionality, empty in itself, directed towards its "objects" which alone provide substance (Sartre). In Heidegger, the attitude to the subject is too veiled to assess, but the injunction that we must be silent and simply let Being speak shows a lack of recognition and trust in the role and powers of each subject to form the questions which make Being speak, the power to coordinate facts within explanations, the power to illuminate what we are presented with by apt choice of words, and the making of comparisons and distinctions.

It is typical of the objectivist outlook to ignore subjects and subjectivity, to treat them as annoying, emoting, sensory blots on a pure theory of the world in itself. These objectivist denials are closely matched by a strangely similar loss of the reality and power of the self, in subjectivist outlooks. Unlike the objectivist, the subjectivist begins with a sense of the centrality of self, but still, like the objectivist, sees the self as something to be disposed of. In wishing to give him or herself entirely over to reality, whether to a lover and love as in erotic romanticism, to sensation as in decadence, or to be lost in the undivided oneness of all things as in mysticism, still the subjectivist, like the objectivist, wishes that there should be only the reality he or she knows and feels and senses, and not himself or herself as an equal reality knowing and feeling and sensing it. To admit the self against such objectivist denials and subjectivist losses is to realize that one is a real object for others. It is to realize that criticism cannot rationally be escaped, that everything can be changed for better or for worse by another separate, critical, even if understanding and not cold, eye and mouth.

Purity of interest

The need for absorption and close persistent attention in maintaining an objective search is one reason for the recurrence of the idea of purity of vision as a condition of objectivity. This purity of vision requires a purity of interest. One is interested in the object for its sake and not for ulterior motives. It is easy to mock this notion, to take it as a clear and excessive expression of objectivism. There are mixed motives, fears, hopes, desires and personal gain in all our interests, as much in mathematics and in the law and justice, in philosophy and poetry, in sports, in hobbies, in professional and any sort of paid work as particularly and notoriously in our interests in ourselves and others. However it is better to distinguish between a purity of interest and purism, than to lose sight of the former in debunking the latter. Certainly, a pure interest, if it arises at all, does so from nothing other than our mixed motives, varied and variable opinions, our fears and hopes, or our enjoyment and delight in what we find interesting. The purist does not want to allow that a pure interest arises from the same soil as a corrupt one. Nor does he wish to face the fact that a pure interest cannot guarantee its own permanent purity. It may be that but for the hope of fame a person would not conduct his or her painstaking scientific experiments, that but for the hope of immortality, of becoming an always recurring spirit in literature, a person would never be so dedicated to writing his or her poetry, that but for the hope of further wealth, a person would lack adequate incentive to keep writing a book, that sometimes but for the sexual impulse a person would not care tenderly for another. But even where or when this is the core, the interest produced need not reduce to the ground of prior desires and impulses in which it grows.

By careless work, malpractice or misconduct, a doctor can lose the wealth, reputation, reputability and respect which may be the necessary conditions of his doing first rate medical work. But, spurred by fears of loss and hopes of gain, he may develop the capacity for a pure interest in medicine. While diagnosing, prescribing or operating, she or he may have the single mindedness and full attention properly called a pure interest. While of that mind, the person will not be moved or perturbed by the announcement that the patient does not, after all, have the money to pay, or that the doctor will be ostracized for treating him. The doctor might work, at that time, with a pure interest, even though his prejudices, fears or cupidities might render him incapable of taking such an interest from the outset when next confronted with a patient with such problems.

A purity of interest is evanescent. What we discover or experience in pursuing our pure interests may fire the very emotions which were essential to the existence of the pure interest, so that they move from being background sustaining conditions into the foreground of our attention and concern. Purism cannot accept the evanescence of purity; it imposes stereotyped surrogates for pure interest. Purism aims to put purity at the disposal of the will, whereas purity of interest is something which needs to be cared for and carefully treated.

It is typical of new intense interest to be pure; it allows no distraction, or at least puts distractions in their place; it is an interest in the thing itself and not an interest in further rewards, spin-offs, or self-improvement. Further, though the capacity for a pure interest is important to the best in objectivity, other equally important requirements make for its instability. It is neither practical, reasonable, moral nor, finally, objectivity inducing to maintain a sole interest. (Not to imply that a pure interest must be a sole interest, but wait.) The practical and logical consequences and implications of these other interests may destroy the unification of one's subjectivity which was necessary to the purity of interest. Some of the facts of oneself which maintained the purity of interest are forced into pre-eminence; or, hopes, fears and desires which could, for a time, work together in a single direction fall apart.

One does not simply have interests. In having an interest, one conducts one's inner life and one's observable conduct along certain lines. It is of the essence of an interest, as distinct from a boredom that one cannot predict more than the outlines of what will ensue when one follows it. To take the simplest example, one may have an interest in a person him or herself. That person may know another; that other person may make one angry, envious, impassioned, jealous or alienated. And these emotions are too self-involving and distracting for the original interest to continue. A new interest, with a new awareness, partly shifted basis and different flavour and style may well emerge. And that will, in all probability, cause its own dissolution. The desire for objectivity cannot properly guard against this by maintaining a sole and exclusive interest in the first person and by insisting on the same from that other. For one thing the obvious conditions for objectivity of outside observation and comment are flouted. But most directly and intrinsically, the interest is instantly changed by its wilful exclusiveness; part of its object is now its own existence and not, as in pure interest, the thing which was of interest.

So the desire for purity of interest turns into purism if sustained in conservatism. This purism is one of the figures in the picture of objectivity as the state of a person who is cold, withdrawn and still. Each of these conditions is a wilful falling-away from respectively, coolness as self-possession, the keeping of the distance needed in order to maintain one's balance and direction, and the at least occasional stillness and restraint of expression and action needed in order that one be both self-reflective and also sensitive to the separateness of the initiatives and qualities of others and other things. We are rightly annoyed by the picture of objectivity presented in these falls. Objectivity appears as dishonest and evasive; the person's pure search for Truth a fraud. We recognize dishonesty, since the purist does not simply have a pure interest; he or she is creating a facade of one, behind the whirring mechanisms which busily reject other interests and reify the interest itself as its own concern. We recognize evasion, because the rejection of other interests, and (emotional) rejection of the emotional basis of the interests of purism itself is an evasion of its own basis and of the reality of the new competing interests which have caused the person to move into the purist stance in fearful self-defence. The objectivist is cold because it is only the acceptance of the new interests which have to be forcibly put aside to preserve this formalized facsimile of a pure original interest, untrammelled by modern concerns, which would generate warmth. He or she is withdrawn for the same reason, and stiff because engaged in a fabrication rather than a living continuance of a deeply felt attachment. (The relationships between people provide the most vivid instances of the structures described, but what is said applies equally to one's interest in activities, inanimate objects, and to topics and studies.) There is a similar phenomenon of puritanism in morality, which, on the view described, is a misunderstanding of and lapse from the purity of interest in others and their concerns, pleasures and pains required for a moral point of view.

It is a continual real puzzle, not just a philosopher's invention, how interested, passionate, partial, prejudiced people can hope to be disinterested, dispassionate, impartial and to put their prejudices aside. To lose our interests does not make us disinterested, but merely indifferent and bored; we do not enquire and we do not find out. To lose one's passions is to lose one's capacity for that close and continued involvement with things and people without which one cannot bear with the difficulties, pains and shocks of discovery and continual acquaintance. Without passion, initial interest and attraction fizzles out and leaves us with only superficial opinion. To have no partialities is impossible if one is interested and involved, and the attempt to rid oneself of them and to reach such a high plane that all things may be regarded with equal equanimity is to move only towards increasing vacantness of mind and to allow oneself to utter only fatuities. Or, since every proposition may be deduced from a self-contradiction, it is to allow oneself the luxury of, or even to extol the virtues of, self-contradiction. Thus the "objectivism" of pure impartiality ends in logical lunacy. As for prejudices, it is impossible in practice that anyone should avoid having prejudices, even in the gross and derogatory sense of the term. In growing up, we catch them as we catch mumps and chickenpox, but the effect is much worse, for the inoculation we are left with in the case of prejudices is against their being rectified by experience, rather than against our reinfection.

In a more refined and philosophical sense, it is absurd to suppose that we should be without prejudice: since proof cannot be endless, some things must be taken to be so if they seem reasonable or evident, even though we know that we may later learn that we were mistaken. Of course, we hope to anchor much of our reasoning not merely in what seems reasonable, but in what we strictly observe. But each person can observe only a mite of what he or she must take as true because others say they have seen it. A person who used nothing from anybody else would be dull ignorant and witless; a prime use of our wits is to decide who we should trust, and in which respects and on what kinds of issues. Further, even when we make observations ourselves, we must record or remember our observations, and so fall again into reliance on things and people other than ourselves to corroborate and aid our memory. We observe things in certain ways among the many possible ways, and from certain points of view (physical as well as intellectual and emotional) from among many possible points of view; we interpret and describe what we observe in certain terms from among many possible terms, and bring to bear certain generalizations and theories from among other possible such generalizations and theories. Happily, we are "prejudiced" in this fine philosophical understanding of the term, for such prejudice is a mark of the intelligent use of our senses. Still, they are prejudices in that they might not be true. Further, they are prejudices in that we can call any one or a bunch of them into question even though we cannot, as Descartes and the early Husserl hoped, call them all into question, or put them all in brackets out of operation in our thought. This is because it is only from an intelligent discriminating base that we can call anything into question, and with no such prejudices we would have no such base for questioning or bracketing and no coherent, directed mode of questioning either. Still, the necessity of always having and operating with some prejudices is no reason at all to refuse the questioning of any one or a bunch of them, when the occasion arises.

So, in short, we cannot decide, simply, to have no prejudices, since we must have some. Further, even when we turn attention to a particular prejudice which we might well do without, we cannot simply decide not to have it, since one cannot simply believe or not believe things at will. Yet Sartre is right and Ryle is wrong. A belief is not just a state or disposition of us, in the sense that its temperature is a state of a mass of water and its elasticity is a disposition of steel. We can actively encourage or discourage ourselves in our feelings of conviction or doubt. We can be protective rather than properly critical about our beliefs; believing that all swans are white, we can evade any refuting observations: one looks warily at anything black, making sure not to look carefully if it looks at all like a swan. If belief is in some ways a disposition, then we must recognize that such "dispositions" are as much a matter of how we dispose ourselves as how we find ourselves already set. In this inevitable formation of meta-attitudes — we are "proud" to believe, we are "ashamed" of believing, we see in the very idea of belief the possibility of being wrong and so, as Sartre says, we less than fully believe what we believe — in all of these attitudes we are not simply possessed of or possessed by our beliefs.

Even if we cannot simply "will to believe", still the normal use of the active verb "I believe . . ." or "I disbelieve" is entirely suitable to our relationship with our "beliefs". When a person says "I am disposed to believe you", he or she is not only recording a fact about his mental set. He is also expressing his willingness to listen favourably and so on. Furthermore, his remark is itself part of his conduct of favourable disposition. When the person decides whether or not to say "I am disposed to believe you . . ." he is not simply scanning his states of preparedness and informing the other person of how the land lies; he is in part doing this because, though wishing for some reasons that he could listen favourably, he might have to confess to "finding in himself" too great a reluctance to do so. (Sartre much underrates this factual obduracy of our own nature in his representation of people as continually and freshly constituting themselves in this state of mind and feeling.) But, if scanning and finding out and informing are things which humans can do, actions they can take, then favourably disposing themselves to listen is also a thing which can be done, an action which can be taken. This is true even though one's given, already constituted self can make on occasion, such action impossible.

Similarly, it is not within one's power simply to cease to believe what one has hitherto believed. It would be a chaotic situation if one could: it would be intellectually pointless; it would leave one quite intellectually directionless rather than liberated and keen minded if one practised it at once on all one's beliefs. Nevertheless it may be within one's power to question them oneself, to encourage others to question them if one feels less than equal to or wholehearted about the task. This can be more than an intellectual game to satisfy the forms of the intellectual life. One can actively dispose oneself towards disbelief, and really subject oneself to the criticisms and evidence which will result in disbelief, if that is how it is to be.

It is objectivity to be prepared to live through phases of such criticism. It cannot be objectivity to be prepared to live continually in such phases.

So, to take prejudice out of that list of interest, passion, partiality and prejudice, it should not surprise us so much, logically or psychologically, that though we are prejudiced we can set our prejudices aside when occasion or the shafts of others move or compel us. And it should not distress us too much that our objectivity is only for the moment. It is the needs of the moment which produce it, or which enable us to achieve it by effort and resolve. And it is our being subject to the needs of the moment which makes our wounded consciousness quickly, too quickly perhaps, seal, heal over again. We need not fear that our objectivity will never again arise when that sharp openness is closed, any more than we need fear, when satisfied, that our hungers and desires will never return. Our life is one of different and only partly interpenetrating moments, and the moment of realizing this is only one of them. (Hegel, in *The Phenomenology of Spirit,* had the brilliant realization of the first of these facts, but could not bear the face of the second.) There is a practical paradox of objectivity: objectivity is at once a shock, a losing of ordinary balance and footing, but a shock in which the shattered panes are elements of a new stability, for in the shock is the sense of perspective that we indeed did have a footing, had indeed made a certain balance, that it was from "here" and "in this way" that we are so confidently knew that "the world just is as we see and balance it": in this realization, if we allow it to grow, we may then more nimbly recover a new footing and a new balance so that we are not just shocked or lost in fragmented wonderment or Sartrean vertigo when it dawns on us that our everyday path had been a narrow ledge on a precipice. If we retain our objectivity in the shock of objectivity, then we can coherently think and judge and listen and look, swiftly making ourselves familiar again in the new strangeness, whose strangeness is made fresh interest by our grip, though more distanced, on our old familiar prespective. So might a bigoted judge see and listen to and hear the case of an accused person with the wrong coloured skin, or who belonged to a social class or age which threatened him, if his or her mind was made to glitter out of its ordinariness by the accurate moral ferocity of a defending barrister. For a moment his/her mind would be fresh; he or she would hear evidence as evidence, not in sentimental guilty "liberal" reaction either, but with a sharp, witty and kind mind, open at the front and closed at the back. (From Michael Frayn, *The Tin Men,* about a very liberal member of the establishment, "He has a very open mind. Open at the front and open at the back.") I shall treat in a similar way the possibilities of our transcending while still possessing our interests, passions, partialities, but for the moment other matters are more urgent.

Disinterest, detachment and involvement

If objectivity requires our interest and therefore our involvement then how are we to be disinterested and detached? John Anderson (an ex-Scot, Australian philosopher) held that objectivity was interested disinterest. This aphorism at once reminds us that disinterest is not the opposite of interest, and that objectivity requires interest as much as it does disinterest. Popular mythology has it that an interested party cannot be objective. If there is any sense in this, then it will have to be true that not all our interests make us interested parties. I would not even remark on the silly notion that one may be objective only if faintly interested but not objective if one is intensely concerned, except that people, usually in bad faith, but sometimes in stupid or affrighted annoyance, having their superficial noses put out of joint when they encounter those who most passionately and intensely want to know something, tend to efface and to trivialize and to neutralize that interest by the smoky rhetoric of, "He or she is too subjectively involved to be objective". True, there are distinctions to be made. An obsessive interest may be intense, but not the best in objectivity. Though the thermal metaphors — being cool, warm or hot — and the place of emotion generally, are yet to be considered, one would wish at once to distinguish from hysteria even the most intense and consuming interest. Conventional wisdom has it that a person is an interested party if he or she stands to gain or to lose money over the issue. First, this fails as a generalization. Though some people are sometimes led by hope for gain or fear of loss into a lack of objectivity, others, such as astute business people, are led by much the same motives into a scrupulous objectivity. Because they desire to profit and they wish their products to be marketable, they assess their products and the market all the more objectively. In another way too, the generalization fails to hit the mark, since if people have enough money and are not greedy for more, or simply have other interests which take over when some level of financial needs is met, then the prospect of gaining or losing money is not going to make them an interested party in the required sense, even if the law or commonsense makes that assumption. In any case commonsense has it that fame, power, the offer or denial of sexual relationships and many other things are as likely as considerations of money to make us interested parties. It will not do to say that one is an interested party in the sense which is supposed to defeat or diminish our objectivity, since it is quite unclear how one would continue the list. To put the same point in another way, the making of such a list, however long, simply evades the issue of explaining what it is to have an objectivity enhancing interest in money, fame, sexuality and so on, and what it is to be interested in such a way that one's objectivity is defeated or diminished. A person's very life may be at stake. As the tide comes in one may need to assess how to climb a cliff. One is a most interested party and that makes one sufficiently objective to find a way; without the extreme need one might never have scrutinized exactly, imaginatively placed onself at various points on the projected route, considered without vanity or false humility one's various strengths and weaknesses, agilities and clumsinesses. A cool detached observer may see no possible escape route. True, the detached observer may see that a ledge is impassable, and the climber, if desperate or merely wishful, may misjudge it. But this shows only that personal involvement (having something to gain or to lose which is most precious) is not a guarantee of objectivity.

So in reality, the question ought not to be whether the person is an interested party in the sense of having something precious to himself to gain or to lose; the question is whether, in this interest, still he or she is disinterested. It is conventional thinking about the various things which are precious to people which misleads us in the first place. It is assumed that financial interest is, virtually by definition, self-interest. The life of the self-seeking capitalist is contrasted with that of the "altruistic" medical missionary or dedicated revolutionary. The cynic who espouses the theory of egoism, that people seek only their own advantage, is no closer to the mark. He can see that the missionary or revolutionary can be as self-concerned as a capitalist seeking to maximize profits, but he cannot see that the capitalist might be as disinterested as at least some missionaries and revolutionaries. (Once we see behind these conventional errors we can, thankfully, move away also from these hackneyed examples, once and for all.)

It is known, and not just a cynicism, that someone doing good works may be as self-interested as someone whose actions are worthless or harmful to others. Someone curing the sick may be interested in the sick being cured, or he may be predominantly or solely interested in his curing the sick. The practical distinction is clear enough. If he is interested in the sick being cured, then he is content if someone else will take over, so long as they are as good or better a doctor. Of course, the usual professional doctor will be interested in someone being cured, but also in his curing the person,

because he earns his living from curing people. We accept this congruence of disinterest and self-interest as necessary and in no way
discreditable in everyday affairs, unless self-interest demolishes
disinterest, as when a doctor will not refer a patient to someone else
who could treat him better. A doctor who was interested in his
having an interesting medical case, and who let this get in the way
of deciding who best would treat the patient, would also fail in
disinterestedness. The voluntary unpaid helper of others does not
thus automatically secure disinterestedness; only if his desire that
he be doing something worthy is detached from his desire that some
good be done can be maintain that direct disinterested interest in
the object of social concern. Such direct interest can and usually
does coexist with self-interest; to act or to think or to feel
disinterestedly with regard to something, then, means either that
one has an interest only in that thing, and acts, thinks and feels out
of that interest, or if one has ulterior interests such as making
money or being sexually aroused or satisfied, then such interests are
put aside, put out of play. This capacity of people to disengage
from operating upon or being motivated by beliefs and feelings
which are nevertheless really part of them is what attracted
Husserl's persistent interest. Without appeal to this ability, neither
disinterest, detachment, nor dispassion, indeed no sort of restraint
can be understood.

The fact that we can engage in such self-controlling, self-
monitoring and even self-abnegating actions has, notoriously, produced many a theoretical will-o'-the-wisp. We may be excused now
for being tired of dragging ourselves out of the philosophical
swamps next morning. If we are tired of drying our philosophical
clothes of Kant's soggy noumenal self, irritated by the hot air of
Descartes' ethereal substance whose sole essence is to think, a little
bored now by Hume's ironic lament that he cannot find himself
whenever he looks for himself, more than a little dizzy juggling
Husserl's three egos, short-changed by Sartre's nothingness as the
source of freedom and creativity, impatiently flicking off the dry
dust of Ryle's dispositions, then we shall look to a more homely
understanding of self-referring action, thought and feeling. At any
rate, it is not my purpose here to provide a model for self-referring
action. We simply scratch to relieve an itch — one self-referring
action — or, another self-referring action (out of a sense of propriety) we refrain from scratching. We no more have to be two
people in one to refrain from scratching than we have to be two
people in one in order to scratch.

There is a considerable danger of promoting something false in disinterestedness as a condition of being objective, if being objective means being such as to best approach and get to get to know the object of one's concern. However much one insists on the difference between disinterest and a lack of interest, the "dis" has a weakening, deadening attachment to "interest" which is the very reverse of what is needed in getting to know, or to care about or care for something. Just as in refurbishing the concept of objectivity, we see that we might just as well have consigned it to the dustbin and begun afresh with new concepts, but for the fact that we cannot eliminate old currency and therefore must revalue it as best we can, so too, in reviving the best in the concept of disinterestedness, it is vital to bear in mind that it would have been much the same, and in some ways more refreshing, to attack it outright, as the centre of damaging myths, the myths that only when we keep our distance, have no partialities, regard all things equally, hope for no reward for ourselves can we know about, care about or care for, understand and judge things best. It is true that getting close, proceeding on the basis of one's partialities, being confident in one's finding of some things to be better than others, and then resolutely preferring them — all of these endanger one's "objectivity". But the general persistent denial of them also makes any objectivity impossible. Objectivity lives on the conditions which endanger it. The objectivist error is to flinch back entirely from these conditions, using, as we can, the excuse that they endanger objectivity. The subjectivist error in reaction to what we rightly see as the aridities of objectivism is to use the fact that objectivity is impossible without what endangers it, as an excuse of making no distinction between, on the one hand, the possession of interests, partialities, loves, hates and a point of view and, on the other hand, maintaining an objectivity in one's interests, partialities, loves, hates and points of view. And just as interestedness, though a danger to objectivity, is vital, so too, disinterestedness, sharply distinguished from non-interest and loss of interest, though itself a danger to objectivity, is necessary to it. To pursue disinterestedness at the complete cost of satisfying oneself is strictly self-refuting, since to succeed in the aim is to succeed at least in satisfying oneself in the success of achieving the aim of total disinterestedness, and thus not to satisfy oneself, and thus in turn, to satisfy oneself as disinterested, and thus, in turn, to destroy the success of the achievement, and so on in a lurching circle, for ever.

Disinterest and love

Even before it could reach its logically self-destructive limit, however, the aim of total disinterestedness can be exposed as irrational. If one loves someone only disinterestedly, what reason could there be for this? Either the one who loves is worth something, or he/she is not. If the one who loves is worth nothing, his love is worthless to the person on whom it is placed. Disinterest is in vain. If the one who loves has worth, then it is irrational for him or her to think himself (or herself) not to be counted at all. Extreme altruism rests on the same irrationality as extreme egoism. As the egoist's "I am I" fails to give any reason why "I" should be automatically or totally preferred, by myself or by any other, so too the same principle "I am merely I" fails to give any reason why my interests should automatically or totally fail to count in competition with any other.

That one's love of another should include disinterest is the just condition that it should, at least sometimes, be an interest simply and directly in the other, and include a care and concern for their interests for their own sake, whether or not one stands to gain anything beyond the satisfaction of knowing that the other person's interests are satisfied. (That last self-satisfaction it is logical absurdity to be so purist as to refuse, though, of course, one may know one might not gain it − or may know that one may die or be left in ignorance of whether one's aims have been achieved.) But though the presence of this sort of disinterest among one's interests (and the preparedness and capacity to develop it) is important to possessing and to maintaining one's objectivity of interest, cultivation of it as a sole kind of interest is detrimental to its own objects. As well, it is irrational for one to attempt and logically absurd that one should succeed in having it solely and entirely as the growth in the garden of one's soul. To be objective requires, as one primary condition, a current knowledge and awareness of one's limitations as a subject, and particularly of the fact that one is a subject. It is that awareness of oneself as a subjectivity, as well as the more obvious recognitions of oneself as physical − occupying space, having mass, requiring force to be accelerated; as physiological − in needing certain chemicals, being poisoned by others, being subject to varying levels of available energy and so on − which constitute one's objectivity concerning oneself. If someone's interest in another is so pure, for instance, that he or she will not expect or ensure that there is a just and needed return to themselves from time to time, then that person's interest is too pure to be fully serious. To take the thought swiftly to its limit: dead, one is rarely of use to anyone. From that limiting thought, one who has been overimpressed by disinterestedness swiftly recovers the perspective that unless they count their interests in and for themselves as important, their living for another is that of a parasite. ("He lives for others." "Yes, you can tell by their hunted look.") It is the other who is made to bear the more serius onto-logical burden of being of worth and deciding what is of value.

However much the pure and extreme altruist does for another, it is not more than the mechanical work of a functionary if the altruist will not make his autonomous decisions about what is of value. And if people are of some value, he will have to find himself of some value. If he pleads, "But I am an exception. I am an utterly worthless knave," then he has nothing to offer anyone. If he is right about himself, he would not even wish to offer anything. His altruism is bankrupt. If one's loving, being interested in and caring about or for another is to mean much to them, then one must not be a person who looks to his own interests only in order the better to consider the other person's concerns or needs. The sense of reality, worth and solidity which one gains from the love of another arises in no small part from the thought that one's lover who has something to give, is prepared to give it. If you can see a lover only as someone who might be enriched by your love, then you do not have the attitude of a person who can properly offer such riches. The attitude is not that of level regard, but of a condescension.

If being disinterested is a way of being interested, and includes our direct interests in others and their concerns, in making money, in gaining or giving or sharing sexual enjoyment — all matters in which the person involved may well stand to gain a good deal — then we have to regard as being as no more than conventional safeguards the exclusion of interested parties from certain kinds of situations and decisions. Their exclusion as "incapable of the disinterestedness necessary for objectivity" must be regarded as a convenient device, rather than as an exact or necessary judgement. If a man or woman is charged with a crime, then neither their spouse nor any relative may be judge or member of the jury. In cases of settlement of damages, neither party could properly be judge or assessor. That one's personal involvement or connection may make one dishonest in announcing one's judgement, rather than unobjective in making one's real judgement, is sufficient ex-planation for this convention of law. To this explanation may be

added the consideration, again one of crucial importance to the
practice of law, but not to the making of objective and informed
judgement in general, that if a judge or member of the jury knows
the defendant intimately, he will find it almost impossible to
restrict himself to the evidence presented in court when making his
judgement.

It would be foolish to deny that if a judge found his or her child
in the dock, he or she might find that their affection and concern
made it impossible for him to form any objective judgement of the
child's guilt. Yet this is not because, universally, or even typically,
affection and close ties make fair appraisal impossible. Indeed, on
the whole, only such conditions are enough to make a person
bother to make fair, careful and tempered judgements outside the
professional arena of the law. A judge (or members of the jury) is
not to try the case of a relation or friend because the public context
of the law makes public shame and punishment inevitable upon
judgement of guilt, and so the judge whose affections are involved
either will be too upset to think clearly, or else too afraid of looking
at the evidence with a clear and open mind in case it should point to
the guilt of someone whom he would not wish to see hurt.

One must name the emotional involvement before considering a
proposition such as that objectivity is impaired by emotional involvement. It is not surprising that if someone is infatuated with
another, he or she fails to have or to wish to form any clear idea of
the reality and complexity of the other person. To be infatuated is
to be made fatuous with respect to the object of infatuation. But if
we know that someone is full of admiration for another, we must
wait to know the details of the grounds and cause of the admiration
before jumping to any conclusions about whether the admirer has
lost his or her objectivity. This is equally true if someone is known
to be proud of another's appearance, achivements, goodness or
whatever. If someone loves another, then he or she wants to know
the best rather than the worst about them. But the person who loves
someone equally wants to know that person intimately, partly
because this is in the nature of love, and partly from the knowledge
that one cannot care much about or for another if one does not
know well what they are like. It is because we are delighted,
distressed, shocked, absorbed by and in the doings and matters
which happen to someone we love that conventional myth has it
that those who love lose their objectivity. This is simply part of the
conventional, false cliché that to be objective is to be uncommitted,
impersonal, uninvolved, moderate, impartial, calm and un-

emotional. Quite unthinkingly, common thought gathers into this bunch, being dispassionate, disinterested, unprejudiced and unbiased. This gathering is an error. The two bunches are of quite different kinds, and a consideration of what it is for a person to love or to hate another shows this. To love or to hate includes having a commitment, it is to regard someone personally: it is an involvement, it is not to be content with the usual common, commonplace moderate view of the person; it is to be prepared to have one's calm upset and, being an emotion; it is to be sometimes emotional with respect to the one who is loved. These conceptual formalities of love preclude it from being a formal and ordered relationship, even though habit, custom, the requirements of society and other practical considerations may make it coexist with, or live within, certain formal structures of conduct.

It is equally part of the conceptual formalities of love that while having a passionate regard, one is still prepared to be dispassionate — that is, to bracket or distance oneself from one's feelings when that is necessary in order to maintain or to develop one's imaginative sense of the distinctness of the other person, the difference of that person in their point of view, to avoid infatuation, and for many other reasons. And while it is silly, a mere idealism, to say that love is only a disinterested emotion, it is vital that the person who loves is capable of disinterestedness. To strive for complete disinterestedness is logically and practically self-defeating; yet to be quite incapable of it is to be incapable of a detached regard for the person's feelings, ideas, ventures; it is to be incapable of accepting the person's past which does not include oneself and that part of the person's present which does not include oneself. And that detached regard is a condition of any serious love or hatred. To be capable of disinterest is to be capable of having this detached regard in terms which are not limited to those which intrinsically involve the way in which one is related to the one who is loved or hated.

As fast as one begins implicitly to extol the virtues of such disinterestedness, however, one becomes apprehensive of any excess of it. As much as one is delighted with a moment of disinterestedness from someone who loves you, you are dismayed by its continuing, for it seems then that the person does not want to be related to you. They want only to be distantly related to your welfare, like the lady who is supposed to have loved and supported Tschaikovsky and yet never to have met him. Pure and persistent disinterestedness is as much a conceit as selfishness, for in wanting only the other person's happiness, and not one's own, one refuses to be happy with the other person, and to be happy on account of their happiness. It is impossible to be purely disinterested and to wish that the other person's happiness even in part exists in the way that person is related to you and your doings and your initiatives to and acceptances of the person. Not to include that latter wish among one's wishes is not to desire to love that person. It is only to desire their welfare or happiness, which it is quite possible to do without loving them. It is no accident that Christian love, which is defined upon the pure ideal of disinterestedness and self-sacrifice, should always be associated with hypocrisy. The common explanation of Christian hypocrisy is that the Christ-like standards are too high for us mortals, and so we fall into a pretence of satisfying them. The real reason is deeper than that, and is inescapable in heaven as it is on earth. Let us once insist on our own presence, our own needs, our desires that at least part of the happiness of the one we love be joint with our own, and we are not purely disinterested. Let us never do this, and we refuse the intimacy, the actuality of ourselves to another, without which there is no love; the other person then correctly appreciates only the too cold, however virtuous, wish for his or her good.

Chapter Four

Liberality and Totalitarianisms

Liberality and commitment

Liberal, free, open, wise, tolerant, dispassionate; from these there is a slide in thought or practice towards "vices": Lack of judgement, lack of resolution, lack of control, promiscuity, cowardly unpreparedness to intervene, lack of care for the better against the worse, and indifference. Perhaps the "virtues" were only smokescreens in the first place.

There is, of course, the everyday background patter and clatter of "liberalism":

"Everyone is entitled to his opinion." (Her opinion?)

"Who am I to judge?"

"Who are you to judge?"

"Whatever you say, it's only your opinion."

Let these saws gather dust among our cobwebs.

The virtues are no mere smokescreens for the vices. To be liberal is to be generous minded; it is to give others a fair chance to put their views and particularly to express them in the style they find natural; it is to warmly encourage others to put their case and to find their place; it is to encourage one's own conflicting tendencies and views to find their appropriate expression and place; it is to be contemptuous of that allegiance to "logical consistency" which is only verbal veneer for unresolved complexity and conflict.

Such real liberality takes initiative in supporting certain values; it is therefore not a neutrality with respect to values. Thus, in being liberal, one cannot regard all attitudes with equanimity.

(Tolerance, non-tolerance and intolerance — these are for later.) To be liberal is to oppose illiberal attitudes and opinions. Typically those who are seriously religious, marxist or fascist (Marcuse when he thinks that tolerance is something we cannot afford in the capitalist state, and capitalists' verbal hit-men like Milton Friedmann who urge that education is to be regarded as an economic investment) despise tolerant attitudes in education. A tolerant evenhanded encouragement of an understanding of the varieties of ways in which one can live and think and feel is thought of, according to one's sect, as "weakening the faith and eroding the moral will", as "failing to confront unequivocally the economic class structure generating and upholding the established order of ideas", as "rotting the fibre of the nation and leading to anarchy", as "frivolous, standard-lowering and trendily progressive, trying to entertain rather than strictly educate" and so on. In malicious fear of free styles of access to ideas and facts and an equal hatred of an unregulated variety of forms of representation and expression of them, people held in those and similar doctrines think that a liberal attitude is weak and inconsistent. They think, "As 'liberal' one cannot stand, as one must, implacably opposed to the evils in people and society". And, they also accuse, "The liberal's liberal halo is bound to slip when he or she is confronted with the lies, dishonesty, unscupulousness and finally the machine guns of illiberalism". It is alleged (particularly by marxists, who want to borrow something from the idealisms of liberality, but transform it into a more hard headed social realism) that when liberalism is confronted with what threatens it, its liberality must collapse. It will expose itself either as a fraudulent evasion from making a stand somewhere, or reveal the colours it hid but had all along; it will show itself just as illiberal as its opponents when its interests are threatened.

Those for whom *being* anti-Marxist or anti-Communist is a real thing, a primary way of being, scorn liberality no less than the Marxists. They think it is soft on communism, that it "lacks the 'will' to stand firm" (not sufficiently "erect"?) against the flood tides that threaten our democratic Western civilization. Their's is a scarcely disguised macho sneer that to be liberal is to lack male sexuality (a sexuality of a kind fantasied from their hysterical condition of real or imagined impotence.) Women don't play any part of initiative in the imagined picture; their role in these anti-liberal fantasies is to be either corrupt, seducing the male hero away from upholding the ideas of the free world (alleged porno-politics) or else to be victims. In the latter role they conveniently justify "our" (that is, man's) raged outrage against the radicals and insurgents who exploit and deceive them. By definition, in this imagined world projected so practically upon the political realm, women themselves lack will.

Take a deep breath. We shall find room for a decent and generous liberality. (We know already to beware of "isms", in any case.) First, truly, it is evasive and feeble to expect liberality to be more than one value among others with which it may come in conflict; to expect more is to elevate it into liberalism. Liberality is in any case more a style and attitude than a content or programme of action and feeling. To be liberal does require some definition in one's subjectivity, at least to the extent that one desires to recognize and to understand the separate and different subjectivities of others, and to deal with people in terms of that. To do so requires a style and attitude sufficiently accepting of others' opinions and manners of expression that such recognition can be secured and such understanding maintained. Also, this accepting and interested attitude must not be entirely or merely functionary, or it is false and self-defeating. If liberal, one is interested and exploratory of others' differences, not just in order to recognize and understand (though one may usually have that purpose too.) One simply is interested and exploratory and this has the consequence that recognition is secured and one can "understand", that is, "stand under", that is, "bear with" the other person's realities and differences of reality from oneself.

Some of the legitimate objection to what would pass itself off as the liberal attitude is an objection to making a thing of being liberal. It is an objection to liberalism, in which the aim of "being liberal" stands between the would-be liberal and the real liberal interest of simply wanting to know, to care about, to allow for and, if possible, to care for and to be cared about by others. This stylized social-workering liberalism of social improvement is particularly liable to fail to see that being liberal is a matter of style rather than of content. Since it is making liberalism itself an aim, it wants to think in terms of liberal policy and liberal opinion. Notoriously, one chases shadows and rainbows when one tried to locate just what this policy and opinion is. If there are typically liberal opinions, these are either merely the conventions of opinion to which those who would be considered liberals must conform or, more respectably, they are the opinions to which most people come, if they adopt liberal attitudes in their dealings with and explorations of their fellows. When we are done with explaining the bad smells of evasion, amorphousness, lack of thoroughmindedness and, finally, fatuousness which always linger around even the living body of liberality, we see that they issue from the rot which sets in when liberal style and attitude attempts to make itself into its own self-contained and complete world in which its own style, instead of the world of things, people and societies which ought to be approached liberally, becomes the object of its attitude.

In style and attitude, liberal people are predisposed to listen with interest to those who differ. They are predisposed to see the good in others who differ, to see the truth in the opinions of those with whom they have some disagreement. Yet there are limits to the possibility and the desirability of liberalism, even when so generously construed. To keep a clear mind, a firm grip on our values and to avoid hypocrisy and patronage, we must at times be prepared to maintain other than liberal styles and attitudes. If we are not other than liberal (though not therefore illiberal, rather non-liberal) we cannot keep a grip even on our liberalism. For instance, one might have a very liberal attitude to what counts as art. But the same seriousness of interest which prevents one rejecting things which might seem too strange, too ordinary, too far from the usual array of things counted as art, which also make one summarily reject some things as rubbish, as boring and unimaginative. Even though some of these rejections will be mistakes, it is more important to make some of these errors than to suffer the loss of direction of enquiring movement, control of perception and confidence in judgement which is conceptually and causally involved in taking on more than the mind and sense can properly cope with and appraise.

Conventional wisdom has it that to be liberal is to be tolerant. And conventional criticism of liberality is either (from fascists, conservatives or marxists) that either the true liberal would tolerate even those who are brutally prejudiced, unjustly violent and simply scoundrels, and thus allow the extinction of the conditions of existent liberality of outlook, or else the liberal must, on liberal theory, be intolerant of the intolerant. Thus, it would follow, liberals must be intolerant of liberals in their intolerance of intolerance. But also intolerant of liberals if they are weak enough to tolerate intolerance.

Liberals can contrive an escape from this theoretical self-immolation if they can effectively distinguish first order and second order intolerance. First order intolerance has as its object all things other than intolerance itself. The liberal might like to define himself as tolerant of all attitudes except first order intolerance. But the distinction raises a problem more serious than the conundrum it was meant to solve. Is intolerance the worst thing in the world? If second order intolerance is to be permissible to a liberal (perhaps even obligatory) why should he not be intolerant (first order) of many other attitudes and beliefs? Is he to be intolerant of an admittedly nasty but minor intolerance of the way someone has her hair cut, but tolerant of those who bash and rob, or more quietly exploit and extort in their business dealings?

The answer is this. We should not attempt to define the liberal attitude to be always the correct one to take, or think that anything other than the liberal attitude is illiberality or intolerance. It scarcely needs to be said that tolerance is not the only virtue, and that like any other virtue, there is not virtue but rather Epaminondas-like foolishness in essaying to exhibit it in every kind of situation. Courage is a virtue, but much of the time it is not called for. One's lack of courage in those situations is not cowardice: the attempt to display it makes one a Quixote. (Similarly, one's lack of mercy in the normal situation when mercy is simply not in question, amounts to no kind of mercilessness.) Intolerance is a particular reactive attitude, which rejects what it does not understand, and does not want to understand it. Not being tolerant does not, in itself, amount to the reactive attitude of intolerance. Intolerance is also egoism whereas not tolerating something need not be from egoism. If I reject something out of intolerance, it is in part because it is something which is not what *I* hold, or because it contravenes what *I* hold. It might be thought that this egoism is inescapable, and that again we must see the fraudulence of liberality. Surely, if I oppose something, it is because it is other than or goes against something I hold. If I oppose it because *someone else* differs from it, or it contravenes what *he* holds, then either I am being merely, as it were, paid advocate, and I am not opposing it, I am merely acting the part of opposing it, or else I have made that other person's concerns my own — perhaps they are mine only because and only so long as the other person has them — they are borrowed — but still *I* have them. We have here the usual slipperiness of egoist theory. In genuine concern, one is, oneself, concerned. Egoist theory makes it seem that in genuine concern one is really concerned with oneself, the one who has the concern. If I oppose something, but not out of intolerance, then I oppose it because of what I hold, and not because of the fact that it is I who hold it. But more is required than this lack of egoism. One must also have a desire (and have acted seriously to satisfy that desire) to understand what one is opposing. It is in these ways and for these reasons, that to be objective in one's subjectivity involves having, among other styles and attitudes, liberal styles and attitudes.

True, being liberal is not enough. One cannot be objective and accept everything. One becomes committed to judging some things true and others false, some right and wrong, some good and some bad, some beautiful and others ugly. One cannot always be liberal, and liberality remains a virtue only in the company of many other different and sometimes competing intellectual and moral virtues. If one is to be objective then one cannot always be tolerant, and one cannot tolerate everything even when one is properly tolerant. But none of this is an excuse, morally or intellectually, for intolerance. Liberality is not only tolerance, it is not universal tolerance, yet it rejects intolerance of the intolerant. It is committed fully against intolerance, and though it opposes intolerance, if true to its liberality, it does this without intolerance.

To understand all is not to forgive all. And to understand all is not to sympathize with all. It is out of fear of sympathizing and being forgiving and thus, it is supposed, of losing one's own position, skidding across the pool of one's tears into the arms of one's opponents, that one engages intolerantly in one's opposition. Oppose and stand firm one must; blind, deaf and obdurate one mustn't and needn't be. Furthermore, it is possible that when we understand, we will sympathize, agree even and not even need to forgive. That is, we might discover the mistake was our own. The nastiest intellectual aspect of intolerance: it is set up as the guardian of purity of interest and commitment. Those who defend sending their children to a school dedicated to upholding a faith, or who proscribe the reading of certain books or the seeing of certain films or the discussion of certain issues will trot out the monsters of evil influence: the drug peddlars, those who use children as subjects for pornographic movies and any others who exploit childish or adult credulity, as "proof of the need for protection from evil". Their censoriousness and repressive bias in selection of what in the world is to be presented to those unlucky ones in their tender care, the self-deceptive, self-protectiveness of their repression of others is dressed up as wisdom and breadth of understanding shouldering its burden of responsibility. Those, too, who think it best to remain at a more expressive level (articulated philosophically by the emotive theory of ethics), a level of disgust, horror, hatred, "absolute rejection of the very idea of . . .", can trot out the monsters of recent history. Idi Amin, Al Capone, Hitler, Stalin, come out in a rush to gag and stupefy the liberal imagination.

We smell the rat we have to trap when we notice that Napoleon, Alexander "the Great" and Julius Caesar don't make it on this list. Once figures have receded well into the past, some degree of understanding becomes inevitable. It must have been as horrible to have been living in a village in Gaul when Caesar came through with his mighty armies, as it was for those in Guernica when the Nazis explored the techniques of terrorist bombing. Perhaps historians go too far in their quiet survey of all of these things being contained within and explained by the conditions and conceptions of their times. We lose much of our sense of the reality of the past, as times that were lived through just as we live through our own, when *The Conquest of Gaul* is more the story we hear, than the groans of those whose hacked bodies crawled off to die. Still, willy-nilly, finally we come up, aghast, for air, and have no choice but to understand the ideals which the Romans upheld, the way they were brought up as children, and the pressures to which they were subject as members of their society. Even if we had been educated to deploring, being disgusted at, hating and rejecting Caesar and what he stood for, curiosity, the perspective of historical distance, the fact that we know about Caesar only through a myriad of details which place his actions in context as we get to know about him would have prevailed. But inasmuch as understanding Caesar in his times involves, at least temporarily, abstaining from the expression of moral attitudes we seem to find so important to maintaining our values and our sense of identity, it equally involves abstaining from an initial praise or admiration for him as a great man of history. Some will, upon gaining their understanding, come to praise Caesar, rather than to bury him in the hall of monsters. Still, there is no excuse to revere great historical figures. The hideous sentimentality involved in doing so renders us incapable of a clear and consistent present use of moral criticism and appraisal. An historian must work against and abstain from employing his intolerance. Yet he must not, on that account, employ double standards with respect to the past.

So, to be liberal in style and outlook is to suffer but to maintain as inevitable some tension between revulsion and understanding of those who are monstrously illiberal. On the one hand, it is scarcely the mark of a deeply liberal outlook to take only or primarily a detached scientific concern for Stalin. But if a liberal outlook must include, even begin with, deploring, hating, having repugnance for and reviling, at least it must swiftly move towards being scathing, sarcastic and satirical: that is, these antipathetic emotions are held at mind's length, a cooler perception is made of the character, motives and strengths and weaknesses of the illiberal monster, and these intellectualized teeth returned to the jaws of one's repugnance. At any rate, if people still will ask mind-and-concept-deadening questions such as, "Is objectivity possible in matters of morals and politics?", it is in some such terms that replies can be made.

There is no doubt it is now common to contrast a liberal with a radical (whether left or right) outlook, and to think of the liberal as someone who would leave things largely alone, attempting improvement by only careful and slight adjustments in the social web. But this is merely conventional thought. A radical is one who would understand the roots of what he or she wishes to change, and who will then take steps to bring about changes, and who will take these steps in terms of radical understanding. So unless one wishes merely to conventionally dub as radical the extreme actions taken by those who are desperate and the actions of extremists who adopt a desperatist philosophy even though they are not in desperate straits ("on behalf of the oppressed"), it must be made an open question whether those whose philosophy and actions are to bring about a revolution by armed force are "radicals", or just one more set of victims of the conventional militaristic thinking and feeling of the systems they oppose. So, though it is common, it is prejudical to call liberals those "who mean well but who will not see or take the actions necessary for securing their ends". Certainly many who call themselves liberals are like that and, as their "radical" critics say, quickly ally themselves with oppressive authorities when the going gets tough and their lives or even simply their ways of life are threatened. Not to idealize liberal attitudes, it may be best to admit that the real, genuine liberal attitude is as really liable to such cowardly self-serving retreats as is real radicalism to taking the initiative in the use of guns and bombs. But there is no need to define liberal attitudes and actions in terms of such evasion, cowardice and abdication from judgement and commitment, as there is no need to define radicalism in terms of the preparedness to enforce one's aims on the basis of their moral superiority.

It is too sanguine to suppose that the most thoroughgoing love of liberality will always commit one to avoiding bloodshed. There is nothing admirable in allowing people to be killed rather than disabling or risking the life of an attacker. And it is absurd and wrong to commit suicide to avoid the situation. That adds to the killing and deaths and saves no-one. It may be only a callous joke, for all that, for the liberal to say, "I killed him, but not intolerantly"! The liberal, unlike the attitude typical of TV cowboys and supporters of "People's Liberation Front's, rejects the glory of cutting down the guilty, yet does he thus guarantee his liberality, or at least his lack of illiberality when he is morally forced to violent actions? It is not clearly so. Just as some people lose their life, a limb, their sanity, their sight, their sexuality in armed conflicts, so others may lose their best feelings; they may know they will be permanently much the worse for the actions they will take; they may become the very kind of people they now despise and fear. Nevertheless this is not necessarily the best and sufficient reason not to take actions with those consequences; one would have to suppose oneself the most important person in the world and one's good soul the most precious possession, in order to think so.

Finally, the question whether the liberal attitude is consistent with taking violent, even fatal action, or whether one says that a person who is liberal can be forced by circumstances to lose his or her liberality whichever line is taken becomes an unhappy choice of terms. Yet, in the clearest terms, keeping the clearest head, we admit that the actions of violence and killing to which a person with liberal attitudes can be forced by circumstance are not themselves acts of liberality nor born of a liberal attitude. They are acts of desperation and born of a desperate situation. At most one can say that liberal attitude and opinion do not unequivocally and universally prohibit such acts. Still, it has the utmost repugnance and horror of them, and the utmost contempt for those who would surround them with the aura of glory. Though we might be easily mocked for doing so, we refuse to ally ourselves with intolerance and the repressiveness of force, the substitution of fighting for arguing and trading, even when we are forced into actions visibly indistinguishable from those taken in a sadistic or aggressive or glorying spirit. In being liberal, one rejects the militarist rhetoric (but not all the militant rhetoric) of people's liberation struggles, as much as one supports the need for radical social change in the face of entrenched injustice. Equally one rejects the cold war real politik rhetoric of Kissingers and Haigs, and Reagan's new smiling old-face of cowboy-fascism. If our opposition to the pseudo-scientific bloody roads to utopia of Marxists is liberal, then it easily and with full heat is opposed to the merciless operations of capitalism in the Third World, and equally to the sullen murderous threatening weather of Soviet-style act and word against all forms of spiritedness. (Their special definition of hooliganism.)

Partiality and prejudice

To maintain our objectivity, we must maintain our liberality, though we must live in an acute consciousness of the tensions within it, and recognize that we must develop and defend many other different and competing values. There can be no doubt that the virtues of liberality are scarcely recognized, partly because they are buried beneath the weak and self-serving forms of liberalism which have just been described, on the one hand, and because of the fears of the repressive and self-centredly ambitious, on the other. The values of liberality are always in constant slide towards a liberalism of indifferentism and cowardly fear both of the feelings themselves which a clear mind and clear perception of people and surroundings and circumstance inevitably produce, and of the actions which may be to our cost and at our peril, which such perception and feeling lay upon us.

It is doubly dangerous that it is now a conventionalized and thus boring truism that objectivity requires impartiality. Doubly dangerous, since to be bored is to be blinded, and thus one is blinded to the importance and striking theoretical difficulties surrounding impartiality on the one hand, and to the need for it, and for no excuse for its absence to be made upon the inevitable mass and mess of our operative partialities, on the other. It is easy to become cynical, too, about impartiality, since those who do not or will not understand it well propose a lack of partiality as if it were impartiality. Any child wants to lift this cloak. Does one become a god in the process of becoming an adult, a parent, a judge or executioner?

To be impartial is still to have partialities and, depending on circumstance and fortune, to have to deal with issues on which one has specific partialities of thought and feeling. Without our distinctiveness of taste, we have only dullness of perception, and therefore not the perceptiveness required for objectivity. And to allow this is to begin to come to terms, too, with the problems about being cool and calm, about having to be involved, warm or hot, which attend all our attempts to keep a fair view while still really looking with intent and direction and sensitive response.

Partiality is essential to any objectivity, though it is equally a sharp risk. Jane is partial to old buildings, and thinks it is very important that they be preserved. Samantha is indifferent to them, and thinks Jane is a crank. Jane drags Samantha along (very emotional, very subjective, that Jane) to see some buildings due for demolition. Samantha has hitherto only glanced at them from the window of her car; she has never dwelt on them, let alone in one. Jane sits Samantha down, gives her a drink, makes her relax. She's not arguing, or citing evidence, or establishing "objectively" the worth of old buildings. The strength, proportions, elegance, restfulness of the old place starts to work on Samantha; Jane says a few things about the history of the building; how it relates to other buildings in the area. Samantha realizes her previous ignorance of or prejudice about such buildings; it is the partial Jane who has been in contact with the object, who is more objective. You might think that Jane is more objective about something than Samantha if, when they know the same things about it, Jane is less partial to it than Samantha. But this is not so. Jane and Samantha may know the same things but Samantha is now indifferent to them. Jane is partial to them and continues to remain in contact with them and the issues connected with them, looking to see whether there is more to the issue. Jane is more objective though more partial, even if she does not come to know more about the issue than Samantha.

The opposite of partiality is indifference, not impartiality, just as boredom, not disinterest, is the opposite of interest. Impartiality does have to do with objectivity; perhaps it is a necessary condition. In part, it means not being affected by irrelevant considerations. Not being affected by the colour of a person's skin when judging in a legal case; not making a difference whether one's child is a boy or a girl when handing out pocket money, praise or blame (except insofar as it *is* relevant to do so). A person is partial to, or not partial or averse to, somebody. Talk of impartiality is different in form and object. One is said to be impartial (or not) about an issue, or impartial in one's actions towards someone. One cannot be said to be impartial (or not) to some person or thing or issue. Partiality is a preference. Indifference is a lack of preference, aversion is a preference against something. Impartiality is an attitude, a way of conducting oneself, a way of *handling* our thoughts, feelings, preferences, etc.; an ideal in the light of which we attempt to control our mind and behaviour. A judge may be partial to the defendant. They may be lovers; he couldn't find a public reason to escape being judge for that case. Perhaps she appeared in court under a different name. Probably he will be made to judge impartiality. He may be so agitated that he cannot even think, let alone judge. But to say that he is partial, very partial, is not to deny that he will be impartial in his dealings and judgement. He may realize that to keep her respect he must control his feelings and actions. If he treats her in a special way, he insults her with the insinuation that her innocence will not become apparent in the normal course of justice. He knows she is guilty? Then the problem is *not* one of impartiality, but of the competing claims of sentiment and justice. He fears she may be guilty? Then the question is whether he can bear his fear, and conduct the trial impartially to its proper, as yet unknown, conclusion. That is, if he wishes to be impartial. If he simply decides to get her off by hook or by crook, that is nothing to do with impartiality in his attitude. It's a different phenomenon, a different kind of action, and subject to a different kind of appraisal.

With all our partialities, still we need to keep our cool, in order to develop and to hang on to our objectivity. Yet this almost truism must be set against the costs of doing so, and the style of steady balance we maintain. Is our proud cool balance merely the vacant stillness of the perfect but unloaded and undisturbed beam balance, or is it a steadiness of cool coping with exhilaration and fear?

In a W.C. Fields' film, two young innocents accept a ride across the USA with a middle aged couple. Continually, the innocents remain cool about situations they cause, which situations and their coolness produce speechless fury in the older couple, who see the real danger in the situation and the innocents' detachment from any responsibility for being the cause, or for being the cure, and the barely amused unconcern of the innocents at their efforts to retrieve the situation. By nicely not seeing any aspect of justice, the innocents remain cool and detached; by not seeing that the possibility of their surviving while in so pretty a state exists only in a world where the others carry for them, but only seeing what they wish to of what is going on, they preserve their illusion of being able simply to see what is going on.

Coolness can be maintained at the price of cultivated detachment; that is, by wilful ignoring of disturbing fact; passion, even to the point where continued objectivity is not possible, may be the consequence of contact with the real situation. Relative coolness in the face of the same situation for two observers with equally good senses, is no measure of their relative objectivity.

It would, of course, be a wild reaction against deadening conventionalism about objectivity to say that coolness is *proof* of objectivity destroying detachment. First aid experts at the scene of traffic accidents have learned to admit fully the horrible situation, while moderating the extent of their felt response so as to allow practical help to be given. But this is not a detachment of indifference but control within involvement. These reflections on involvement, emotion, coolness and partiality now leads us from this transitional discussion to the next main theme.

Control and cold fixity

We need some sense of control of ourselves and even some degree of control over others and other things in order not to feel an inflated need to fully control and therefore to overcontrol ourselves and others and other things, when coming to know them. Such needful control is not "mastery". As Hegel famously shows, the "master" is debarred from proper knowledge of the "slave". Self-control, too, is not self-mastery. If we must take on "mastery" of ourselves or others, we won't have the responsiveness or sensitive tact which is needed in order to deal with people or things as they are themselves. It is by a deliberate coolness which is predicated upon rather than maintained by ignoring perceived fact, that we can achieve the control which is necessary (where involvement and emotion would otherwise be too great) for retaining contact without "forcing" things. Control allows efficient use of resources; it allows us to find direction, and gives us the steadiness for focus and the ability to unfocus when clarity would be damaging. (Obsessive focusing.) The absence of control, then, causes a long of momentum; either by dissipation or downright destruction of the thing in motion. (These thermal and these dynamic metaphors are to be focused on later. At the moment, the point is to touch on their connection.)

Sometimes it seems that objectivity is possible but repulsive — a lessening and a degradation. In much the same mood and outlook it also seems to be quite impossible — sometimes a will-o'-the-wisp and sometimes a receding horizon. Both of these opposed feelings arise from the same error. We need a relief from overinvolvement, agitation, lack of perspective — the sheer overpoweringness and sometimes simple exhaustingness of what we see, what others do, what we do, what we think, the news we read, the generalizations

and specifications we realize. So we withdraw, either or both intellectually and emotionally from what and who and how we know.
Thus we achieve a kind of calm, but either a tense or frozen calm.
Thought and reflection are possible in this state; we can transcend
the situation, either going above it, considering it from a great
height (the attitude of affected superiority), standing beside our
position (obliqueness, wit, or downright evasion in perception and
response). But this kind of calm is both unstable and infertile. Since
it is achieved by a lessening or cessation of initiative, the person's
security in his "objectivity" is highly subject to the disruptive influences of others. Insofar as we make our own way, in the many
senses of that word, we have the momentum necessary for being
able to receive the stimulus, opposition and shocks of the differing
views of others, without losing the sense that though we are subjects in our objectivity, so is anyone else; we can be influenced
without losing the direction of enquiry and coherence of outlook
essential to any discovery, including the discovery that we had been
mistaken.

To be "objective" in a good sense is to be in touch with the
"object" of concern whether that "object" is a human being, some
other animal, a machine, a static object, an "abstract" problem,
concept or a theme. This being in touch requires having some consciousness as well as sedimented knowledge of the manner and
motive of your approach and touch, and in turn this requires that
you often be reflective. To be accurately reflective you must be
steady and calm. Not that being calm and being reflective are the
same. You can calmly and reflectively sip your tea, or calmly but
neither reflectively nor reflectingly send a poor wretch to the
gallows. And you may engage or indulge in violent, fractured or
distorted reflections when upset, excited, desirous or angry.
Though these uncalm reflections may equally bear witness to some
reality, accurate and persistent reflection from which we can learn
requires steadiness and calm.

When upset or agitated one must calm oneself, if another is not
there who can and will do it. It is probable that when you must
calm and steady yourself, that you choose the less thoughtful and
unreflective course and do no more than restrain your bodily
actions and expressions. This is the obvious lapse since, in the
nature of the case, one is not in the best reflective control of what
one is doing. In this state of forced restraint rather than of calm
steadiness, one is highly disposed to various forms of behaviour,
rather than being flexibly prepared to engage in chosen conduct.

We are, as Ryle said without understanding much of what he was saying, "disposed" to behave, as a fragile glass is "disposed" to break when tapped. This is most easily recognized in someone who is restraining himself from what he would do (strike, grasp, abuse, admire, tremble, communicate his fear), and is much the same, but with a duller more muffled effect when a person is seeking calm and steadiness in a more central and internal fashion, but by stifling himself, distracting himself or deceiving himself about his feelings, thoughts and wishes.

Thus, while actually most uncalm, and without calming and steadying oneself, one can wilfully force or forge a kind of outer (and even inner) mock-up or toy steadiness. This may be necessary. We can vitally need states which we do not happen to possess or know how to produce; the state in which we find ourselves may be the very one which puts out of play some usual capacity to control or to change our state. But though we may need these forms of superficial moderation, they should be recognized as the makeshift and inadequate devices which they are; the danger lies in the fact that these fabrications easily and quickly become styles fixed by habit and recognized as adequate and satisfactory in social convention because convenient. Their defect is that our energy and concentration are too much diverted into maintaining the unstable balance of impulse and restraint, so that we are too tight to allow the flexible even roving eye without which we get only fixed and barren perceptions and reflections which mislead us into an empty, one might say a para-occupied view of the world. This view they promote is thus ineluctably egocentric. It is the freely moving "eye" which allows us, though it is not sufficient by itself to guarantee us, both clear perception and a strong but unshocked sense of the multitude of separate centres of consciousness around us.

The fixed gaze and totalitarianisms

Objectivism is marked by this fixity of vision. Physicalism is an example of such an objectivism. In a different work, one would analyse the details of errors in argument and concept within physicalism. But here my task is to characterize the outlook, the false consciousness of physicalism — the kind of vision which makes plausible and inviting the view that in reality there is no more than electrons, positrons, neutrons and protons, etc. Physicalism can seem an inevitable consequence of taking seriously the discoveries of modern physics. The physicalist view is a philosophical fixity of thought which is so intense that it cannot think of itself as thought; it can think only of the object of its thought, and so feels itself to be utterly "objective", and everything else to be soft minded; it is angry in this last accusation, for the very existence of soft-mindedness is enough to upset it ontologically. Hard-mindedness is, logically speaking, as much of a problem for the physicalist view as soft-mindedness, but it hides its own existence in its hard minded insistence that there is "only atoms in the void", "only electrons, positrons, etc.", only "mathematical points embedded in force fields" (Quine). Physicalism is a hard unyielding intellectual stare, as the hard unyielding social stare is the rude dramatic act of making out that the one stared at is an excrescence, an object stupidly "there" over and against the world, and which aims to make its victim and perhaps the starer him or herself forget the subjectivity of the starer.

Impassivity is the more glutinous alternative to brittle, fragile, icy or glassy calm. Icy, brittle calm is a little more intelligent than impassivity, for it is only a pretence of living death. Impassivity is a living death. The brittle calm is also more vulnerable than impassivity, though at the same time more aggressive and fear provoking in its fearfulness. In forced steadiness, one implicitly fears the blow which would shatter; one cannot be confident of making the intelligently elastic response which those with real steadiness and wide knowledgeability can make upon accepting a blow to their body or ideas. They can reply temperately even if countering with passion. In contrast, the rigid minded and cold eyed, sensing that they bring a glass jaw to intellectual bouts, must defend their view tooth and nail. The fear cannot but turn into a resentful paranoia, too, since if the objectivist is nettled out of frigidity or impassivity by sharp active criticisms the subjectivity in objectivism floods to the forefront. He betrays his objectivism in betraying the very subjectivity which it was the point of his stance to hide and his opinions to deny as fundamental. The objectivist thinks and reacts to criticism, "How dare you make me forget myself!" Indeed, how dare one expose the denial of passion as a passion for denial.

The objectivist cannot stand swift moving, live, even temperately passionate argument, seeing in this only "subjective involvement". The blind feeling of inward icy calm is that there is only one's own view, and that everything else is illusion. (All lies! All lies!) This goes then with the notorious feeling that those who disagree become, in so doing, one's opponents and that they must be (as

Lady Caroline Lamb said of Byron) "Mad, bad and dangerous to know". To be fair to physicalism, one must remark that any view might be held in an objectivist manner. Ironically, Husserl comes closest to objectivism in his attempt to represent a total transcendence from ordinary subjectivity into transcendental subjectivity. It is just that views such as physicalism, Marxism and Christianity are convenient Aunt Sallys; since they define themselves as all embracing totalizing views, encompassing everything else as subsidiary.

Extreme fixity of gaze, physiologically with the eye, and intellectually with the brain, fails to effectively record information. So the insistence on "One Truth Overall", as one has it most crudely and socially in Christianity, Marxism and "scientific" physicalism, always carries the insister to a precarious perch overlooking nihilism. Those who value their intellect and senses are right to react against the cultivation of a Christian wide eyed innocence and vacant mindedness necessary to the reception and containment of mysteries and contradictions. This deceptive and contrary conceit breeds stupidity coupled with the cunning of serpents which those "innocents" must practise to make their way both in debate and in material institutional power against the world. Those who would cherish being sensitive, sensual and sensible and who will follow the implications of these powers of understanding will not believe there is a God. They will not yearn for a unified limit of all goodnesses, since they will observe that there are many kinds of good, that the realization of them all, equally and in combination in one being, is a theoretical impossibility and, most centrally, that the only realization of these goodnesses which can be openly appraised and inspected is that which is to be found in humans, other animals, their artefacts and art objects and their ways of life and institutions. Yet those who reject a Christianity they once possessed must not scoff at the Christians' fear and warnings of nihilism. Christianity (and Judaism) have already backed themselves into a corner with respect to nihilism. Christianity cannot find value in humans and their affairs as they exist in themselves; it must refer these to an unseen and mysterious source and background, otherwise, it thinks, everything would be permissible; nothing would be preferable to anything else. It is because Christianity itself is on the brink of nihilism that it can only see those who leave it as destined for nothing. It is because it really does offer nothing beyond its illusions and confusions except the simply human wisdom and errors of the Hebrew prophets and Jesus and his followers that it cannot offer any vital and direct understanding or appraisal of those ideas. It is because the Christian voice has to be the true voice of God that it cannot dare to recognize what it is saying. It is because of all this and more that to reject Christianity can seem to leave one with nothing.

Where Christianity exploits our moral uncertainties and fear of death, Marxism exploits our most ordinary love of justice and hatred of oppression. Then it tries, by being "scientific", to rise so far above these ordinary emotions as to see ordinary morality as mere "bourgeois preoccupations which only serve the interests of the ruling class". But, severed from our bourgeois moral preoccupations, what reason have we to work for justice and to relieve the oppressed? The revolutionary absolutism of negating all the values of capitalist society, of despising reform as still embodying the values of a society which is yet to be and which must be transformed, is what breeds the illusion that one can get beyond the complex, localized and theoretically and practically conflicting values which always divert the locomotive of revolutionary progress into side tracks and dead ends, which anarchistically uncouple the guard's van, opportunistically detach and divert the dining car for those with more gustatory than revolutionary spirit and appropriate even the whistle for the musically rather than the practically minded. There must always be such a task for the guardians of the revolution: "So much to do, and so little time!" (Peter Seller's rising rock star). Of course the revolutionary thinks that he has found by negation a place for all of these apparently diverse values. He claims that freedom of expression, the culinary, the musical arts and the rest are to be engaged in, allowed, encouraged, insofar as they aid the revolution. Yet this, however dreadful in historical practice, is merely ridiculous in logical theory. If all values other than those of bringing about the revolution are justified only insofar as they aid the revolution, then of what value is the revolution? What was supposed to be wrong with the old society? That the poor had too little bread, too few musical instruments and too little leisure in which to play what they had, and that everyone, rich and poor alike were locked in a state of cruel competitiveness? Well, then, if the revolution towards a better society is to maintain its moral validity, then the military values of the revolutionary (those of unquestioning loyalty, endurance, self-denial, indifference to the suffering and inflicting of pain, injury and death and, in most general terms, living for the future rather than for the present) must be recognized to be in real and continual conflict with the values which are supposed to justify and to necessitate the revolution.

Finally, some ontological or metaphysical reflections. What has been said about the need to easily change one's perspective and horizons would have to be recognized by anyone who was freely perceiving and thinking; the trouble is that the seeking of a single minded unifying framework for everything has for a very long time been lauded as a virtue; a virtual virtuous requirement of the serious search for Truth. Those who did not have this ideal were mere subjectivists or relativists. This permanent obsessiveness about one frame of thought and values is the degenerate aftermath of what should have been a temporary phase of intense single minded search for and construction of some unifying theory. Those who attempt to make a permanent extension of the moment feel that, if there is the slightest departure from the unified ideal, everything will crumble.

Consider, to leave the political examples, Hume's obsession with a proposition which he himself argued to be unprovable, that every event has a cause; think of Sartre's counter-obsession that if for even a moment we lost our freedom we could never again regain it; reflect on the ideas of recent materialists that it is just too extraordinary that in a vast universe of only basic physical particles, there should be, in just one corner, this phenomenon of consciousness. J.J.C. Smart, who expressed this feeling particularly well, confessed that he had no strict argument on the matter, but that to accept the existence of consciousness flouted his sense of the plausible. The answer to the feeling, then, lies in reminding ourselves of the plurality of facts and conceptual forms, and in regaining a free capacity to shift our perspectives. Smart has, in his imagination, placed consciousness as one thing alone against elementary particles. The feeling of utterly unique contrast thus produced is a distortion. Smart would have been as unable to translate the statements of the geological history of this planet into statements of elementary physics, as to translate statements about one's consciousness into those terms. No-one would say, no-one would have motive to say, that there are, on the one hand, the vastly complex movements of elementary particles which make up volcanoes and other land forms and, on the other, something else, the eruption of volcanoes, erosion of mountains, formation of sedimentary rocks and the rest. Nor would anyone deny that these changes and movements have an explanation in the terms of physics. Yet it is as hard to bring a volcano as to bring consciousness into a picture which allows no character or description except that contained within basic physics. The record and description of the geological history of the earth cannot be reduced to or replaced by any multitude of descriptions of the elementary particles; the perception of the objects and events in the formation of the earth is not identical with the perception (necessarily indirect, through instruments) of elementary particles; the theoretically imaginative thought of the phases of geological history is not the same as the theoretically imaginative thought of the movements of the particles which compose the objects whose movements and changes constitute the material for that history. It is foolish to deny that volcanoes are composed of the elementary particles, and equally foolish to suppose that a story in terms of elementary particles presents *the* reality of things, whereas a story in the large scale about volcanoes and lava flows presents only a superficial appearance of the world. There are no degrees of reality. The same conceptual points hold for the emergence of forms of life. The biological history of the world is the history of what is composed of elementary particles, but is not told in terms of those elementary physical particles necessary to and constituting the stuff of that biological development. So too for the "emergence" of consciousness. It is not to the detriment of the importance of the emergence of consciousness that the sense in which, undeniably, it emerges from earlier forms which do not involve it is just the same *sense* in which volcanoes emerge from earlier phases of the earth too uniformly hot and liquid to allow volcanoes. The difference of importance is not in the sense of "emergence" but in the greater importance to us of consciousness. Smart foxed himself by thinking of just one thing, consciousness, set over and above everything else considered in the terms of just one preferred science. He felt he had a sense of extreme objectivity, of entirely transcending the anthropomorphic point of view, and just thinking of the universe as it is, just electrons, positrons and the rest, and then thinking, "The rest of what we talk about and seem to feel, see, touch and so on must be some sort of experiential or conceptual sham".

What he describes is just an example of a very common loss of objectivity which we suffer when an interest fixes our mind in its own terms, makes us lose our sense of ourselves as subjects for the objects we are considering, and inhibits our freedom of intellectual movement from theory to theory, from outlook to outlook. It makes us feel that something must be so, that it couldn't possibly be otherwise, instead of allowing us to look and to find out whether it is so (Wittgenstein). If we look first and think afterwards, we happily accept the multitude of differing kinds of description of things which is warranted by observation and experiment, and any of the differing kinds of explanation which have their own case to recommend them, just so long as they are not in logical contradiction.

Fixity of sensory and of intellectual gaze must swiftly turn into a boring vision, simply because of the lack of variety. We cannot value things in the conditions and to the extent that they bore us. This is one reason why value seems an enormous problem within single frame fixed perspective outlooks. Within such outlooks it seems that it can be conquered only by evasion, obscurity or heroic acts. Christianity loses sight of the intrinsic value of the sensual, sensible world and even of people in their own right. Christianity has to reimport from a mysterious realm and from an absolute "being" whose "goodness", "wisdom", "justice" are utterly different from our own and yet, inconsistent with this, sufficiently the same so that if human justice, for instance, is modelled on God's, it will be justice and not something entirely different. If it is a pure and absolute thing beyond our comprehension, it will say nothing about our human problems of justice. Let it touch the human problems as when God's edicts (through the voice of the Church) attempt to advise the state on war, abortion, sexuality or violence against repressions. The "Voice" is then as ordinary, rough and questionable as that of human justice. Like every other voice, it involves questionable competing claims. Thus it will not answer the doubts and uncertainties which threaten our everyday moral sense and confidence. Only when we get to heaven will we realize the true values which have somehow (somehow, indeed!) underlain and underwritten our everyday preferences, priorities and indignations and admirations.

In similar style, unhappy with the contradictions of value in present society, we are supposed, in revolutionary spirit, to transcend these in revolutionary action towards a later state of society when, and only when, real moral perception can inform us of the extent to which we did well to embark on the enterprise at all. Without evasion, but with no more satisfactory resolution, the physicalist throws the whole game to the ground, and denies the truth of all statements of value, since they are not to be found in the temple of physics. If clear and consistent he will claim that all statements of the value of physics are false, and that therefore there can be no reason to prefer it to irrationality. It is no use and it is too late for him to cry "But physics is true!", for, if nothing is really of value, then neither is truth.

Emotion and Emotionalism

We must be involved in an issue, with a person, in an activity, in order to become objective about it, even though being involved is not all there is to objectivity. Thus we risk the appearance and actuality of bias and emotionalism. The immediacy of impingement, if we succeed in securing it, tends to induce strongly held and confident, even passionate, opinion. Such holding of opinion entails the equal conviction that those who differ are wrong, and have gained their opinions secondhand, or that they have made some error of perception, inattention, mistake of logic, or ignored some relevant fact. Such a conviction is extremely annoying to those who differ, particularly if the confident person is correct — and those who differ are being brought to realize that their opinions are secondhand or have been carelessly observed or thought out. They are liable to feel and to deceive themselves into thinking that the person who is involved and confident in his or her closeness to the facts is arrogant, dogmatic, one-eyed and biased. Arrogance, vanity, conceit, narcissism — these will be considered soon. At the moment, it is dogmatism which is to be distinguished from confidence, strength and persistence in opinion and attitude. It is emotion as warmth, involvement and wholeheartedness in argument and discussion which I wish to distinguish from emotionalism.

To be convinced that something is so, is to be convinced that those who differ are wrong. The denial of this is illogicality, not a lack of dogmatism. Still, the way in which one's ego becomes involved when one argues with those who differ may quickly cause a degeneration in one's stance. What proceeds from confident knowledge becomes stated in dogmatic assertiveness. It is a strange thing this: even where we have knowledge, we tend towards speaking from shady ground and from suspect motives. Even where we can be right, we would rather get a short term ego boost. "I say it is true because it is I who have thought it." How stupid, when in any case I know it to be a fact! The dismay for the ego is that as known fact, it slips out of my private possessive grasp. *My* contribution to the world becomes *"my contribution"*. In the long run it is better to learn the pleasure of disinteredness. It may be exhilarating to sweep people off their feet, but if you don't go on carrying them, they are let down. Then beware. To begin to speak out of your conviction, instead of out of what convinces you, is to sweep yourself off your own feet. The inflated ego has become a clown's balloon, eluding his own grasp. To become dogmatic is to come to force one's ideas onto oneself and onto others, to stick to them strongly and to want others to hold them on account of the fact that one holds them and that they are precious possessions and part of oneself, rather than because of the power and clarity given by their source — the original resolved attention to the appropriate object.

To be objective about something is to put oneself in the best attitude and position for getting to know and to understand the thing. To suppose that this should be done without emotion is to suppose an absurdity. At best it is a confusion with the wise injunction to avoid emotionalism. We should be goggle eyed if asked to love without sentiment, but would understand if we were warned against sentimentality. The emotion with which we think or perceive is included within the manner in which we think or perceive, and it is nonsense to suggest that we might perceive or think in no manner. The normal manner of perception and thought is with some emotion. We perceive or think with interest or curiosity, in elation or depression, warmly or coldly, with love, hate or indifference. Abnormally, as actions and words may be passionless, as an aberration from the normal keenness of meant deeds and the meaning of felt words, so, too, thought and perception may suffer the lack of emotion. It is a dispirited state of low perceptiveness. It should be conceded that there is a curious feeling of "objectivity" connected with emotionless thought and perception. What shall we say about this feeling of emotionless thought and perception? It is out of linguistic propriety that we say emotionless thought and perception. The emotion is still there in the same way that feeling is still there when we feel numb. It is a curious and relatively uninforming feeling, not a complete absence of feeling. Certainly it would be an illusion to suppose that this "objective" emotionless thinking was intrinsically more logical or far seeing. Someone's spirited, fervent, cantankerous, generous or mean minded remarks may show one, with sudden upset, realms of implications and of gaps in what has been proposed which were undreamed of by an emotionless mind. We can speculate whether all emotionless thought and perception have an emotional meaning which the person or observer, through shock, torpor of mind, suppression or repression is not able to recognize or to describe. Certainly it is often the case that apparently emotionless conduct often expresses repressed emotion. A person might think, perceive and speak emotionlessly when someone they love suddenly dies. A person feels that his or her love or anger has no right to exist, or that its existence is too much of a danger and speaks of it, if at all, emotionlessly. Suddenly it glows or blazes with one or the other, and it is only from this point of clear emotion that objectivity begins.

If there were strictly emotionless thought and perception, in which we think about and perceive things which affect us in no way at all, neither with boredom, curiosity, love, hate, like or dislike, it would be a very rare thing. It can scarcely from the daily stuff of getting to know things as they are. It might be said in reply that objectivity is rare. It might be accepted that spurious objectivity is a state of repressed or numb emotion, which must be repudiated because the person is not really in touch with things, neither with their own feelings nor with the objects of those feelings. Yet it might be insisted that a real objective thought and perception would be entirely devoid of feeling.

To follow this last line of thought is to follow one of the natural tendencies of thought and to be influenced by one of the inbuilt suggestions of the word "objectivity" − that we be as objects treating objects, or at least treating things as if they were objects. Now, to follow this as a policy is to lapse into spurious objectivity, that of repressing or pretending not to have the subjectivity which is our own personal identity. If we ever happened to find ourselves with a completely unfelt thought or perception, this must be a mere matter of chance. For to restrict the field of objectivity so that we may be sure to find ourselves unconcerned, unmoved, uninvolved, is to make objectivity useless to us. Our real problems are how to relate objectively to things and people as they are, not to them as they would appear to be if we imposed extraordinary conditions upon our relating to them. So we need an objectivity which operates within our concerns, our emotions and our involvements. Objectivity is something we can aim at. We can improve ourselves in it. Though, for these reasons, objectivity is not to be identified with the absence of emotion, nor is the absence of emotion to be taken as necessary to objectivity, the occasional existence of more or less emotionless thought and perception is valuable as a contrast to ordinary life and acts as a clue to our discovery of, or as a guide, to the forged but not spurious creation of our detachments within involvement. It is these controlled detachments which are essential moments in our maintaining a sensitive grasp and judicious appraisal in our involving contacts.

Objectivity requires balances between detachment and involvement. These balances must be balanced; sometimes half-detached, half-involved; sometimes fully involved, sometimes wholly detached; oscillating between detachment and involvement; a persisting insisting detachment, or an insisting persistent involvement. Objectivity requires balances between, on the one hand, valuing things as good, as bad, as evil; as right, as wrong, as unspeakable. On the other hand it requires, no less, taking things neutrally no matter what they are like, merely to see without moral judgement what they are and what they are doing and why they are like that. We cannot write a coherent history if we will not judge its figures, but we cannot find the array of facts for judgement if we will not put off judgement for a while. But not forever. We need the power to relinquish and to regain our valuing and disvaluing them. If one makes the conventional identification of the neutral attitude of neither valuing or disvaluing with that of being scientific, then it follows that the scientific attitude is one part (but just one part) of being objective.

Objectivity requires balances between being in control and being controlled, whether by other people, other animals or unliving things. Again the balances must be balanced. Sometimes half-controlled, half-controlling; at times one wholly controls, at others one is wholly controlled, whether by one's own thoughts and feelings, another's or by the unliving once alive, or the merely inanimate. To be objective we must be free to think, feel and act as we would, but it requires no less that we relinquish freedom in order that other things and people have or find their proper place without warfare. Only if we sometimes relinquish freedom in this way, become subject, can we perceive what they are like in their unconstraints and discover, too, what our reality is for them in their loss of constraint. There are more balances. Our emotions must expand and be expressed or we cannot real-ize ourselves; we will not be real and will not know what we are or why we act. Equally, our emotions must be restrained in expression and even constrained in themselves, for the calm we need as observers or as agents, or because those around us need calm to be observant. And, no less, we may need to be upset before we become observant. Faulty, broken isolated and isolating observation may be the only alternative to none.

It may be in bad faith that the having of emotions with respect to something or someone is reckoned incompatible with objectivity. Someone's vulnerability to error or bias is made the butt of disparagement, rather than any actual proven error A fear of emotion emotionally confuses it with emotionalism. "You are looking at this emotionally" might be a fair comment on someone's having substituted emotion for argument or observation. Equally it may be an unfair attention to the emotion with which someone argues or observes. It is then the "deplorer of emotion", frightened by the force of the argument, who fails to consider the argument presented or the observation made. Because one detests an opinion, one might emotionally bring forward reasons against it. By itself this does not constitute emotionalism. One substitutes emotion for argument when one's detesting something, instead of the reasons for one's detestation, becomes the reason against it.

Reasons for thought and action may be started with or without emotion, but cannot float free of all emotion. If one opposes the logging of a rare rain forest, the reasons being the beauty of the forest, the lives of the birds and animals which depend upon it and the delight some humans take in these things, then these may well be miscalled emotional considerations in contrast with the practical reasons for logging — the profits which will be made, the employment which will be created, the mechanics' work on tractors, the furniture which will be built and the newspapers which will be printed. The illusion of emotion and sentiment being set against practical unemotional considerations is dispelled as soon as one enquires into what makes considerations practical or economic. "Furniture" sounds with "solid", "manufactured" and "saleable". What is the upshot of the practical activities? People sit in the furniture and read in comfort the magazine from the paper pulp. They invite their friends and are pleased to make them at ease. They ask their enemies and are pleased to show their superior status. The points of importance upon which practical activities depend are no less a matter of sentiment and emotion than taking pleasure in walking in a forest, or watching what moves, or simply caring that what lives there should have its existence whether observed by people or not. If people profit financially from destroying a forest, what is the advantage of this, if they do not enjoy the feeling of power from simply having money, or the admiration they accord themselves or receive from others for being astute, or if they do not enjoy the objects or services they can buy? To call reasons for action emotional merely because the facts given as reasons would not be reasons but for the emotional involvements of the person concerned is to categorize all reason as emotional. This is not to say that emotion automatically turns fact into good reason for some action. Emotion itself, too, many be good or it may be bad.

The role of emotion is equally vital when it comes to reasons for belief or for opinion or for thinking something to be so, as it is in the case of reason for action. Emotion, though it may lead us into error, in wishful or in apprehensive thinking, also fuels sharp minded enquiry. In exasperation with our own or someone else's vague or inaccurate grasp of the facts, in bafflement at how living things can arise from non-living chemicals, in curiosity about the workings of an ant colony, we come to terms with what confronts us. The necessity of emotional involvement for gaining knowledge and understanding, when expressed in these terms, seems so obvious that it is hard to understand the currency of the embargo on emotional involvement for those who would be "objective". If we conceded the insinuation of a common colloquial meaning of "objective" of "having no emotion connecting one with the issue under consideration" then we should have to declare objectivity to be of no general advantage in gaining knowledge, or in being reasonable, or in attaining or maintaining understanding. An understanding of this myth of objectivity as emotionless may be gained from the fact that objectivity as a valuable attitude and de-meanour is a tactful contact. This tact requires restraint and con-trol of emotion. This can suggest, by a thoughtless extrapolation, that an absence of emotion is necessary. This extrapolation is a reaction to excesses of, or abuses, of emotion. It is like Descartes' reaction to the facts of perceptual illusion in which he spoke, for a while, as if the essence of things could be known by pure intel-lectual intuition, rather than by sensual involvement.

There are two main ways in which the emotion necessary for serious objectivity degenerates into the emotionalism which is its antithesis. Where "You are merely being emotional" is a legitimate criticism, the emotion which normally warms and motivates good thorough argument, or careful, exact perception, or constructive general theory, becomes the reason for the arguing or perceiving. One argues or perceives or theorizes for the hate or love or other emotion one feels for the other protagonist or position; the emotion one feels for the issue or object or person which is sup-posed to be the "object" of consideration becomes the object of one's desire instead of the force behind one's enquiry. In senti-mental altruism, for example, one argues or perceives for the good glow one obtains from being concerned with the issue, for the feel-ings engendered towards or from the person with whom you argue, or whom your perceive.

The degeneration into emotionalism does not consist simply in one's own feeling rather than the original object of feeling becoming the object of concern. If that occurs knowingly and with proper consideration, then objectivity has simply found a new object; objectivity has not been lost. If it is one's feelings which are to be the "objects" of an objective interest, then they in turn must be under the focus of an interested concern. So, I can look objectively at the anger I feel to a protagonist of a different point of view, and ask myself and others why I should feel like this. What are the causes? Is the repulsion legitimate? What is it about the other? What is it in me? What is it in the issue? In doing this, one's concern has a new clear object, the feelings one is investigating. Understanding these may then help one's original problem of objectivity. The feelings involved in making that further investigation are the new horizon — and unexamined.

There are feelings which lie behind any enquiry. For the most part these are employed in the conduct, in one's own mind or publicly, in which they are expressed; they burn as fast and brightly as they are generated. The uncovering of them, as elements in themselves, often leads to a delighted sensation of specially added objectivity! "Now I really know what is going on!" You see what your "objective" enquiry expresses; you detect its tone or character. Certainly, you know something which you had not realized before, you tend to think that something was other than you had previously thought: "Not the genuine article". This is the wrong response to a recognition of hitherto unnamed feelings behind an interest. Suppose that you fall victim to such a loss of objectivity from the shock of new objectivity. "Fall victim" is the right phrase since, in the nature of novelty, at the time of the new recognition you do not recognize the further feelings and motives which lie behind your surprised acceptance of that new realization. Hence, if the finding of a hitherto unsuspected character to an enquiry were in itself to undermine the validity of that enquiry, then that new discovery itself must on further reflection be declared only to appear valid, pending discovery of the hidden currents of feeling and motive behind it in turn. In maintaining one's objectivity, it is equally important to heed these cautions and to give due weight to the realization of motive and feeling, and perhaps of bias, though one is cautioned not to overreact.

Anyone who, from the Freudian discoveries and conceptual innovations of unconscious motivation, generally impugned the objectivity of everyday thinking must face the fact that in observing and construing the unconscious in someone's behaviour and conduct, one is not considering the unconscious motives one has for doing this oneself. Even if, with the help of an analyst, one searched out the unconscious reasons for that last search, and so on. If objectivity requires a *complete* understanding of what you are doing in engaging with the "object", then indeed, objectivity is impossible. A will-o'-the-wisp; a shadow which moves as fast as one attempts to stand on it.

It is not the existence of emotion, nor simply the existence of unrecognized emotion, which constitutes the emotionalism which is at least a diminution of objectivity. Emotionalism is the substitution of the interests of one's emotional life in pursuing some interest in the place of the interests of the person, thing or matter in which one was to have taken an interest. Once this substitution has occurred, then the emotion felt makes it appear as if it were only right and reasonable that one should exclude reasoning, compromise, detachment or a careful consideration of another's view. It would be disloyal, soft, compromising to think otherwise. Not all emotionalism is intense; it can be all the more dangerously covert when quiet. Yet, once the shift in purpose of discussion, enquiry or perception has occurred, the emotion generated in discussion or in perceiving, which has become the aim as well as the ground of the discussion or perception, is led back as in electrical positive feedback systems, to generate a more emotional discussion or perception. Since the aim of this, if one is being an emotionalist, is the having and the enjoying of emotion, the output of emotion is reintroduced as an augmented origin of discussion or perception. Unless interrupted from outside emotion increases exponentially into hysteria. What is important about hysteria to our concept of objectivity is not so much the banality that hysteria is a loss of objectivity and is infectious, but that the fear of becoming hysterical and equally the fear of appearing or being maliciously misrepresented as being hysterical, is a main inhibitor of free discussion, and of an open minded exploratory attitude in perception. Those with a keenly logical mind who can enjoy and maintain strenuous and thorough argument must be the first to recognize that the logical force of an argument and the adequacy of the grounds for the premises are to be distinguished from the emotional style with which it is delivered. Sometimes this distinction is wrongly taken to imply a derogatory attitude to an emotional style of argument. The correct logical lesson: it is illogical to pick an emotional style as an indicator of bad argument. Further, an argument may not only be emotionally presented but also, more seriously, put in what are conventionally known as emotional terms: murderer, callous, generous, cunning. Yet if these are apt epithets and the implications are well drawn, charges of emotionalism on the basis of their presence in reasoning are simply trumped up; the charges are evasions of what is being put forward. The feeling that one is losing one's objectivity when presented with forceful moral arguments, for instance, may be nothing more than the feeling that one is being subject to moral considerations. As, in general, the refusal of one's subjectivity which has as an example the refusal to be subject to reason, is irrationalism however dressed up as commonsense or hard-mindedness, so the refusal of moral reasons is moral irrationalism, however dressed up as keeping only to the facts or to being scientific.

Moral reasons can be challenged; the necessity to be subject to good moral reasons as to any other good reasons is not a plea for blind acceptance of current or conventional views. The challenge to what one resists as bad reasons must come from other moral considerations, from the making of different analogies, and take its form in the insistence on certain facts rather than others as vital to the issue.

It is natural that one slides into a discussion of moral reasons when considering being emotional and being objective. Though moral considerations may be, on occasion, presented or thought about as coolly as any others, still it is obvious to a child that were it not for our emotional involvements with other people, with activities and with things, moral considerations would be a set of idly whirring cogs in the mechanism of reason. Our system of moral ideas would be one of those mechanical curios in museums which busily go into fascinating motion when one presses the right button; the illusion of the reality of the old pumping mechanism produced by a hidden new electrical device. The mechanism pumps nothing. In a little while the light goes out, the machine is motionless and all is as it had been.

Chapter Five

Confidence and Autonomy

The Importance of Being Confident

Being objective requires, at times, pure mental resistance, a refusal to have one's position undercut by the fact of its being questioned and one's being forced back simply to a reiteration. This is a truth dangerous to utter. For the most part we are too complacent rather than too questioning, and the assertion of this truth may be made in abuse of the need in the circumstances to question the questionable, and to be doubtful because of the lack of any answer but reiteration.

Yet, however embarrassed we may be when it comes to the point, to have to fall back on reiteration, still the declaration that to do so is always irrational is our abdication from, not our subscription to, especially high standards of reason. If we are to come to serious and reasonable conclusions, then we must be equally serious and reasonable in our premises. Sometimes we gain our premises by direct observation and, quite reasonably, we have to insist upon our premises. We insist that we have used our senses well and carefully, that we have been judicious in appraising just how much can be asserted on the basis of what we perceived, and that the epithets we have chosen are warranted. The fact that, in general, we could possibly be mistaken must not be taken to deter us from confident judgement, and to sticking to our line, if we are ever to be confident in any judgement, or to stick to any line. The fact that "we might have put things differently, given the same visual, auditory, olfactory . . . stimulus from the same object or situation, had we been born into a different culture, in a different age, or even that we might ourselves learn something different by tomorrow which, had we known it now, would have cast a different light on the matter" — none of this is information from which we can infer any degree of present error or even of distortion. To know that we may be regarded as the dark ignorant past in centuries to come, or as the golden age of wisdom and high educational standards or, more drastically, to know that we cannot know the very terms and ideas which may be developed by which we will be appraised — to know all of this may call for a wry smile in the midst of our confidence, but if we attempt to move the smile into any articulation of how we are mistaken, our feeling of superior intelligence above our involved confidence will collapse in a slack jaw. The very "ignorance" of the future perspective from which our confidence will be appraised must leave our rational confidence undisturbed.

Our lack of knowledge of a future perspective is described as ignorance only by metaphor. When we are ignorant, we ignore something. We ignore what we have already some slight apprehension of, and which we decline to investigate further. We ignore people when they come to us with information and advice. We are ignorant of science or art if we have not come to terms with the best which has been developed in or own or other available cultures. But to say that we are ignorant of ways of thinking which have not been developed and which we cannot even imagine, let alone predict, is to abuse a metaphor. We do not ignore these things. We can only wait to see if they arise in our lifetime, or struggle to new ideas for ourselves. And of course there is a paradox. If we have no right to be confident now because we cannot tell how our ideas may have to be cast out or modified from future perspectives, then in those later times when those new perspectives have been developed, we would have no right to criticize the past, since we could have no confidence that still later perspectives might not show that our supposed new development, our elightenment, was an illusion.

Finally, we do not learn from history only how foolish it is to suppose, from the present obvious truth of our science and the quality of our art, that things will always remain thus, or that we will never be forced to radical revision. An equally constant fact is that we are informed by past discoveries, inspired by art of the past and sometimes simply corrected in our thinking by what has been done in the past. It is equally likely that our present best confidence *is* the truth which people yet unborn will need, as that it is the dark age of ignorance which they will despise. We cannot actually entertain the thought that what we know best and most clearly is really dark ignorance. This inability is not dogmatism, but rational consistency. We can call something ignorance only from the point of view of what is known better. And, in the logical nature of the case, there is no vantage point from which what we seem to know best can be thought to be, let alone reasonably suspected to be mistaken.

In these conundrums, we are caught at once in depth and foolishness.

By imaginative construction of theory, and detached and careful measurement of the results of contrived experiments, we know the mass of an electron. From a scientific point of view, it is hot air to say that all of these results, so carefully checked and rechecked, might be spurious merely because they might be explained by and thus support a quite different theory of matter. We have no such theory, nor any inkling of what it would look like. Whether electrons are to be thought of as wave forms or as point masses might be a matter of indecision, but try to imagine having no structural theory of the atom, and no atomic theory of matter. We cannot imagine how any scientific development of science will overturn the whole idea of atomic and subatomic structures. Yet, if we look from the perspective of the changes which have occurred from the time of the early Greeks until now in the conception of the basic elements of matter, or even of there being any such fundamentals, it seems only reasonable to suppose that in centuries to come people will find to be natural, scientific or basic, ideas or models of nature quite different from those which now seem irreplaceable.

This by itself does nothing to establish any degree of uncertainty concerning our scientific theories. The very point that we cannot know what scientific advances there may be in the next decades or centuries equally reminds us that we cannot know that there will be scientific advances at all. Perhaps people will continue to be "scientific" as we now regard the quality of mind, but will make a lot of mistakes, and be much farther from the truth than we now are. They should have left well alone we would say could we travel in time and appear among them. Or perhaps they will find no safe alternative sources of energy, and the industrial society now necessary to the advance of science (that is, for instance, precise quantitative chemical research, studies of the behaviour of subatomic particles, space exploration and the like) will collapse, and the arts and crafts of modern science will die out, not from yielding false results, but from becoming useless and inapplicable, as did the arts and crafts of making sailing ships.

When, from the fancy of these unknown historical vantage points, we return to the midst of our present scientific (or social, artistic or philosophical) outlook, and regard again our confidence in mechanical and electrical inventions, and the belief in industrial solutions to present social problems, of war, famine, boredom, hopelessness about the future and so on, it seems that we must be closing our eyes to all that lies beyond our present society. Yet the point is that we cannot close our eyes to the future of scientific discovery or any sort of creativity since, in the nature of the case, we cannot see it when we open them. To the extent that we hope to bring about a certain kind of future rather than another then, tautologically, that must be brought about from where we are; that is, to think seriously of bringing about one thing rather than another is to evince a confidence in our grasp of the character of where we are, and our ways and means of dealing with what we find "ready at hand". (As Heidegger likes to put it.)

At this point, it will develop our sense of perspective about confidence and doubt to think again about the method of radical doubt in philosophy. Descartes' method of scepticism, is to "withhold (his) assent from matters which are not entirely certain and indubitable". This is coupled with his criterion of uncertainty, that a matter is uncertain if one can find the least reason to doubt it, and with his specific strategies of doubt: "One's senses sometimes deceive one, and one cannot never entirely trust what has once been deceptive"; sometimes one is asleep and only dreaming when one takes oneself to be awake, perceiving and thinking; at the very farthest edge of radical questioning, one can simply imagine the possibility that an intelligent deceptive power is causing one to perceive and to think incorrectly, and equally causing one to find no effective means to discover such deception.

It is generally instructive to discover what one must simply insist upon in order to maintain one's realism concerning those things, including other people, which one perceives, engages with and thinks about. One can proceed a little way by criticism internal to Descartes' method — that is without any assumption of realism except that one can think straight — and show that his method and examples of reasons to doubt are, according to his criterion of doubt, doubtful themselves. This shows that one is not logically forced to a position of scepticism. Briefly, the internal criticism is that, first, if one cannot trust the senses for the reason that sometimes the use of them has led one to error, then one cannot trust the use of the senses which is supposed to have shown up that error. To the rejoinder that Descartes need not assume that his tower, which appeared round at a distance, was really square when he came closer, since he need only note that first it appears one way, then another and that it cannot be both, there is a crushing reply: unless he took for granted the permanence and stability of the things he perceived, and that they persisted apart from his perceiving them, there would be no reason to think in terms of one appearance being inconsistent with another. It might seem that pure reason unaided by the senses might tell us that no tower can be both round and square at the same time in the same section. Still, without our coordinated sense of sight, of mass and of resistance to change, and our capacity to retain what we have seen and felt as we go on seeing and feeling, there would be no reasonable presumption that there need be any "answer" whatsoever concerning "the" shape of the tower. It might be just round-at-a-distance-for-me and square-close-up-for-me.

Similarly, if from the *fact* that sometimes we dream, we conclude that we never know we are awake and thus really perceiving rather than just dreaming that we are, then we have concluded that we cannot tell that we do ever dream. The reason for doubting that we are awake falls to the ground. If it is said that really all we can tell is that sometimes we seem to be awake and sometimes we seem to be dreaming, and that, without ever knowing that we are or have been dreaming we know by pure reason that it must be one or the other, and the sceptical problem is that we cannot tell which, there is a crushing rejoinder: without reliance on the sense of being in contact with reality which is separate from our own consciousness and which we sense as having its own power of resisting or agreeing with our wishes, we have no reason to draw any distinction at all between dreamt and actual experience. The presumption that there is something to know here, something about which we might be deceived is itself founded upon the ordinary (naive if you like) taking of experience to be "of" or "directed towards" things with their own character, some of them being people and as capable as oneself of experiencing or dreaming.

Finally, suppose that the "possibility" that a "demon" might deceive one about even what seems most evident is taken to show that we do not know or must be any whit less confident of what seems to be so, either to reason or to sense. In that case the possibility of universal deception shows equally that we do not know or cannot be confident, that it *is* possible for any demon (or accidental force for that matter) which could deceive us systematically even about what seems most evident.

In all of these rejoinders to general scepticism, I have simply persisted in the objective mode. As Anderson, the ex-Scot Australian philosopher, would have said, I have refused to "modify the copula". I have simply declared what is so; where I have argued, I have simply declared the premises and simply employed the logical sense of the reader and myself. As, of course, did Descartes when he gave "reasons" for doubt. Which precisely is the general critical reply to general doubt. If general doubt has no base, it is baseless. If it has a base, it is not entirely general doubt.

From this security, we experience a drift of thought: "Sometimes, indeed, we have been mistaken or misled when we have been most careful, most sure . . . so we can't be quite sure that we are now misled . . . if that means, as the critic of scepticism says, that we can't be sure that we have been misled, then everything is quite unsure . . . we can only say that this is how things seem to us". But now we have drifted, as Hegel says, onto the "wild whirligig of reason" off which we shall be cast violently to ground again. If everything is unsure, and thus even that we do have our reasons for being unsure is unsure, then our unsureness itself cannot be a matter of reason. I insist upon that quite surely. I step off the merry-go-round before I am thrown off. The difference between the general sceptical and the critical but realistic and objective attitude becomes an existential one, a question of what sort of person one is to be; a question of what style and attitude of thought and life one is to choose. In philosophy, as in all pursuits, one can be and must attempt to be critically general; one cannot be and must not attempt to be generally critical. It is not the insistence on what appears to be true, as true, which is dogmatic or irrationalist or a retreat into "animal faith" (as thought Hume). It is the pretence (for it is not logically possible that it should be more than that) of being general critical, that is of criticizing all propositions, which is the final irrationalism. It is the abdication of reason. One would have to hold that one must never say, "This argument *is* fallacious", of "This premise *is* false", or "This observation *is* badly, hastily, mistakenly, made".

Without reason and doubt, judgement is an idiot, to be sure. But without judgement, reason is a squawking parrot. The universal critic retires to his lair: "All I can say, all you have the right to say is 'It seems to me that . . .' ". We smoke him out: "Does it indeed 'seem' to you? Is it in just the way you say, that it 'seems'? Perhaps when you thought it seemed to you that a golden butterfly flashed in the sun, nothing seemed at all. Your senses were blank. Preposterous? Do firmly judge that, then? Perhaps when you thought it seemed a butterfly, really it seemed a camel . . ., or rather like a whale"? A lunatic supposition you say? Then you firmly judge it did not seem so? So now judgement is firmly judged to be necessary. A good deal is known and if someone questions it, then, for the most part, one can do no more than insist that one has one's wits about one, has paid attention and stands by one's account of what one perceived and/or thought. If someone is to criticize, the criticism must be specific. It cannot be merely the throwing up of a possibility.

What complicates the matter and allows universal criticism even to seem like the higher ideal to which we fail to rise only through slackness and adherence to the practical necessities of life is that at times it is right for the maintenance of our openness of mind and freedom of imagination, and to free ourselves from immediate bondage to our place in society and in history, that we should simply entertain the possibility that we are wrong where we most seem to be right. There *is* a sense in which one cannot argue one's way out of remaining permanently in that intellectual attitude. Yet it is quite wrong to infer that it is only by an irrational act of faith that one can leave the state of universal doubt, since the reason one cannot argue oneself out of the state is just that the very process of arguing is already a case of *not* being in that generally sceptical "Perhaps I am wrong at every point" frame of questioning mind. Arguing is inferring, moving, from some place where one is to some place where one is not yet, or arriving again more securely where one had already been staying with inadequate rational confidence. (Or, as Ryle has reminded us, the rehearsal or recapitulation of such inferring.) Most importantly, to infer is to move *from* a place one has observed oneself to be in or to which one has previously argued.

The generally sceptical mode of comment upon experience as found in Descartes, or the general abstaining from objective judgement on the content of consciousness as found in Husserl, each of which aims at a higher, a more absolute objectivity, an absolute foundation for certainty and agreement among all who think seriously, ends inevitably in the most profound subjectivism. To be equally cautious at every point is to pay no special attention to the dangers. To bracket off the apparent objects of every enquiring attitude is finally not even to be in a position to judge the quality of character of the bracketing activity. "But who is to say which are the dangers?" We are, and we must. John Austin, an Oxford realist, said, "It is the sceptic who is credulous". For if we attempt not to believe anything until we come upon utter certainty, a foolish proposition is no more to be disbelieved than a wise one.

The importance of being not too confident

For all this insistence on the necessity of judgement, of deciding that certain matters are so and others not, as a condition of reason and not a mere dogmatism, the subjective mode has its place in all our attempts to deal with what we see and think. To deny this is to deny the place of wondering, pondering, mulling things over, softening one's line and attitude to be receptive to what one does not yet understand, to what seems perhaps, to flout outrageously what one knows clearly and full well. It is to leave us no room for beginning to approach perplexity, complexity, conundrums and paradox. It is no accident that it is philosophers who have had the most trouble in locating and evaluating the different and necessary roles of judgement and speculate indecisive thought, since it is the specific task of philosophy to approach and come to terms with perplexity, conundrum and the rest. So philosophers are most subject to the ambivalent calls of "clearly and definitely sorting out the puzzle", on the one hand, and "pondering, meditating, wondering, being sensitive to the depth of the problem" on the other.

Certainly this acceptance of the pondering or deeply unsure frame of mind is made difficult too because the overuse of the subjective mode is an irritation, an evasion from coming to terms with issues, a subtly conceived way of seeming to be humble when really we are arrogantly blunting or averting the point of another's (or even our own) observations or arguments. So, when we feel that someone is overusing the subjective mode, saying, all the time "In my opinion . . ." and "It seems to me . . ." and "I cannot but feel that . . ." and "I really do believe . . ." and "On my theory, this would be regarded . . .", we want to cry out to restore a sense of "the issue", "the argument", "the object", a "detached regard for the truth": "Who wants to hear that it's your opinion?". And: "Well, is it so, or does it merely seem so?". And: "Does your *feeling* make it so?", and: "Of course, 'on your theory' this is what would be said. A defender of a flat earth could say as much. So can the superstitious and religious." If we make a critical point and a person just says, "Well this is what I believe about it . . ." or "On my theory this is how it is", this seems only an evasion of the criticism. It seems that we are being faced with egotism, not humility, since the person's believing something is being put forward as a good enough reason why they should believe it, and why they should ignore criticism. The evasion is that while they plead merely their personalness, their having of belief, that belief is itself irremediably objectifying; it is the belief that such and such *is* the case. The humble use of the subjectivist mode leads them quietly, but all of a sudden they are flung on the Big Dipper of objectivity. It is better to pay the entrance fee and at least be prepared for the thrills.

It is in our reasonably annoyed but not fully comprehending reaction to these pseudo-modest self-indulgences and evasions expressed in the abuses of the subjective mode that we easily fall into objectivism — into the bemused fancy which represents itself as hard-headedness, that the "truth", the "object", the "fact" or whatever can simply be dealt with without any subjectivity being essentially involved or considered in one's theory of knowledge. So Karl Popper, in *The Logic of Scientific Discovery,* (Part One, Chapters 1 to 5) thought that "thoughts", "feelings", "sensations", "experiences" had no relevance to scientific knowledge. Such confusion lies quite immediately in the refusal to recognize that knowledge, that conceptual epitome of exactness, truth and proof, is, too, a subjectivity in that, in knowing, a person is necessarily subjected to things; his or her mind must be modified, must be allowed to change, to restructure, to absorb, to fit and to make adjustments. To acknowledge the subjectivity of knowledge is not to allow that it is all equal to "mere opinion", or "has nothing to do with the truth" or that "there is no reason to decide between fact and fiction". It is to acknowledge openly that in knowledge as much as in pondering, speculating, meditating and wondering, it is necessary that one's *mind* is involved with the issue, that objectivity arrives only with a subject. Seeing that some such involvement is a logical necessity for objectivity, it is logically absurd to advance it as a detraction.

It is natural that we fall into objectivism in reaction to subjectivism because, in impatiently asking someone to forget his or her having of opinions, feelings and thoughts, and instead, to attend to the issue, we forget that our request for a greater objectivity is a request for a change to a different attitude; in the objectivist illusion, it is as if there could be a coherent request for a change from having an attitude to having no attitude whatsoever, and "just getting on with the business of the facts" (or the theories, for that matter). (Need I say that getting on with the facts is one specific attitude among the many of which we are capable?) In asking for objectivity, we are asking for a change in attitude to an investigatory from a self-congratulatory, self-defending or simply self-absorbed attitude. We are asking for a change in immediate object of attitude from one's having of beliefs, feelings and so on, to the object of those beliefs, feelings and so on. One can hear how "object of attitude" slides rightly into "objective attitude"; it takes some care to pronounce the difference. The sense in which the subject disappears is simply that one loses oneself in an engrossing pursuit. Here is a paradox, for the subject who was lost as object of scrutiny and concern, now emerges as wholly present because wholly engrossed.

There is another illusion which might tempt one at this point, namely the intellectual apparition of making a special thing of losing oneself so as to gain objectivity. The *aim* of losing oneself is only a thinly disguised new self-concern, in which one's concern is with oneself, the concern being in the form of losing oneself. This concern has a self-refuting character similar to the absurd action of deliberately attempting not to think anything. No, in a return to objectivity, one is returned away from a concern with one's beliefs, feelings and thoughts as one's possessions, as merely nice, disturbing, or prestigious things to have. In regaining a proper objectivity concerning the objects of one's mind, one is simply concerned with their objects, and the preoccupation with oneself as having the beliefs, feelings and so on, falls away. This proper objectivity involves no denial or minimization of the fact that a concern with a mathematical problem, someone's future, what someone is thinking about, *is* a concern, *is* one's own concern with those matters. Also, it is inevitable that in one's involvement with things, one's involvement itself surfaces as a matter of interest and importance to oneself and to others. If we have fully accepted that our objectivity is a quality of and an artful use of our subjectivity rather than an escape from it, then we will not be too squeamish to thoughtfully consider the personal and idiosyncratic character of all pursuits, whether they are of scientific rigour, or the creation of art or theory, an understanding of one special person, or human nature broadly or whatever. We will not, as did Popper, too swiftly bundle all those unwanted phenomena into a world separate from the worlds of mathematics, arguments and theories, and the worlds of material objects and physical events. (Popper's "three worlds" in his *Objective Knowledge*.) Nor will we be shocked into a Feyerabend's childish pronouncements (*Against Method*) that no real lines can be drawn between good and bad thought, between a scientific and a superstitious outlook (See almost any part or the whole of *Against Method*; the first three chapters and Appendix 4 illustrate well what I am attributing to him.). We will have too much understanding of the confusions and evasions involved in saying "Everything is equally subjective" to have any interest in saying it or in listening to it. Briefly, such sayings are the false observations gained by a startled and transfixed gaze which, so long used to the scientific attitude of considering the object and ignoring the human conditions of considering it, can do nothing but stare at those conditions when finally they can no longer be repressed. That "everything is subjective" (as it is commonly put) or that "anything goes" (as Feyerabend puts it) is an expression of the irrational loss of intellectual confidence which occurs when one's gaze (intellectual or sensory) is thus shifted from the object of one's first concern where one knew one's way about and did not have to think about how one knew it, or what was involved of oneself in knowing it. In no longer attending to the detail of what one knew and of one's care and methods in knowing it, one comes to think of that knowledge as like everything else. This loss of confidence is like falling out of a friendship so that one no longer wants to, or perhaps cannot, focus on all that there was to that person, and all that there was to that friendship. Thus we cannot avoid falling into an easy cynicism that everyone is alike or no-one is better than anybody else.

I have claimed that confidence and persistence in concern and interest are necessary conditions of objectivity even though one can be hard put, at times, in practice, to distinguish these qualities from dogmatism. In drawing these lines, it helps if we will observe that a reasonable confidence allows one to include within one's observation and judgements what still is, in tone, an openly concessionary and further-observation-and-discussion-permitting "It seems . . .", "I feel that . . .". In dogmatism, one thinks that the facts, the principles, the theory, speak for themselves. In confidence, by contrast, one is prepared to speak for oneself, to carry a view and to accept the personal responsibility for carrying it; the full confidence that one has gained the object allows an easy acceptance of the personal character of what is involved in gaining it. One does not fancy that what one holds as true speaks for itself, and so one does not angrily suppose that one who disagrees or who does not see it is turning a deaf ear to the world. Rather it is I, myself, who have not done an adequate job of explaining, of leading the person to the right place at the right time in the right mood.

There, in that last phrase "right mood", lies at least one essential part of the need for recognizing the subjectivity in one's interest in any "object". If you do not, then you do not see that others have to handle problems of subjectivity different from your own in gaining an approach to or understanding of the same object which you know. Not to know, or stupidly to deny this, leads to, is virtually tantamount to, dogmatism. It is the view that all that is needed for recognition of the truth is attention to one's proposition; if one assertion is not enough, then the matter must be dinned in, regularly recited, as in religious catechisms, or Mao's *Little Red Book*. Dogmatic insistence wants to create the facade of a perfect objectivity in which subjectivity has no place: "these are the facts", "this is the true theory". Difference of opinion threatens to destroy the facade. Furious insistence only exposes one's own subjectivity. To bring about reasonable agreement, one would have to explain carefully to those who differ what it is that one thinks, and why; one would have to respect their understanding and knowledge in order to have any chance of success in this endeavour; most vitally, but viciously for dogmatism, one would have to risk the discovery that one had no good explanation, that the other person had a better case; even if one succeeded in gaining agreement one would have come face to face with the different hue which this same truth had in another's mind. It is superficial to say that the dogmatist just won't bother to explain himself, to offer adequate evidence or to lead his hearer to the right place to learn for him or herself, just as the dogmatist has, supposedly, learned. It is essential to the dogmatic preservation of the illusion of "pure truth which speaks for itself", that he himself has no "close encounters of the third kind" with those of alien belief. The very heart of the matter is that one can preserve one's dogmatism only by refusing any close encounters by oneself not only with one's opponents but with the very matters upon which one is dogmatic. For even if, upon close encounter, it turns out that one's belief is correct, that one was a happily lucky dogmatist, the character of one's belief, what it means to one to have it, will change utterly; in recognizing the previously dogmatic character of one's belief, by contrast with the way in which one's opinion is now subject to its object, one realizes how the previous attempt to be entirely beyond subjectivity (to short-circuit the processes of understanding, coming to terms with, arguing about and enquiring into, in which we cannot escape our subjectivity, wishing instead to be in the immediate realm of pure truth) was only our total engulfment in subjectivity. There was present, in the dogmatic "truth" nothing more than one's desire, one's rigidity, which distracted attention from itself by loud assertion which purported to be about something other than itself.

All of these reflections may raise again the thought that finally one is left with nothing but dogmatism when faced with radical scepticism. The sceptic says that we can never get beyond our pure subjectivity for, when dreaming, we can think we are awake and practising all our fine arts of objectivity. In the midst of or "objectivity" comes the thought that "It could be just like *'this'* though we are dreaming". Let us see what happens. It is time for pondering and wondering, then. Suppose we were to maintain our objective mode of thought and speech. We say, "If I don't know when I am awake, then I am in no position to say what is possible in dreams. The very claim that certain experiences are possible in dreams betrays the presence of the very objective attitude which was being argued to be unjustifiable." To which the subjectivist answers, "Dogmatism dressed up as clear minded insistence! The undogmatic conclusion is that we cannot know what is possible in dreams, and so, for all we know, it is possible that we are dreaming and that such a complete apparent reality can occur in dreams."

Again, we can see how we can maintain our realistic style. What of this phrase "for all we know"? Who has determined the limits of what we know? If we know we are awake then it is false that for all we know, we are dreaming. The subjectivist is assuming his subjectivism. I am awake, for I am typing these words, and could not be doing so like this if I were asleep and only dreaming. I might be dreaming? No. For in that case I would have to be asleep, and I am awake. A circular argument? No, a set of interdependent insistences upon what I *find* myself to be doing. That someone might dream that they are awake and insisting that they are not dreaming does not touch my realization of my waking activities now.

There are other examples of how the general possibility of error, delusion, dreaming and so on do not touch the individual case. Suppose I am to add up a few numbers, the sum of 7, 5 and 4. The answer is 16. Now someone says, "But you could be wrong. People make mistakes adding up numbers. You yourself, probably when tired, or hoping that you had 17 dollars in your pocket, or after adding dozens of other numbers, have made mistakes. So admit at least the possibility that you have made a mistake and that the answer is not 16. Or else stand convicted of dogmatism!"

I cannot admit the possibility, for I can find no crevice in which the possibility can lie. The "possibility of people making errors when adding even simple numbers" cannot be brought to bear on my present addition in any way which introduces an understanding of how I could be in error in *this* addition. The same is true of the general possibility that a person should be dreaming that he was awake and utterly confident that he was awake and that in no way could he, right at that time, be asleep and dreaming.

Fine style! But a headache, that nags like a tooth, now enters. The fool, the ignorant, the unthinking or the dogmatist can all use this kind of retort as a tactical line to evade questioning. To doubts and to questioning they all reply in equal vein that what they know puts all questions out of court. Their dogmatic retorts show only how easy it is to talk with an empty head, or merely for effect; how easy to lie or to be in error. An example: someone asks me how much money I have in my pocket. I might reply, frivolously, not giving a damn what I have, "Twenty dollars". I might give the same reply for effect − to be thought rich or to be thought poor. In neither of these examples need I be lying (to put a precise point upon it). I do not care about the facts. Alternatively, I might specifically and deliberately lie, knowing just how much money I had, and misrepresenting the amount. Or I might be in error. In all cases, let us suppose, what I say is "Twenty dollars". No method of doing something or of saying or otherwise representing something is proof against simulation or counterfeit. To refuse to give the lie to the sceptic from what one knows because a fool would use the same form of words foolishly, and the rogue roguishly, is the greatest foolishness and not far from roguery. So far from upholding the strictest philosophical standards, it is the abandonment of judgement.

It helps, in keeping one's footing, to remember that questioning, no less than asserting, may be simulated and phoney. The fatal weakness of the Socratic philosophy lies in its self-imposed inability to separate serious from groundless questions. It is easy to pose a question when there is no doubt or ignorance, just as it is easy to *state* that you know something when you lack any substance behind your words. To sum up these attacks on scepticism shortly: unless the generally sceptical questions are groundless, the statement of a generally sceptical position (that we cannot really know anything, etc.) is false. Certainly this is not a proof that the sceptic position is false. It is a philosophical dream to suppose that there could be a proof of its falsity other than one which involved the assertion of something we knew. It is absurd to search for a philosophical disproof of scepticism which consists in a form of words whose use assumed nothing of the honesty, judgement, observativeness and seriousness of the one who use it. Do not protest against proofs whose premises are statements of knowledge only when uttered by people who have that knowledge.

Open-mindedness and conviction

The right avoidance of dogmatism might be identified with an open susceptibility to the ideas, attitudes and intellectual and emotional pressures of others. But to be so susceptible no matter what the circumstances — and no matter what ideas, attitudes and pressures, on principle, as if that were one's general moral and intellectual duty to oneself and to one's fellows — is to be in a deep well of cobwebs. Like John Locke with his abstract idea of a triangle, which had to be an idea of something "neither equilateral, isosceles nor scalene, but all and none of these at once", we should have to be equally susceptible to dogmatic, to strict and exacting, and to loose and amorphous ideas and to the idea that we ought not to be so susceptible to any or all of these, singly or at once together. Yet to be never susceptible to influence from unexpected events and sayings which puzzle and intrigue us and which as yet we do not clearly understand and cannot exactly judge or appraise, or to hold ourselves apart from experiences whose content or significance we cannot yet fathom, is proof of vanity, rigidity and dogmatism.

We shall have to admit and attempt to discover the real difference between the set of attitudes in the cluster of myopia, moribundity, purblindness and dogmatism, and those in the set of clear minded persistence, intellectual fidelity, having an open eyed (but not wide eyed) steadiness, and using deliberate and selective focus in thought and perception. In the devil's dictionary, it is written simply that my right confidence is your blind dogmatism. We need a better lexicon than that. The reason for having two distinctively different clusters of ideas is not merely, if at all, that one wishes to attack others who differ from oneself, and to praise oneself for being oneself. The difference lies in detectable differences of attitude, style and motive in thought and perception, so that it is possible for the penetrating criticism of another to make someone recognize his own rigidity, dogmatism or myopia, or to recognize in another a superior intellectual seriousness, persistence, and an intelligent selectiveness which is not in any way a proof of bias, or mere protectiveness of his own views.

The motive for dogmatism and the rest of that cluster is fear — an avoidance of desire, interest and satisfaction — whereas the motive for persistence and strength of mind is desire. A desire simply to know, or to be able to better cope or handle something, to understand more fully or to be or feel closer to something or someone. To be dogmatic is to think, perceive and argue (dogmatism cannot abide discussion but may be deceptively keen on argument thus appearing very logical) out of the fear that one could not cope with views at variance with or in opposition to one's own if one were to consider them sympathetically and with an intent to understand the best in them. It evinces a fear that one would be moved from one's position if one saw and grasped what was being offered, and expresses alarm that one would be at sea or adrift when moved from anchor.

In understanding the causes of so foolish a stultification as dogmatism, one should not underrate the fear of such an epistemologically trivial seeming thing as embarrassment: to be embarrassed is to be unsure and to feel foolish in the face of a situation or feelings which make one unable, for the moment at least, to determine what kind of person to be. Whichever way one goes, one feels partly untrue, strained and unreal. Too much embarrassment, or a lack of understanding of embarrassment by the person who suffers it, or the lucky onlookers who may grin, leads to a loss of objectivity for it leads to panic flight from the situation or one's own feelings. But embarrassment itself plays a key role in one's maintaining one's objectivity, for it is, in part, the shock of new recognition, and is also a more sensitive state in which we are unable to ward off things in our habitual fashion. In embarrassment we have a heightened sense of the impinging otherness of things and other people, and also of aspects of our own self which we have been disinclined to own.

While it is masochistic and mawkish to launch oneself deliberately into embarrassing situations except for reasons which make one have to suffer embarrassment, and while it is weak minded simply to succumb to embarrassment when it occurs, it is a measure of one's objectivity that one can accept its inevitability and the importance of its function as, necessarily, a brief phenomenon, in accommodating oneself to unexpected fact and feeling. As lust is an erotic love in which we fancy we can dispense with social friction, so dogmatism is a persistent strength of intellectual purpose in which we fancy that we can dispense with the embarrassment of the discoveries which any genuinely persistent search will bring. So it is natural that we use the bodily metaphor of stamping one's foot when speaking of dogmatism. The dogmatist must make only a pretence of intellectually walking; by stamping he symbolizes the self-defensive, self-stultifying pseudo-action in which he is engaged. As, if he actually walked, he would, like it or not, come to be somewhere else, and it might or might not agree with him and it might or might not flatter his appearance, so if his show of strong minded persistence of thought were actually a movement of thought (that is, thinking) then he would, like it or not, come to be somewhere else intellectually, and it might or might not agree with him, and might or might not flatter the intellectual appearance which he has built up.

Rational persistence and strength of mind, and dogmatism, are alike in involving some selective partial closure of mind and feeling and restriction of view by focusing. They differ in that when we lack dogmatism this selection and partial closure make a deliberate and knowing act. In knowing what we are doing, we do not mistake the heightened vividness of vision and exactness of understanding which can arise from selective focus and intensified interest, for a discovery of what everything is really like. Such a feeling of total discovery is the live original feeling behind what becomes the conventionalized dogmas of physicalism, historical materialism and religion. A first flush of delight at new discovery of realms of thought and feeling becomes a belief that one has discovered the fundamental nature of reality lying behind mere phenomenal appearance (physicalism), behind bourgeois mystifications (historical materialism), or behind the physical and fleshy mere window dressing for the real spiritual Department Store (religion). When not dogmatic, we realize that our total absorption still represents a partial interest. We are ignoring a great deal because our energies and time are limited, as our capacities to project ourselves accurately and successfully to others are also limited; we realize similarly that our capacities to receive ideas and information from others and from things are limited. We know that we have to judge selectively among friends, acquaintances, books, movies and television shows; we choose what and how much we can absorb while still maintaining a capacity to come to terms with these things and not to be swamped or, at least, not to suffer more than brief dumpings in the sensory and mental surf. To put it briefly, we are not dogmatic in our restrictions of interest, in our refusals to consider every possibility and in our determination to proceed in some chosen direction, when these restrictions are our recognitions of our limitations as subjects. If we are not dogmatic, we recognize that what we gain in experience, opinion and knowledge by following the direction we have chosen, and the restriction and selection we have made, may require us to change direction and enlarge or diminish focus; to make an abrupt and disconnected shift and to look from somewhere else, or through someone else.

It might seem, then, that dogmatism can be identified in part as the attitude of sticking to one's initial attitudes and working rules, and in our expectations and opinions, despite experiences gained by the use of them. But the difference cannot be made so easily. To give up one's chosen and formed attitudes at the first sign of trouble is to make it pointless to have them. We need some resolve and commitment and not only receptivity and susceptibility (Heidegger's "waiting for Being to speak") because reality (things, events, people) is diverse, complicated and confusing and does not explain itself. We have to take a line so that reality begins to take some shape for us.

It may sound empty and banal to say that we should cling to initial commitment and opinions until experience makes them too difficult to maintain. If the difficulty of maintaining an initial position arises as we make our best efforts to understand how what we have been committed to could be so in the light of what we have now experienced, if we can no longer believe in the stories we must tell or the constructions we must place on experience in order to maintain even bare consistency between what we have thought and what we now experience and are inclined to think, then it can only be reasonable to change our commitments of belief or attitude. This may all sound too psychological. Whether we must or cannot believe something . . . what has that to do with reality?

The feeling that the fact of our having to, or being unable to, believe something, has nothing to do with what it is reasonable for us to take things as being, is erroneous. The feeling arises in part from the fact that, in a dialectical situation, if someone does not believe what I do, and asks me to establish what I say, or to explain to him why, either, I believe it or why he should (which need not be quite the same) it is useless for me to answer by saying that I cannot but believe it. (To concede the point I say "useless", though there is at least the vanishing point of support given by unshakeable conviction. A witness who easily becomes unsure under questioning is less credible, other things being equal, than one who is utterly convinced.)

From a detached point of view, we concede at once that someone who cannot but believe something "may be" entirely mistaken. The conviction may arise from wishful thinking, paranoid observation, unquestioning trust of another because of his total dependency on that person, or from a sheer error of thought or perception or both. Yet when we find unshakeable belief we do always look for some fact which at worst is misperceived or misthought. If someone has an unshakeable belief in God, which belief is not interested in logical strategies to expose the fallacies in the five ways of Aquinas, or somesuch, then an atheist who counts himself as reasonable and as engaging reasonably with one who differs, must come closer to the nub of the matter than he could be berating his opponent as irrational. Unless he is going to count himself and the religious virtually as members of a different species, he must, as much for his own intellectual satisfaction as for maintaining contact with one who differs so radically about what the world requires of commitment in belief, present his own account of the facts to which he thinks the religious respond unnecessarily or inappropriately.

When we come up against unshakeable conviction, we have to come to terms with it, if we are still to argue and discuss. We have to make it yield something in its terms, and give a little ourselves. (Otherwise we'll be stuck in Feberabendian incommensurability.) For example, when the religious insist that "one cannot go on if there is nothing beyond the grave", an atheist can agree, but he retains a radically different understanding of the feeling of there being nothing beyond the grave. He or she takes in hand the feeling of nothing beyond the grave, and finds in it a total loss of objectivity, a loss of sense of the reality and value of things and people other than oneself. Life is barren if one cares for no one but oneself and nothing but one's doings. For if, on the other hand, one does care for one's children, friends, lover, spouse, and for people one is simply acquainted with or knows of, and is interested in certain kinds of things going on — philosophy, sailing, painting, music and so on — then it is false to say that there is nothing beyond the grave.

What is beyond the grave is the lives of the people one cares for or cares about now; the continuation of the things one now thinks is worth doing, and right or good that oneself or others should do, the objects one considers valuable, and the rain forests, koala bears, tigers and hedgehogs which now one believes ought to be protected and to continue to exist. If it is supposed to be a sufficient rejection of this natural answer to the nothingness beyond the grave to say "But what is this to me when I am dead and not there to enjoy or even to know about it?", then one's *present* egotism stands immediately exposed. The "emptiness of all things if I am to die" is a mask for "only my life and its concerns so defined as to exclude essential reference to the concerns of others or of other things is of any value". Apart from the moral reprimands to which one is fairly liable for such a travesty of fairness and consideration for others and other things, that "only my life is of any value" is a blatantly false and irrational thought. If now, while alive I have an interest beyond an egotistical one, in philosophy, then I am glad that philosophy goes on in places as well as those which involve me. If there are people whom I care for or care about, then I am glad that they are alive, and not glad merely that they live in some relation to me. If I knew that I was to be cast up on a desert island or lost in space and never see them again, still I should, if they really were the objects of my concern, care that they should live and be happy. Grief that one will never again see someone one loves is quite distinct from grief that the person is dead. Such direct concern is a fact. We know it while living, and have it for the living. When we feel, "There is nothing beyond the grave . . . all is barren and futile", we merely panic at the thought of death, and forget that we care about things and people who will continue to live and exist after we are dead.

You think, "There may be a great deal, but there will be nothing for me"? You may reply, "That is foolishness. There will be neither something for me nor nothing for me. The point is that there will be nothing *of* me, but plenty of and for others." The unshakeableness (by pointing to lack of evidence, etc.) of belief is not a kind of proof of belief, nor any evidence that as expressed, it is true. The belief of some, now exposed as false and irrational, that "life is empty if there is nothing beyond the grave", is unshakeable. They will take care not to consider the false implication of their belief. Or be unable to do so. But it is foolish to suppose that unshakeable belief records nothing. Why should anyone waste their energy, their reputation perhaps, their time and effort, over absolutely nothing? There is some fact which sticks in the gullet of those with apparently irrational beliefs, and it is part of the objective attitude to discover and clarify this fact. In these and in other ways, we can deal in reason with belief respecting the emotion behind it, and accepting that emotion dwells in our own reason, and yet unequivocally criticizing "belief".

The idea that conviction is irrelevant to the problem of knowledge and reasonable belief is an oversight of the fact that we are human beings — human animals, enmeshed in an environment of causes. We may have some freedom to act in respect of those causes, if we can identify them and take some degree of detached regard towards them. Yet we have almost as little liberty of belief as we do of action. We cannot believe any moonshine as we please. We may desperately attempt to push our stalled car up a grade just too steep, but we do not attempt to move Mount Everest to northern Wales. An over-hopeful runner may strive fruitlessly towards at 4.30 minute mile, but he does not strive to run as fast as the car in which he drives away from the track. In the same way, though we may easily be too idealistic in our beliefs about the possibilities of social reform, that more disputes than at present can be settled with understanding and good humour than by acrimony and war, still, when we try to believe that pain and suffering will cease to be part of the human lot, or that people will no longer suspect or practise any harm on each other, we fall into the mouthings of empty words.

We have to pay some reasonable attention to strong conviction and commitment because belief is not so easily come by, and none too easy to maintain. In contrast, loud protestation is relatively cheap, and may be nothing more than the way in which a person dins his own ears so that he has no time or quiet to think.

Opinions may come pretty cheap; thoughts are passing and free as the breeze. But beliefs cost us dearly. They may not seem to matter much until someone attempts to change them. At the extreme of confidence: I have four fingers and a thumb on each of two hands. G.E. Moore had only to hold his out in the light of an evening lecture and challenge his philosophical audience to doubt it, for "the harpies and ghosts of idealism to go shrieking back to the dark corners of philosophy" (John Wisdom). True, some states and degrees of commitment strong enough to be called belief are upheld by little more than hot air. Living according to them, people come to disaster or death, believing (as in the US in the twenties) in the inevitable rise of the stock market, or that God will protect them from deadly snakes. Yet for the most part, the end for such credence is less dramatic, as the air cools and the balloon slowly subsides.

Despite the pitfalls of belief, personal objectivity (that is, one's own grasp of the arts and skills of being objective) requires what might be called belief in that it requires confidence in one's own point of view, even though points of view may be twisted or ignoring and yet confidently held. At any rate, the confidence which is necessary but not enough, requires not the counterfeit — wilful assertiveness — but a continuance which it would be difficult to divert or destroy, maintained by constant resolution of thought and feeling and, finally, belief, in the face of new experience, and in the context of actions taken on one's initiative; actions which should be right if one's point of view is fair and well balanced; actions which should be safe enough if one's beliefs are as well founded as one is confident they are. Again, as with belief, it is a false prejudice that confidence is irrelevant to knowledge and reason because one might decide to be confident about any irrational thing. We are confident only if we often resolve — if we do not leave things to pile up unconsidered and unjudged in our minds, if we do not do the intellectual and other work required to come to a new single-mindedness after new experience and thoughts disturb an old confidence. Yet though we can continue confident only if we often resolve, we cannot resolve to be confident. The attempt will breed only wilful assertiveness. At most we can resolve to take the steps we have come to know are necessary to secure or to maintain it.

Confidence is important to objectivity, and essential to reason, partly in that we have to clarify our minds and come to new adequate ideas in order to meet the double demands of consistency on the one hand, and of not supressing new fact and thought on the other. Further, it is important, since it is in confidence, rather than in the pseudo-objective ultra-caution in which we can see only the endless possibilities of error, that we proceed far enough and firmly enough that our ideas may be tested. There yet is another reason. It is in confidence that a person is able to maintain his or her perceptive realization of the existence and character of another's point of view; it can be fully and vitally recognized without being found to so threaten one's own outlook that it must be suppressed. It allows a person to maintain his or her view of another, to allow and to take seriously the judgements, unpremeditated responses and the active initiatives of another, without having one's judgement and view and interests pre-empted, or feeling that they are about to be.

Privacy and confidences. Autonomy and subjectivity

In maintaining objectivity and the confidence necessary for it, and in avoiding a vain, arrogant or dogmatic stance, one continually strikes new balances between developing and pursuing one's own point of view, and being touched by, allowing oneself possibly to be moved by the points of view of others. Though such contact and influence may disturb into fresh activity one's imagination of the point of view of others generally, or someone else in particular, it is not to be confused with an imagination of another's point of view. Well informed and realistically refreshed by close flow between other's point of view and one's own, one's imagination of the place, outlook, feelings of another, are a necessary condition of the gaining of knowledge and the possession of understanding of another. It is, therefore, a necessary condition of one's understanding of oneself, since a person himself or herself is at once an interiority and an exteriority, a subject and an object, perceiving and perceived, feeling and felt, acting and being acted upon, creating consequences and suffering them. On the one hand, to aim for objectivity by assuming the superiority of another's view and description of my character and actions because that view is external, because it is made from a point beyond me, is to forgo my autonomy. Paradoxically, it is to forgo my ability to appreciate, appraise or even finally to understand what it is that is said about me from beyond myself. To suppose that objectivity concerning oneself comes only from others also is to forget or not to actively realize than others are themselves people. What they say about me is not me-myself but proceeds from their feeling, understanding, knowledge and ignorance of my past, and of my direction towards the future. What might seem to be a summit of respect for others in taking immediately, literally and with full seriousness and as correct, what they indicate by look, touch, word or action of what they think of me, is a disguised degradation of them. It is to degrade others to take them so literally and seriously, even if one does not understand oneself to degrade them. For to give the view of others *that* much respect is to forget that they are people. If I can be so subject to error on account of my subjectivity that I should come to think that it is only those who see me who see the truth about me then, if I pursue consequences consistently, I cannot in any way trust the view others take of me, since it too must be rooted in the very subjectivity in them which is supposed to vitiate my own understanding of myself when found in me.

Those who fail to question the natural tendency to tie together the notion of objectivity concerning oneself and the external observed view of oneself are bound to oscillate hopelessly between a virtual solipsism: a conceptual conceit in which one thinks that what one really is what one is for oneself, and a total collapse of one's inner sense of oneself in which the regard of others which shows such a wicked difference between oneself and oneself for others is taken as the revelation of the truth about oneself.

Sartre, to take the latest and best and most brilliant explorer of this fact (who still cannot adequately diagnose it) is fully committed to the idea that one's consciousness intrinsically germinates self-consciousness — that to be conscious of something is to be incipiently aware of one's consciousness of it. Reflection is always in the offing and only needs to be given its head for us to be fully conscious of our mode of consciousness. It then comes as an experiential shock to one's outlook, such a dialectical intrusion that we shudder from head to foot, to the core of our soul, when we are looked at (spoken to, and so on) by someone who appraises us when we are so absorbed in what we are doing that our own self-conscious appraisal is at a minimum. (*In Being and Nothingness,* Part III, Chapter 1.)

Since, in such shocks of intrusion, irreducibly and unreflectively, without argument or guesswork, one's own consciousness is that one's self is the object of appraisal by another, the idea of solipsism that consciousness is its own certainty of itself, crashes. If one does not trust in the character of one's own consciousness, then the solipsistic certainty is gone; if one does trust it, then one has learned that one exists for another as truly as one exists for oneself.

Sartre writes as if (or perhaps simply to describe the world of those for whom) one's consciousness or what one is for oneself, is at the mercy of others. (And they are singularly lacking in mercy.) He is much aware that he is involved in treating others as at once superior and as inferior beings. He speaks of the "Other" as if it were the all seeing eye of God, that ruthless bastard of the nursery and Sunday School who has the power but will not restrain it, to see our every innermost thought and feeling. An "Other" as God not only can see one's soul intimately as it is for oneself but knows it as one cannot know it for oneself, from a point away from oneself, but still just as intimately. To some extent Sartre mocks one's foolish tendency to treat, first oneself and the "Other" as an all seeing God. At least he gives equal weight to our conflicting and equally foolish tendencies to treat others as hidden from us, and ourselves as exposed to others. Our sense of objectivity concerning ourselves sometimes finds its home in self-intimacy, and sometimes in the sense of the superiority any person other than oneself has in being able to look at us from a real distance.

There was a great obsession with the problem of other minds in British and, in a different way, in European philosophy from the twenties of this century until about the sixties when language was at last acknowledged to be a public concern and so the would-be solipsist was convicted on the charge that he broke his own beliefs in saying anything, even to himself. It is only in Sartre that the alternative and equally gripping feeling came to extended articulation, that it is the existence of oneself, the nature and character of one's being-in-the-world, one's being-with-others, and one's being-with and being-by-oneself which cannot be known by oneself; that in the nature of the case one lacks any distance from oneself; one's reflectiveness shatters the consciousness which it was to illuminate. In this realization, the separateness of another seems to give him or her a total metaphysical advantage which we as object of that removed regard can in no way either ignore or destroy.

Yet we need neither collapse before another's look nor deny that what another observes and says of oneself cannot touch one's real, one's inner self. (That last alternative is the indefensibly skewed position that one is really one's mind and not one's body, taken up in order to preserve the possibility of a modicum of privacy.) True, seriously to accept that as living, thinking bodies, our thinking self is no more a different thing from one's body than is one's living body from one's body, we have to allow that, like it or not, we are present to those who observe us.

When we are "ourselves", both in unpremeditated and in meditated actions, we may be perceived to be what we are by those who intend or chance to look, though they may have to bear in mind what has been going on and what we have been doing. They may have to ask what we mean to be doing, and what it is we expect will be happening. (When we are not "ourselves" others must, at best, guess at and infer a state of mind, even when we do speak and answer.) When are we "ourselves"? We are "ourselves" in a wide variety of circumstances: when engrossed, careless or unguarded, and equally when deliberately expressive and exactly communicating with the precise gesture, expression and word.

It is a romantic error to confuse the clear revealing of oneself with a betrayal of oneself in loss of control. We are beings who seek control as much as we are beings who yearn to lose it. We are "ourselves" as much when, deliberately communicating, we employ our learned skills and our awareness of ourselves and others, and activate these sophisticated possessions at the very moment we need them in response to and in reactivation of what is given by the other to whom we "speak". This "speaking" is by word and gesture, by attitude, and equally by projection and by reserve. Even then, we cannot say that the others will perceive exactly or correctly, or that they will see all there is to be seen which is relevant to the idea they form. But it is wrong to say that they catch merely our metaphysically "outer garment" at such times. This is further supported by the fact that, for ourselves as much as for others, we "find ourselves" in our expressive and publicly deliberative activities, no less than we find our more private selves in our withheld thoughts, feelings, desires and speeches.

None of this argues against the possibility of degrees of restraint and deceptiveness in our expressions and actions. Yet it is as well to pay the metaphysical price of a loss of the possibility of absolute privacy, since only on that condition can we consistently regard ourselves as able to speak to another in body or word, and accept that we have answered or approached an "objectivity" worth having. Such an objectivity is an attitude which is a readiness to listen, to absorb, and a determination to stick by and to insist upon what (it seems) one knows. It requires a confidence which is, at one and the same time with equal priority of value, a confidence of one's own and a relation of confidence between oneself and others. Because we are as much to be observed as we are observers, because the character of what we do is as much to be known from its outward appearance as it is from how the one who acts, thinks and feels concerning it when engaged in it, because our sense of our solidity, our being real in the world and not a mere consciousness and consciousness-of-a-body rather than a body which is conscious — because of all this one's objectivity stands in essential relation to one's knowledge and understanding of oneself. For all of these and for many more reasons, one needs to live with another or, at any rate, relate closely with another or others, if one is to develop and to maintain one's sense of reality and one's sense of one's dimensions and those of others — the complexity of desires, fears, hopes, memories and expectations which are coordinated in even simple actions and the priorities and seriousness of one's commitments to aesthetic, moral, political and other values and ideals.

One might, out of a too narrow or conventional understanding of the phrase, object against the idea that objectivity requires living together. Taking up the sexual connotation, according to which living together is commonly contrasted with being married, it is enough to point out that people may live together who are not married, and people, whether married or not, may not live together, even though they are in the same house. And some who live alone according to the conventional sense of having no one else who resides with them, may live closely with those with whom they work. Certainly, just as much as people need to live together in order to develop or to maintain their objectivity, they may well need to separate their lives to some extent and in a variety of ways in order to maintain the perspectives and measure of each other. This is not to deny that, with great courage, people can live on accumulated capital. Cast up on a desert island or put in solitary confinement, they live on self-observation, observation, and a synthesis of memory and imagination of observations, reviewals, appraisals and enlightening acts of others towards them. One remembers how one has appeared and imagines how one would appear.

As there is a tension between the need for tension and the need for harmony between people who live together, there is a tension between the facts that on the one hand people need to relate, to realize themselves and each other in their words and acts towards each other and in the presence of each other and in their reaction to what just descends upon them unplanned and unforecasted, and, on the other hand, that one retains, keeps to oneself, even disguises what one thinks, feels or is doing. This is done, partly to maintain their own sense of themselves and their limits and to sharply clarify differences which must be established no matter how close they sometimes are and feel themselves to be to another. Also some confidences, disguise and secrecy are kept up in order to respect the differences of another, and in recognition of the fact that the interest and significance of what one thinks, has seen or has done, will not be the same to the one who hears as it is for the one who speaks.

People need to "live together", to fulfil some of each other's needs, and yet they have to avoid such a symbiotic relationship that neither is sufficiently himself or herself to have anything to offer. If they are to remain someone whom another would wish to live beside and to be close to, they must be able to keep, at times, separate confidences. Each preserves an unspoken but shared knowledge and awareness that the other is aware that she or he is aware that . . . each may and does keep some separate confidences.

"Confidence" and "confidences" — a double meaning of the word. We may explain the common force of the term from the idea of keeping a confidence. To keep confident, one must keep confidences. The confidence of one's own resides with the confidences which one is not to share with another. It is the understanding *that* one will keep confidences which is shared. Part of one's confidence, one's sureness that one will keep confidences, the secrets secreted in one's mind is the sureness that the other will keep confidences. Part of the sureness that another will keep the confidences which are between you is the sureness that he or she will keep his own confidences and those which are between him or her and others. One must be confident that the other will keep confidences; of others, safe from your intrusion; of yours, safe from others' intrusion.

Our confidence that we can and will keep a confidence is a feeling of our integrity. This is at least part of the feeling which allows us to express our needs and to respond to the needs of others without losing a sense of our separate solidity and its limits. Without this we cannot strike the needed balance between on the one hand, an autonomy of our inner life of restrained or otherwise hidden or unexpressed and undescribed thoughts, feelings, memories, hopes and fears and the stories, the history and the explanations we give of them and, on the other hand, the openness of oneself to others — one's expressiveness and capacity to accept and respond to another's expressiveness. Without the first more secret autonomy, no agreement can be struck. Someone must be bold enough to speak first, but he or she must have developed and distilled something to say. Without this inner autonomy, disagreement is no more than the debater's echo of things overheard and impassioned words said for effect or jerked out reactively, and agreement is confusing, dulling collusion. Yet without one's recurring and extended moments of spontaneous and deliberate communicativeness there is for oneself no measure, no dimension and no enrichment of one's inner life. Simply, for oneself, there is no striking effectual life and no feedback for one's inner life; for others, one does not exist except as a negativity — one who keeps to himself or herself and is caught in either the high conceit that no one else is worthy of his or her thought and feeling, or the low conceit that what he or she has is not worthy of anyone else's interest. (As in Peter Cary's *War Crimes*.)

The angle from which I write, that of describing, clarifying and to some extent recommending the possibility of and need for certain kinds of objectivity, results in a somewhat angular light being thrown on other matters. This is inevitable. I have argued that to be objective in any sense which brings us into closer and clearer understanding of things and people, one must choose, select and persist in a certain direction. One cannot simply remain sceptical or uncommitted. So far so good. But the tendency to distortion in such an investigation is that all things seem to be placed in the service of objectivity. Certainly, as did Charlotte Bronte's Jane Eyre when St John proposed their marriage as a great enabler of a joint missionary work, we recoil against the idea that one's love of another is only one more deed in the service of God. Yet now, it seems, I have been writing as if love were in the service of objectivity. From my words it seems as if the value of our closer personal relationships was that they allowed us to transcend privacy without loss of autonomy. The effect is only a trick of the light. In a book about love and affection the very same observations would have place objectivity in their service.

The need for consistency and for broad-mindedness

Autonomy and conceit, vanity and a due regard for one's own worth and self-perspective, arrogance and the need to render the views of another in terms of one's own in order to understand them — these and the drawing of lines between them loom as the next objects for our partial objectivity. But allow me to interpose some words to double as concluding these points on points of view, confidence and privacy and to introduce the need for the next stage of enquiry. I have written about the need for a balance between one's confident autonomy and one's respect and consideration for views different from and incompatible with one's own. Yet we are incoherent rather than broadly understanding if we suppose that we might attain an objectivity so broad minded and transcendent of our mundane involvements that we ourselves might be able to think to be true even one proposition which is contrary to our own current opinion. Granted, this tautology of reason is easily abused as an excuse not to enter into debate, dispute and exploration. And even when, in all reason and good conscience one cannot be moved, debate, argument and disputation still play some role in enabling one to understand how others can be in a position where still, uncompromisingly, one will not stand. Yet, for all the potential value of debate, for the most part it is the audience rather than the disputants who increase their understanding of the nature of the issues and the motives and reasons of those who engage in them. Those forced to conflicting debate for the most part forgo their capacity for cooperative exploration and creativity in ideas. In so far as one learns from verbal conflict in which one is involved, it is by later reflection, virtually as "audience" of what one has been forced or triggered into saying in order to maintain one's point of view, and by a subsequent realizing of the whole intricate detail of the different world of words within which an opponent of radically different point of view moves, that one has at least the materials for understanding the point of view of another with whom one still maintains a sharp or large disagreement. There is little diference, for example, between knowing Bishop Berkeley's arguments for idealism (that all that exists is ideas in the mind) and learning the intricacies (the broad outline is not enough, that still leaves one only with the astounded gape, or Dr Johnson's kick at a stone) of how one's language of stones, fish, wine, people, the babblings of brooks and the babbling of children, is all systematically and totally recast into a language of ideas, their qualities and of the minds which have these ideas. Similarly, in coming to understand fascism in an argumentative sense, we come in the same movement of mind to discern and to apprehend at what point the fascist will describe as "our sloppy-minded indulgence" of "parasites", "decadent louts" and "effete artists" what we would characterize as our tolerance, our fair respect for their opinions and their practical capacity to maintain their different lives.

This is not enough. To just disagree with those who radically differ from us in view and opinion is to make everything seem equal after all. They hold their opinions and we hold ours. Naturally we think we are right, but everyone equally has their opinion. This is too loose a liberalism. We must remember our lessons about confidence and insistence. We look again at the facts, at our hearts and our dictionaries, and come to some preliminary judgement. We propose our ideas to those we think most capable of seeing flaws in our reasoning; we approach those who know facts of which we are ignorant, or who have perspectives upon and conceptions of the facts which might easily escape us. If we are lucky — lucky in our own emotional resources to absorb and to balance all that we must and lucky in the goodwill and abilities of those with whom we must cooperate — then all that we know and feel and think may resolve into some judgement in which we feel confident. At that point, to say that we might be wrong after all, is an empty form of words. It is false modesty. It is a kind of conceit since in effect it is more of an immodest attempt to hedge our bets so that we won't have been entirely wrong if we do turn out to be wrong than a concession of a perceived flaw. To stick with the clear judgement that something is so, until something definitely overturns it or requires its reformulation, shows the more genuine humility before the facts. The more confident and open assertion places oneself most liable to a confirming or disconfirming confrontation with the facts.

No fine intention to be broad in understanding and wary of one's own dogmatism and myopias is excuse for remaining with inconsistent views. To countenance inconsistencies in the name of the dialectical process, or the baffling complexity of nature, or the finitude of our minds before God or to promote social harmony is to inflict schizophrenia upon ourselves. Where we cannot choose between inconsistent positions, we must be resolute in believing neither. We must be equally resolute in pursuing our thoughts or experiments or questions until we can decide upon one side. If that is impossible we have to reformulate the whole matter and dispense new and clearer terms. We no longer pick at old knots whose string is now too ragged to untangle into clear and usable lines. For if one is to be objective, and if to be objective is at least to attempt to be correct in one's attitudes, to attempt to be right in one's opinions, to strive to see clearly and to perceive distinctly and in close response to what presents itself, then one must strive for consistency. This is a simple and undeniable truth. To be inconsistent in belief is to be wrong in at least one belief, or in one part of a belief. (Sometimes inconsistenty lies in separate and inconsistent opinions, sometimes in a fusion, a confusion, of one spuriously integrated inconsistency.)

We need these reminders of the obvious need for consistency. We kick against the pricks of material and psychological reality: the aviation mechanics impatiently force an engine back into the strained mountings of a Douglas DC9 and some hundreds of people are killed when the engine tears off at take-off. In a similar way we feel the complexities in the web of our desires and needs and either pretend not to care about the inconsistencies, or wilfully force some single consistent judgement upon them. We kick against the logical, arithmetical and geometrical limits as we do against practical and physical necessities. In these absurd objections to the logic, the geometry and numeracy of the situations which we have to deal with, there is a subtle, though childish, interplay between wilfulness and unwillingness or sullenness. A child (an example I have, orally from Ryle) wishes to ride downhill all day and yet to come back home in the evening. A baby wants and takes a bite from its biscuit and wails that the biscuit in its paw is not whole. The jealous possessive lover desires the satisfaction which can come only from "a love and respect freely given" (Sartre) but is desperately dissatisfied at having anything less than full possession of mind and body of the one by whom he or she would be loved. A lover wants the delight of security within an abandonment in the mind and heart and body of the one who loves him or her, while refusing to recognize and to maintain the conditions for the person to be able to offer the support without which the joyful abandonment is a fall into existential terror; a collapse of each falling through the other in hysteria, each grasping at ghosts in machines, rather than sustaining each other as free spirits.

To be inconsistent in belief is to be mistaken, and to attempt to realize inconsistent desires is to live in error; it is to be logically bound to frustration. It is one form of self-destructiveness, of being a loser rather than just unluckily happening to lose. This truth is simple. There would be no issue to discuss if it were not for the complexities surrounding any attempt to realize it in practice. Not to realize these complexities leads one swiftly to a spurious "consistentism" in which we rigidly fix on propositions we neither fully understand nor can clearly know or see to be preferable to their negation of contrary, "just to be sure at least of consistency". This is a form of objectivism. In reaction against the dishonesty and aridity of that "consistentist" objectivism we are liable to fly to one form or another − sensualist, religious or anarchist − of irrational embrace of inconsistency. The deep inconsistency of these wallowings in subjectivity is typically disguised as a special kind of consistency, one which consistently takes its view to the limits, unafraid of consequences. For example, to be out and out sensualist is to regard as puritanical or life-denying the restraints, disciplines, submissions to fact and the powers of convention and other social pressures, the rigours of reasoning, experimenting, and the risks of pain and hardship involved in caring about anything, let it be oneself, others or even the hypostatized states of sensory pleasure, considered as valued existents in themselves. To be healthy enough and to have a free mind to enjoy, simply, even the pleasures of smell, colour, sound, requires one to take seriously the values of science. To take any or all of these matters seriously, as matters to be right about for their own sake, is to be inconsistent with the exclusive embrace of sensualism. So a spurious purism of interest in sensuality is born, which can be no more than an unworldly aestheticism. To be consistent in one's religious outlook is to force all one's forms of life and the awareness that goes with them — poetical, scientific, philosophical or artistic — within a merely spiritual context. It is spurious to plead that anything less would not be consistent with one's religious commitment, since the problem just is whether a religious commitment is consistent with all of what a person knows, both of and in himself/herself, and the worlds he or she discovers and in which he or she moves.

There may be a legitimate complaint behind the remark that someone is too rigidly consistent. It goes with the person being dogmatic and narrow minded, and not merely irritatingly insistent. The latent complaint is that the person refuses to stir from an original commitment and an insistence on following every consequence. When we criticize such people as overconsistent, we want them instead to regard consequences of their commitment as tests of their original position. An "overconsistent" dogmatist bravely or loudly stamps into every consequence as a commitment merely because it follows from that to which he or she already holds fast. That is the very least flexibility we ask for. We want more movement from our consistentist. We want him or her to extend the range of premises, of ideas, of descriptions of where he or she is and of what is seen from there. A true view is at least one developed by consistently working from where one began. But it is more than that. It is a well balanced, broadly described and freely articulated view. A person who persists in seeing things and describing them from one angle may issue statements no one of which is false; considered individually each is true of the facts reported, but the whole array of statements may be far from representing a true view of the situation; a person who baulks at widening and varying his or her angles of visions and increasing the range and diversity of terms in which observations are made displays a positive contempt for the truth, and a one hundred per cent mark for truths is no adequate defence.

PART II

Chapter Six

Objectivity as Style and Attitude

Style and imaginative detachment

Objectivity is a style of our subjectivity, gained sometimes by a more or less intelligent and knowing use of our emotions and thoughts, and even of our prejudices and our propensities to these. Sometimes we adopt this style or attitude of mind and sometimes we are cast into it by circumstance, by news, perceptions or events or by consequences of our actions. That sometimes we should have to strive to attain that same state into which we are sometimes cast against our will (or just non-voluntarily, with no aid of our will) is a phenomenon typical of the components of objectivity: a central part of any objectivity is the realization that the possibilities of control are limited, that what is desirable, even crucially necessary, is most often beyond one's power directly to produce, and that the very possibility of our resolute action itself depends on what we simply happen to find ourselves with and among.

The getting of objectivity and the holding on to it require emotions of curiosity, love, hate, desire and fear, as much as they require the moments of crucial control and restraint in the expression and harnessed use of these emotions. As emotion is something we must handle and at any rate accept in any real objectivity so, too, involvement or to put it more dangerously — the involvement of oneself, is necessary to any objectivity which has something to do with the best understanding and knowledge which we can gain. The various kinds of detachment, away from involvement or within it, which are essential to objectivity are themselves involvements of a new kind. We briefly detach ourselves from conversation or argument in order to think with greater single minded concentration; we detach ourselves physically from the people or things with which we are involved, in order to be caught up among the trees, grass, sky and wind.

To become detached from one's loving or sexual involvement with someone is to become sexually or lovingly involved with another, perhaps oneself. Or, if the detachment leads only to pure restraint, then it leads to an involvement in restraint. It can require as much energy and concentration and consume and absorb one's life as much to not do something, as to move mountains or to make the house shine like a new pin. So long as we live, our energies ebb and flow. As they flow, they flow somewhere; our choices concern their direction, and that only to a limited degree, and whether the energies are to flow or to ebb. Even in that last choice — whether to live as well as our circumstances permit, or whether in suicide or suicidal living, to make them ebb to nothing — we are not pure wills outside of the thoughtful, understanding and misunderstanding organism which we would vainly pretend to "own" or to "have". All along it constitutes us and gives rise to our possibilities of will and of allowing and of our mere passivities.

The contemplation of these facts alone, however, is fatalistic. Though our powers of objectivity are not those of Kant's noumenal self or Husserl's transcendental ego — we are not gods or ghosts outside or within ourselves — nevertheless the image of self as "ghost" disconnectable from "body", though crude and unreflective, is not entirely inept; it arises from our experience and actions of real imaginative detachments from things and displacements from ourselves. We can form an "objective" view of ourselves as "living in a certain period of history", or "having mass which requires the greater mass of the lumbering steel train which carries dozens of us", of "being a member of an economic class", of "being a biochemical organism", of "being something which will still remain when we are dead and totally subject to others' disposal and to bacterial decay", of "being observable by others in our everyday dealings and as much to be known to others in our observable expressions, behaviour, conduct and various dispositions, as we are to ourselves in our own heed of these matters and in our more inward sense of our thoughts, feelings, motives, inclinations and the rest". We can form these "objective" views. What it requires of us, as well as information, observation and inference, is the active use of our imagination. We can imagine how we look from the "outside": how we look from above or behind, and how our expressions, clothes and bodily attitude are liable to strike another. We can distinguish the impression we do make or which we are liable to make on others, from the feeling or meaning which we take ourselves to express. This realization, that if there are others ("the Other", as Sartre too gravely and mysteriously puts it) then equally one is another ("the Other") for others, lies centrally in our sense of objectivity. This is as true nationally and socially as it is in personal relationships. We know that there were people two hundred years ago who regarded themselves as settling a new land. We call it "Australia". From their written soliloquies and speeches on occasions for the expression of national sentiment, and from what we know of the common propensity of most humans to ponder, wonder and to speculate about the unknown future which will arise partly in consequence of their own actions, we have the right and the rational obligation to regard ourselves, not just as Australians in the eighties (in itself something of an historical synthesis in any case) but also as the previously unidentifiable objects of wonderment and speculation of those who sat down under the angophera trees to look at the harbour and said, "I wonder who will be here, what they will be doing, and what they will be like in two hundred years time!" Equally we place ourselves two hundred years hence, as best we can from what we know, and imagine ourselves as people in some more or less new culture's past, and wonder what they will know and think of us. Similarly, from our experiences in travel, from knowledge of fact, and then in active imagination, we go beyond the idea of Indonesia, Britain or Hungary, as "far countries" and suppose, infer, fancy or know to some extent what it is to look to our country from those places. Travel and learning provide the information and images by which we may reverse the direction of perception; we imaginatively place ourselves as the object perceived or thought about, and "look back" at ourselves as perceivers or thinkers. We imagine, perhaps concretely and factually, others we know as thinking of and looking over at us. Travel and learning do not in themselves constitute this imaginative reversal, but stimulate our imagination to an involuntary or non-voluntary understanding, or provide the materials upon which we work with a deliberate effort to "transcend" our limits of time and place.

In a similar way, our encounters and dealings with, and our studied information about, others may provoke an involuntary or non-voluntary understanding of them as people, as separate physical centres of consciousness with their separate lives of which

we know only small fragments. Or alternatively, from these encounters and this information one may deliberately imagine these
separate lives of others, and think of oneself not as an ultimate centre, but as one of the many objects and subjects of those lives. Yet,
whether produced without volition or whether formed deliberately,
this detaching imagination is not reduced to the conditions which
make it possible. And endless series of involvements with people,
an incessant taking up of causes, or an unflagging asking of questions and posing of problems do not add up to the objective attitude in which we seriously and distinctly think of, and put to
ourselves, how what we do and how the expressions of what we
think and feel and perceive will be thought of, felt and perceived by
another person. We may, after or amid such involvements, find
ourselves to our surprise with such an attitude; we may be found to
make the effort of forming it. In neither case do the involvements
quarantee the imaginative and inferential process by which we
guess at, wonder about and know something of another person's
inner life of restrained, hidden and disguised feelings and thoughts,
and by which we keep a distinct sense of how that life continues,
just as one's own does, when we are not in the company of or
relating to that other person. (Objectivity requires the capacity for
certain kinds of detachment within involvement. The next three
chapters illustrate this by describing various attitudes of mind
which are notoriously damaging to and lacking in objectivity — attitudes in which this imaginative detachment is lacking.)

"Truth", "facts", "objects"

Some people are impatient with an emphasis upon "the subject"
when discussing objectivity. Objectivity as it interests or should
interest philosophers and scientists, they say, is the objectivity of
facts or of truth, not the objectivity of people. Of course it is very
reassuring to speak and to hear of "the objective facts" and "the
objective truth". Yet the reassurance is evanescent before reflection. The phrase suggests that objectivity is a special quality of
facts or of truth. Which facts? Which truths? It can make no sense
to say, "It is a fact, but not an objective one" or, "It is true, but not
objectively true". To speak of the objective facts is simply to speak
firmly or dogmatically of the facts; perhaps there is a slight hint
that the facts concern objects, but this hint moves to embarrassment when one asks whether, in that case, there can be no 'objec-

tive facts' concerning people. Is psychology condemned in advance to a lack of objectivity, or is psychology ordered to proceed on the false, and therefore scarcely "objective" assumption that people are only objects? Furthermore, a debating point lies open here: if one is foolhardy enough to maintain that "ultimately" there are only objects and that none of these "objects" are more than mere objects, then again the point of speaking of the "objective facts" is entirely lost. The "objective facts" still reduce to the class of facts. Similarly, to speak of the "objective truth" may sound especially firm and realistic, but as fast as it offers reassurance, it opens the conceptual room to doubt. If "objective" makes a division between some truths and others, then there are non-objective truths. Is this not a sop to the intellectually half-hearted who like to be able to say that they have a truth, but that it is pointless for it to be objectively criticized, because it is a subjective truth? What is called a "subjective truth" can be allowed to be no more than a claim subjectively arrived at, which may or may not be true. It is not a truth which may be claimed to be so simply because it is thought to be so.

Perhaps, then, objectivity is a universal feature of facts or truths. Perhaps we should insist on the objectivity of truth and of facts, not so as to divide them from the ones which lack objectivity, but just to emphasize what every truth, every fact, must have or be. What can we make of this? Today, as I write, it is sunny. In what does the "objectivity" of this truth consist? Simply that it "really is" sunny, that I do not just fancy it, that I am speaking not of the fact that I think so, but of the fact that I think to be so. There is some inclination to explain the "objectivity" of the truth that it is sunny by saying that the condition one speaks of is "out there" (gesturing to what lies beyond the window) and not "in here" (gesturing to one's head or breast). This inclination is utterly confused, since there are objective conditions in the sense of conditions of objects "in here", just as much as "out there". Then the would-be defender of objectivity as "out there" must contrast it with what is "in here" in something other than a material sense of the phrase. What is "in here" as subjective in contrast with what is "out there" as objective is in here not as one's liver or oxidation processes are "in here" but as one's mind or feelings are "in here". Now the defender of objectivity as a universal trait of truths defeats himself, for he is committed to saying that there are non-material, non-objective truths; he must say that there are some things "in here" in a non-material sense. The conditions which make it true that there are feelings, a mind, "in here" are not, by his own distinction, "out there". There is no profit in dividing truths into those which concern what is "in here" or "out there" or in finding material and non-material senses of "in here". The explanation of the objectivity of truth in terms of what is "out there" is a failure. There are "things" "out there", "things" "in here", "things" "down there", "things" everywhere.

There is another tempting and more subtle explanation of our tendency to explain the objectivity of truth as its having to do with what is "out there". For almost all statements or thoughts, it is plain that the truth of the statement or thought lies in the fact that something other than the statement or thought itself exists. So I can point to something other than my statement, and say, "Without that (a goanna eating a fly) I would not have uttered or thought something true when I just said or thought 'That goanna is eating a fly' ". This story, however much it in turn is also redolent of redundance, at least can be told as well concerning thoughts or statements which concern thoughts, feelings or statements. The thought that my toothache or heartache is getting worse is not itself a toothache or heartache. The thought that my thoughts about Einstein's concepts of relativity must be very confused is not itself a thought about Einstein's concepts of relativity, though I cannot have it without having some thoughts about his concepts.

Though true, this story of objectivity offers very little. It says only that it is true that this goanna is eating that fly, if and only if, this goanna is eating that fly. And so on. When Tarski formalized and generalized this notion, it was felt to be a major advance in the understanding of truth since it enabled us to avoid self-referential paradoxes about truth. But it does not increase our understanding of objectivity.

We might attempt to amplify the notion of objectivity as the fact that thought and experience must involve something other than themselves. However, the claim that there must always be something which exists separately from the statement of it in order that there be "objective" truth creates more problems than it solves. While we might be glad to be rid of "This statement is false", which, if true, is false, and if false, is true, we are less sure that "This statement is true" is either false or meaningless, even though in the nature of the example there is nothing other than itself to make itself true. Furthermore, when Descartes thought that he was at least in some way conscious, and that he could not doubt that fact since his very doubting it was a form of consciousness, the consciousness which makes his thought that he is conscious true, may simply be the thought that he is conscious. It has not proved possible to show why his thought should not be self-sustaining and still coherent. His thought that he is conscious, that he exists as a conscious being, cannot be false for the very reason that he thinks it. It has as good a claim as any to "objective" truth, and yet concerns nothing other than itself. His ego-centering thought is certainly true; it is not a whim or fancy; it can be seen to be true on the basis of our understanding of concepts, logic and the intimacy of one's experience of one's own consciousness. Logically speaking, and speaking from the point of view of immediate consciousness, nothing outside itself is needed to make it true.

Furthermore, while it seems quite clear that logical and mathematical truths should win the accolade "objective" it is much less clear that they concern something "outside themselves". We can understand the mathematical law of induction, that *if*, if a property is held by any number n then it holds for $n + l$, then it holds for $n + 2$ and so on for the infinite series of integers. We do not understand this via the thought that some double conditional relationship exists apart from the existence of any thought, nor do we understand it from any idea of what numbers are apart from their being intentional objects of thought. Nor do we get any closer to understanding by saying that numbers and the relationships between them are created by thought, then to exist as separate things. None of the endless disputes between intuitionists, constructivists and formalists in mathematical theory disturb the clear sense of the necessity and possibility of objectivity in mathematics. This objectivity which is possible and necessary in mathematics is the objectivity which is required of us. It is we who have to set aside prejudice, conventional thinking, wishful thinking and evasions into obscurity. The sense of something apart from us, when we struggle to find or delightedly realize what must be the case in logic or mathematics, simply is our sense of being measured by the difficulty of a problem.

Serious harm is done by the thoughtless use of the pleonasms "objective facts" and "objective truths". On the one hand, if you simply ask a person whether it might ever be right, or be the best of various undesirable actions, to steal or to kill someone, they may be prepared to carefully consider the character of the examples you bring forward, measure their intuitions against careful thoughts of conflicting considerations and certainly treat the matter as something to be discovered. On the other hand, if you say, "Are there objective moral facts?" we are liable to stagger and to lose our balance altogether. We may be pretty sure, on careful reflection, that it would be unjust and cruel for someone to be treated in a certain way. But if objectivity means the existence of what we consider quite apart from all thought and feeling about it, then we are not so sure that there are "objective moral considerations". This is because it is spurious to speak of objective, as distinct from supposedly other sorts of considerations, as it is spurious to speak of objective, as distinct from any other sort of fact or truth. There are serious or frivolous considerations, there are supposed considerations which are not real — a harm one alleged, it is discovered, does not occur. In this sense, there are "subjective" considerations in any study or enquiry. The set of such "subjective considerations" is just the set of our mistakes and misunderstandings.

Ironically, the wish to regard objectivity as a property of objects, a property of "numbers", of "external moral orders" and the like, is an example of one of the most common kinds of notorious "subjective" attitudes. To be to some extent objective in whatever we think about or feel or do — this is up to us; it is our problem to be solved by skill, art and endeavour. By trying to find special realms of objective things to study, we are trying to shift this responsibility from ourselves onto the things about which *we* are supposed to be objective. It is easy for us now to see the "subjective" projection in which Berkeley were engaged when he called matter "stupid, senseless and inert". He spoke of it as might an irritated schoolteacher to a student he had failed to inspire. It has not been so clear to us that when we are inclined to speak of "objective matters of fact" we are engaged in a similar projection, and that we should, if we use those somewhat hackneyed terms at all, speak of "objectively, and in a matter-of-fact attitude, dealing with the matters".

Objectivity is a characteristic of one's approach to or attitude to things. To be objective is to have an attitude such that one's understanding of and opinions about a thing are drawn from and worked out in continual interchange with it. At least this is the first requirement. From this can develop the reflective imagination by which one is aware that oneself is equally a periphery to the consciousness of others as it is a centre of its own consciousness. Conditions which interfere with the interchange of subject and object thereby diminish the objectivity of the subject: it is to these conditions that we now turn our attention.

Chapter Seven

Self-involvements and Connections with Others

Vain, narcissistic, conceited, full of pride, arrogant, envious, jealous and malicious — it is when a person is involved in these special and partly avoidable styles that he loses his objectivities. These lapses, moralistically called "vices" occur within our unavoidable subjectivities of thought, feeling, emotion, motive, reasons, hopes, fears, desires and intellectual limitations. It is these lapses into the various species of self-absorbed outlook, not the subjectivities themselves which threaten objectivity. There is no obvious list of opposites for these terms. For cool we had hot; for involved, detached; for dispassionate, passionate; for biased, true; for prejudiced, judicious. But in respect of this new set of detriments to objectivity it is negative action which is required of us — the actions of not being vain while nevertheless concerned with our various kinds of appearance, of not being narcissistic while nevertheless maintaining a healthy self-love and so on. There is no set of virtues corresponding to the "vices" I have mentioned. This is because they are malign forms of virtues.

Being vain

It is neither a vice nor a detriment to objectivity to be interested in how one appears. This is partly because one may wish to appear as one is: being athletic, one may wish to appear athletic; being just, one may wish to appear just. One may fairly complain of being unjustly regarded if one is regarded as worse than one is, but only if one has taken reasonable steps to appear as one is. One must take care to give the right impression. To spurn all such necessity, to "high mindedly" consider oneself about all such considerations is arrogant, for it is a refusal to consider the point of view of others. You cannot fairly expect others to think that you are honest or kind just because you are; they must gain evidence that you are so. Furthermore, many forms of appearance are valuable characteristics in themselves; it is not merely, in all cases, that the quality one wishes to give the appearance of possessing is valuable. To put on a sprightly appearance is to be, at least briefly, sprightly. To concern oneself with one's physical appearance so that one look well is to succeed in being, even if temporarily, beautiful, elegant, pretty, grand or whatever.

To think that one shouldn't have to bother with appearance is, I have claimed, a kind of arrogance. A writer who says, "Just so long as when it is finally deciphered, my premises are true and well founded and my inferences valid, it matters nothing that my arguments appear obscure or irrational" is arrogant if he thinks he ought to be believed or respected because of the actual truth and validity in his writing.

The notion that appearance is of no value in itself, quite apart from its tendency to lead or to mislead people about the character of something which appears, is a kind of vanity. It is the "vain conceit" that one's own reality, is constituted by the way it appears to a point of view unique to oneself, untutored by any other. In this attempt to secure one's self, one's identity and one's views of oneself inviolate from the "prying fingers and eyes" of others one begins to come up against the vanity of vanity, how vanity is "in vain". For this attempt to keep one's self as large as possible, as unthreatened by what would seem to reduce it by destroying its conceits, is founded and founders on the assumption that one is ontologically thin. Even a poor piece of rock is ontologically thicker than oneself when considered in vanity. A pebble has a past, which it does not and need not recollect; it has a future which it does not and need not expect. It has an indefinitely complex physical and chemical structure. Perhaps, with no help or conceit of its own it is a compelling statue of joy or of grief. It toils not, neither does it spin, and yet its nature is inexhaustibly complex. Suppose I conduct myself along these lines: what another says about my past is "irrelevant because that is not how I remember it", what another says about my future is "irrelevant because that is not how I project it", what another says about my present attitudes, feelings, beliefs or the meaning of my actions is "irrelevant because I am the one with the attitude, the feeling, the belief, I am the one who acts and it is only up to me to declare on the intention of them". If I take these attitudes, obviously in self-aggrandisement and self-protection, then I succeed only in demeaning myself, for I relinquish ownership of my body except as a fluctuating private body-image; I abdicate from the reality of my past except as a series of intermittent flashes which cannot be collected or interpreted; I forgo the future except as spasmodic apprehension. For if I ask not "What memory images float back to me?" but rather "What did I do? What did I see? What was said to me?" then I invite answers which I have never thought of; I call forth observations which I never made, and I am answered in terms which are not my own. Turgenev, in *Fathers and Sons,* remarks of the father that his head is full of memories, and that he never remembers anything.

This is not to say that one gives up one's own position as self-critic, self-judge and self-observer; it is not to deny the force and necessity of my own avowals of my own intentions, feelings, motives and reasons. Objectivity walks a fine line between vanity and loss of autonomy. To be vain involves already taking into yourself the apprehended observation, criticism or praise of others instead of giving it its own independent and separate due. But objectivity requires the capacity for stout resistance to criticism, too. If objectivity involves the ability to see yourself imaginatively as from an outside standpoint, either as you would see yourself from a distance, or as some other specific person you know would do or, more impersonally, as the public would do, then this means being able to provide criticism or praise of yourself in place of the criticism or praise which might be given by another. Briefly, to become objective requires autonomy, and autonomy requires a measure of replacement of being criticized by others by self-criticism. To a large extent the ability for self-appraisal is learned from reflection upon the appraisals given by others, and from one's thought about the role of the other person and their standpoint and assumptions in making their criticism or in delivering their praise. Equally one gains the ability for self-appraisal, and an understanding of what it involves, from one's attempts at appraisals of others, and from their reactions and responses to these, and from one's further reflection upon and discussion of these incidents. Then, of course, quickly the pupil disciplines the teacher, the child instructs the parents and perhaps the one criticized by others learns to criticize himself or herself better than those who criticized. So we become to some extent thoughtfully impervious to the praise of some people, or to some kinds of praise; we become determinedly resistant to criticism and derogation by some, and to some kinds of those dispraises, without thereby being conceited or vain. A person might well be judged vain too hastily simply because he or she placed his or her self-appraisals ahead of those given by others, for a person is a fool and lacks autonomy and is incapable of serious reception or delivery of appraisal who simply accepts the greater validity or force of outside criticism simply because it is "from the outside", "independent" and so on.

Though, on the whole, we do tend more to reject the fair criticisms of others in favour of self-praise, it is easy to see the lack of objectivity involved in going to the other extreme and giving others the final say just because they are others. A person is stupid, flattered, rendered fatuous as one who is flattered, if he accepts the praise of others just because it is praise and from others, in place of heeding and searching the implications of his own disquiet about the possible lack of clarity or evidence of his opinions. If one's appeal for objectivity is to "the outside opinion of others", it cannot be logical to heed it when it is unfavourable, and yet to ignore or to doubt it when it is favourable. Such a stance is self-demeaning and self-confining. It is not a strict self-criticism but a false humility. Equally, to reverse the attitude and to accept praise just because it is from others is to be open to flattery or to sincere but ignorant or overimpressed admiration; it is limply to fail to judge critically the worth and informedness of one's observers. Unless one already pays them the respect of such critical appraisal, you have not put them in a position to render you "outside criticism". That you render them such "outside criticism" is your due to them as much as their's is due to you. For all this, to accept criticism just because it is from others is to dim one's lamps no less. For though it is easy to see the foolishness of accepting praise just because it is from others, it is not quite so easy to see the equal stupor in accepting criticism or disparagement in this way. To lack firm reasoned resistance to this, and to waver only because our answers do not take hold in the minds of critics, is to be as open to malicious, uncomprehending or simply ignorant remarks as is a conceited person to flattery. Not only that. Sometimes people who are equally well intentioned, informed and intelligent find themselves with thoroughly opposed views. If neither can meet the criticisms of the other without falling back on the beliefs which are in dispute, what are they to do in the name of an objectivity which pays full and immediate respect to the outside criticism by others?

Swap their opinions: "I'll have yours and you have mine"! Then begin the debate from opposite corners, with instantly the requirement that they now swap again?

The attitude of vanity is distinguished in two main ways from that proper sense of one's privacy and individuality which we call autonomy. First, a vain interest in one's appearance differs from that given from our own autonomous judgement and, secondly, vanity involves a prejudice about the role and force of the observations and judgements of others, whereas autonomy, the good, involves an open judgement and a certain kind of even-handedness. First, the special and fatally confused character of the kind of interest in appearance characteristic of vanity: vanity is not merely an interest in one's appearance, nor can it be defined simply as an intense such interest. A fashion model and, in a different way, an actor or actress must be vitally concerned with the appearance of their bodies and dress. Yet they are not thereby defined as vain. A judge, interested in maintaining respect and understanding of the law, is concerned that he appear just, as well as being just, even if at the last resort, when there is a conflict of interest between the two, he will choose to be just rather than to appear to be. Philosophers, interested of course in fostering and maintaining the values of reasoned discourse and steady speculation, will desire to appear reasonable, and if reasoning leads them to put forward views and arguments which they know are liable to appear irrational, obscure or simply very strange and therefore an affront to conventional reason, will do their best to present their observations and reasonings in the most reasonable appearing light. If it is the values of original and mind provoking thought which they wish to encourage, they will endeavour to be striking and dramatic in presentation. None of this concern with appearance is vain and, if well executed, it need not be in vain. Vanity is a kind of self-stultifying interest, and this explains both any observer's great impatience with it, and the immediate sense of the phrase "in vain".

A person may dress only to please himself. He may be thought egotistical to care nothing for the opinions and tastes of others; he may be too self-centred, you might say. Still, he may not dress in vain. He may please himself. In irritation to his imperviousness to the tastes of others, some will call him vain, but other criticisms are more apt — insular, too self-contained, inconsiderate about whether he affords aesthetic pleasure or distress to others.

Another person might dress only to please others. Though some will criticize him for a lack of autonomy — for a lack of a sense of identity and his own worth — for a bad kind of humbleness at the core of his outer finery, others will see in him the most obvious kind of vanity. They notice the time he must spend looking anxiously or with serious concern at the mirror. They remark how he persists in enquiring of his friends how he appears. For all this, though many who are vain about clothing, dress to please others, simply to clothe oneself to please others is not thereby to dress in vanity, or in vain. A person who has a clear mind and a clear motive — professionally as a model to earn a living, professionally as a business person or politician to create the right impression, professionally or in an amateur capacity to arouse desire, or simply to secure admiration — such a person who knows what he or she is doing may take the utmost concern about their appearance and maintain an accurate measuring of success and the means which are found to ensure it. In the midst of what may be regarded by some as a thoroughly frivolous or selfish concern, they maintain that critical self-distancing look into the mirror, that observing searching glance and harking to the expressions of others so as to gather the nature and sincerity of admiration or derision, the unguarded involvement with the responses and initiatives of others from which springs a lively sense of their reality, and their reality as other than oneself, and an imaginative displacement away from their own point of view towards the mind and view of the others. Such an intense and serious interest in how one appears to others is an example of a full objectivity, not of vanity. What is said here applies in much the same way to the wearing of opinions and attitudes.

Vanity is to be understood in contrast with simple self-interest and equally in contrast with an exclusive but clear headed interest in the interests of others towards others or to oneself. To be vain is not merely to wish for the interest, praise and esteem of others concerning one's bodily, intellectual or other appearance. Such a wish, in itself, is a reasonable consequence of proper self-regard. And vanity is not simply a self-absorption in which one cares nothing for (or is scarcely even aware of) the impression one makes on others and the judgements they form. Certainly it is not only an innocent lack of awareness of the impression one makes which avoids vanity. To be vain is to attempt to maintain the unstable synthesis of a desire for the esteem of others, while making oneself at the same time sole arbiter and interpreter of the standards and judgements of others. In vanity, one desires the independent admiration of others, but implicitly or explicitly rejects the observations and judgements of others just insofar as, and just because, they disagree with one's own. In self-absorption, the door to the conscious life of others is closed. At any rate it is well lined with muffling substance whereas, in vanity, one desires and heeds the knocking, but suspiciously checks the credentials of the visitor as an admirer before admittance is granted. A vain person is like someone who thinks that all swans are white and appears to be very scientific, searching the world through to check on his opinion. However, he looks at something to see if it is a swan only after he is quite sure that it is white. After many years he says, returning from many distant lands, "I never had seen any but white swans".

Is everyone vain then? How can one prefer the opinions of those who disagree with one; how can one prefer the tastes of those whom one finds distasteful, or who finds one's own tastes repellent? Doesn't everyone keep to the company of those who largely endorse their opinions? The answers are that it is irrelevant that people prefer opinions which agree with their own, and false that no one can sustain the company of those who disagree. Certainly, to think something is so *is* to think that you are correct in thinking it; it is to think that those who think to the contrary are mistaken. This is the demand of consistency, not of vanity. Yet it is spurious to offer this as a reason for listening to or encountering only the expressions of opinion with which one agrees. One cannot but think one's opinions are correct, but one listens in case one finds one has been mistaken, or in case one finds oneself with reason acceptable and credible to the other which will convince him of your own case.

On the one hand we have vanity — the desire for the recognition and admiration of others, coupled with the desire to "flee the Other", as Sartre would say. On the other hand we have retrograde humbleness, in which a person desires recognition and admiration, but capitulates before criticism, wishing at all costs to "be on good terms" with those who differ, and to avoid confrontation and unpleasantness. Uriah Heep, in Dickens' *David Copperfield,* cringes before his "betters" in what I call retrograde humbleness (to distinguish it from a praiseworthy state of mind which is still sometimes dangerously called "humility"). He does not have a steady observing regard for the virtues of others, and therefore no chance of respect or admiration for them. Such a person must hate himself for the loss of self-respect involved in this attitude. Also, though he must be irrational to do so, he must hate those who induce it in him. If "The meek shall inherit the earth", it is because their buried, murderous resentment will out.

The praiseworthy state is dangerously called "humility" because there is an inescapable tinge of implication of inferiority in the notion. A good composer might be said to have a "due humility" in the face of a great one. Well, the attitude which is due does not make the good composer feel worthless. He recognizes that he has talent, and recognizes that another has genius. Yet his *feeling* is not inferiority. It is one of admiration, joy and delight at the work of genius. So a person can keep his or her dignity in the face of greater people, and survey with equanimity achievements which are beyond them. They are proud, not humbled, to recognize greatness and, if there is competitiveness at all, it is no dishonour to be beaten by such an opponent.

It is part of the instability of vanity that although the person who is vain wishes to show his face in order to be admired, vanity is not admired and so he cannot show himself as he is without evoking contempt or annoyance. Vanity must hide its face as fast as it shows it, and it is from this need that the complex evasive structures of vanity arise. In being vain, a person must attempt to resolve in some direction the tensions (the "contradictions", you might say) of vanity. Within being vain, this resolution is necessarily in vain. It is only by a chance circumstance or in dawning realization of the futility of the enterprise or, if shocked, shamed or sharpened into some sort of objectivity by the complaints of those victimized by the vain, that one's actions and feelings in vain, move one out of vanity. The most obvious defence tactic of vanity is to be surrounded only by friends. Such, the vain hope, will give them the satisfaction of outside esteem without the threats, pains and dislocations of cross-cutting criticism. But beware. Friends, real ones, will tell you what only a friend would ever say. You have V.O. Not all your repartees are so witty nor your opinions so wise as you would think. Your profundities are empty pomposities and your tenderest endearments are disguised self-seeking grasps for a permanent and unreserved affection which only a self-pitying and neurotic fool could ever have thought his due even from those who loved him or her best.

So he flies to friendly acquaintances, becomes a member of a group of collusive sycophants. It isn't so satisfactory. He must pay his dues of flattery, which can be irksome enough but, worse, he cannot then escape the sense of his own artifice and falsity, and thus wears too thin the pretence that what he hears from the others of his little in-group is real praise, real admiration, spontaneous applause. Admiration among the vain is like honour among thieves.

He may retire to public lie . . . life. . . . A person may develop his abilities as an entertainer, politician, magician of one sort of another and be admired or even be an object of a public affection directed at him at a distance, by those who have no personal attachment to him and no intimate knowledge of him. A person may not deliberately or self-consciously aim at this solution: indeed it is not likely to work too well if one thinks of it as "solving the problem of vanity", rather, one would just gravitate to it, not knowing its hazards. From the point of view of living in vain, there are many advantages to the public life. One is not expected to, indeed it is thought quite inappropriate if one does, express sincerely one's thoughts and feelings. Even with great actors, comedians and statespeople for whom real feeling informs and motivates their work, it still must be a mask which is presented to the public, however much there are real and serious concerns determining the expressions of the mask. Without this realization, the actor "tears a passion to pieces", the comedian is a maudlin sentimentalist and the politician is a fanatic. So the advantage to vanity of public life is that something may be presented for admiration to others, for which the person behind it can take no small credit, and that the public, even the learned discerning public, do not and are not supposed to know the person intimately. Thus he does not risk exposure of his self to "the sting of reason, the splash of tears" (Garfunkel in "Still Crazy After all these Years"). If a person is successful in public then until he meets his Watergate he may project from his personal reality only what he judges the public will admire.

Yet the disadvantages for succeeding in vanity are very great. The person's conceits about what will please an audience must quickly be shattered; if he clings to the conceits then he regards the public cynically as fools to which he must pretend to pander in order to earn his money, to be famous or to be admired. This cynical regard for their praise is all very insubstantial gruel to the ego, for what is the use of being famous among those one despises; what is the satisfaction in praise from "fools"? If he loses his conceits merely in order to make his tastes and ideas fit the demands of the audience, then he moves, in his consciousness at least, into retrograde humbleness. "Who am I to question what the public wants?", he fawns and yaps. What is left to him then, if he understands the fore-ordained vanity of these routes? If he listens to the criticisms seriously, taking his own ideas seriously and listening seriously to the critics and also answering them when he can, finally allowing himself to be persuaded to change when he cannot answer after all care and searching so that he can have a proper pride in the changes to which his need to meet the public brings him, then his vanity has died. Who will mourn its passing?

Where vanity will not yield and where self-conceit is implacable, it turns into arrogance, vanity's final line of defence through outright aggression.

Becoming arrogant, from being vain

Arrogance is to be considered in its own right. But for a moment, consider it as an aggression to defend vanity. In public life this translation from being vain to being arrogant means lying about what one's opponents say and do; one "arrogates" to oneself the right to determine the words upon which the public is to judge them. It involves more or less drastic choices from among the well known array of repressive actions: preventing one's opponents from speaking or from being heard, torturing them to make them say what you want them to, imprisoning them to "prevent them polluting the minds of the public", depriving them of property, threatening, harassing and bullying them. In private life it is usually limited to lying, shouting people down, ignoring them, refusing to listen, deliberately misconstruing what is said, pretending not to understand, calling people "emotional and subjective" when they get upset at such treatment, and wilfully forging ahead in one's own way against protests and against one's own inner uneasinesses. This oppressive and self-deceiving behaviour goes by such titles as "maintaining academic standards against the invading student barbarians", "defending Marxism against corruption by bourgeois elements" and "defending the sanctity of the family against moral decadence."

Look again at the good qualities present in, though betrayed by vanity. It is a foolishly self-abnegating purism to be anything other than happy about being admired for one's qualities and achievements. The purist may attempt to say, "Just admire, love, respect, be impressed by my music, my mathematics, my comedies or whatever. I am not vain. I refuse your admiration of me for these arts of mine." There is already a vain self-concern in this attempt to extricate oneself so entirely from one's works. Remember, if he thus escapes all praise, he escapes all blame when his works reveal male chauvinism, racism, irrationality, blithe unconcern about the welfare of others and so on. Now "Just look at my works, don't look at me" begins to ring a different bell. In any case, how can we admire someone's works of art without admiring someone for producing them? True, we should be very cautious in what we suppose about that person in the rest of his life, apart from producing such art. A novelist may expose in his or her work the wrongs of cruelty, prejudice and insensitivity, and yet in his or her own life display these very faults more than most. It may be his or her awareness of them which helps to give them the sense of urgency to work. But even if, as is unlikely, a person were admirable in no respect apart from his or her art, and the art was good, that person would be properly creditable at least in producing it, and has no right to refuse admiration for having produced it.

In being vain this right desire to be justly admired collapses into a different form. The difference is that a person comes to do good work (if it is good at all) in order to be admired, and would rather be sure that he was admired than that his work was good; furthermore, in being vain, a person desires not just to be admired, but to be envied. He may no longer even desire to be admired, for even when the reversal of object has occurred, and it is the admiration of him for his work, rather than that his work be so good as to command admiration which has become the aim, the conditions of satisfaction are still liable to be too rigorous for his vanity. This desire to be envied, though a natural consequence from the instability of vanity, is conceptually very strange. Envy is partly a malicious feeling, and it is strange that anyone should desire that others bear him malice. But it is not so strange that people wish to feel in a position of superior power of prestige — perhaps wise reflection persuades some of us of the limited satisfaction to ourselves, and the dubious moral premises, and the insensitivity to rights and feelings which are involved in any thoroughgoing pursuit of it, but at its simplest such a desire is the partly realistic response to our wish to "have our own way". We cannot have that without some power, and with most of the "ways" we wish to have, we need to get people to go along with us, or not to obstruct us. As a desire for power (the power to attract admiration and the powers consequent upon gaining that admiration) vanity is understandable and not intrinsically foolish; the foolishness of it, the "in vainness" of it lies in its dual and conflicting demands — that there be a fully separate admiration and respect from someone who is free and equal, and that it should be within one's power to control and to compel this praise.

Being envious, to defend one's vanity

This last desire is outright inconsistent, and the desire to be envied is one of the various possible stratagems employed to prevent the inconsistency becoming so blatant that vanity collapses under its own weight, leaving its owner back on the gritty ground floor of reality. To be envied is to be regarded by one who is, or who feels himself to be, in an inferior position in respect of the regard. To wish to be envied for something is to wish the person who praises you to feel inferior on account of it. This "inferiority" of regard requires some care in definition. A music critic, for example, who cannot play the violin at all, is not bound to envy the performer whom he reviews. Indeed, envious criticism is as likely to arise from one who is an equal or better performer, if that person doubts his or her ability, or feels that the musician he or she is reviewing is venturing on his or her territory or stealing the thunder. A critic confident of his or her critical abilities can criticize fairly, not feeling an inferior musician for the reason that in being a critic he or she is not being a musician; he or she is not defining him or herself in that "mode of being". An extraordinary degree of objectivity is required of one performer to be a fair, accurate and detailed critic of another performer's ability, and that objectivity is supplied, if at all, by the strength of the direct interest in the "object" (how the music is played). That is, if a person is interested in playing well, then at most an interest in being better than another is only secondary; since the performer's objective musical interest in playing well, he or she has as much an interest in and therefore is as ready to love and admire the playing of another as he or she is interested in his or her own playing. Yet, for all that this objectivity of interest and love is possible, one person must clearly change their frame of mind from being a performer to being a critic, in order to be objective in criticism, and must equally change in frame of mind, no matter how valuably informed from the period of being a critic, in order to be objective in musical performance.

It almost goes without saying that the point of the desire to be envied, considered as a stratagem of vainness, is to have the advantages of admiration without the risks. We gain the sweetest praise from those we consider to be and those who consider themselves to be of equal or greater power and ability and perceptiveness. When they give it, this is delightful, but we cannot count on getting it. So vanity is sometimes expressed in the attempt to overwhelm the audience, to sweep them off their feet, to carry everything before one. The trouble is that if you sweep people off their feet, you have to carry them. And so the risks return. If you don't carry them they become disillusioned; if you do carry them then you are confronted with reality again: you must go beyond any self-delusion of vanity to consider what will, in fact (not just in your conceited imagination) entertain, impress or delude them, or whatever you mean to do to them by way of self-aggrandisement. To be brief, either one attempts to live "vainly" without the reality-recognizing "humiliating" fact of stratagems, in which case that way of being founders upon the existence of the "Other"; or one employs the stratagems, but then the private comforts of admired vanity are necessarily lost. One has had to objectify oneself, to imaginatively project beyond oneself to understand how one appears and why. In this, the "project" of maintaining a consciousness in vanity founders on the social, conventional, psychological and geographical and economic facts also which have had to be truly recognized. This latter consciousness is what is often called, and more often calls itself, with a slightly bitter laugh, "realism". The person "has learned by bitter experience what price has to be paid in order that he be liked or accepted". The trouble with his so-called realism is that still he is not fully aware, if this is his consciousness, that this somewhat cynical realism is the consequence of a non inevitable vainness or conceit in the first place.

Attempting to live "vainly" without stratagem founders upon the existence of others, not simply because there are others and the "realist" must understand that he cannot expect people to be unself-concerned enough to praise and admire without stint, without due reward and incentive. This is still a thoroughly conceited supposal. Compare: if you expect people to be happy with you, you will sometimes be disappointed, and sometimes even cruelly misused. Nevertheless the expectation of happiness is not essentially idiotic. It is feasible. It happens, both to one's surprise and also as a result of one's arranging that it occur. Similarly it is not impossible or absurd that someone be sad with you, grieve with you, eat with you, sleep with you, travel with you and so on and on. But you can't expect people to share your vanity or your arrogance in this sense of being vain with you or being arrogant with you.

When a person is said to be "arrogant with you", this means only that he or she is being arrogant in his or her thoughts and actions *towards* you, not that you join in a common arrogance. You cannot "arrogate with" as you might "laugh with". For to be arrogant is to arrogate, and to arrogate is to attempt to take over and to make over the other into your own warp in your own terms. The relationships between the arrogant must be warring. If collisions are avoided, it is collusions, not intimate agreement which are possible. You can say, "What a conceited pair! And how they are collusive, and encourage each other's conceit!" Similarly, "How they aid and exacerbate each other's arrogance towards others on political or other issues!" Conceit and arrogance can join people in their attitude to other things and people, but it can't join them in their relation to each other. For to be arrogant to another is to arrogate to oneself the nature, importance, validity and terms of the other person's point of view, of his or her thoughts, feelings, motives and evaluations of things. To be vain, to live in one's own conceit, is to refuse a direct interest in another thing or person for its or his or her own sake, but to take an interest in things or people only as it is expected that they will earn admiration or envy for oneself. Hence, though people may be collusive in vanity or arrogance, they cannot be joined in understanding, in those attitudes.

Being envious and being jealous

Envy and jealousy deserve consideration in relation to objectivity in their own right, as well as for their connection with vanity. Arrogance, the self-appropriation naturally coupled with vanity, will find its place. To be envious is to bdesire what another has, on account of the fact that the other has it. Envy is traditionally linked with malice. To envy rather than to admire, respect, vicariously enjoy or to be happy with or for someone is to be in a frame of mind ready made for malice. On Hume's cycle of the "bad" emotions, emotions cause those which most resemble them: grief and disappointment give rise to anger (against the cause of the grief), anger to envy (of those not similarly disappointed) envy leads to malice against the successful, malice to grief, and so on around the bitter cycle again. (*Treatise of Human Nature,* Book II, Part 1, Sec. IV.) In contrast, joy naturally throws one into love, love into generosity, pity, courage and pride. (These patterns are oversimplified, of course, and Hume is the first to admit it. Nevertheless he is close to the mark in reporting how things proceed without either a determined and understanding will and understanding of oneself or others, or else lucky or unlucky changes in circumstances.)

Hume's cycles can be made to appear yet more conceptually and casually obvious as one considers in more detail the character of the successive falls or rises. Envy is potentially malicious because an envious person does not simply want that for which he envies another. Only a radical alteration in attitude can break the link between envy and further misery, since there is no coherently describable object which can satify the demands of envy. It is, in this sense, literally "unobjective". In envy a person cannot enjoy the thought of another's success or joy of any kind, since he feels diminished, inferior, cheated and resentful at the success of the other. Thus he is cut off from a large measure of the pleasure most easily available to us, at the least expense of effort and least requirement of circumstance. People are lucky if they always have a lover; often enough they find even themselves undesirable or unsatisfactory. But as Hume says, people have a natural sympathy, and when they observe or hear of lovers in their state of love they are interested, excited, curious and inspired themselves to desire and to love. Naturally, such vicarious enjoyment has its limits of satisfaction but, compared with the emptying gnaw of envy, it is bliss. This is so even though we should observe that the joy of sympathy, if we make a thing of it in itself, degenerates into mere voyeurism. The same goes for material possessions. A person interested in architecture is glad and interested to hear of some house a person has had built. His interest being directly in the object, it can encompass a pleasure that someone has built the structure and owns it and uses it in the way that the architect's care and imagination deserve.

Not only is a person deprived by envy of a great many of the simplest and most immediate satisfactions; he must also suffer pain, for he feels diminished by the other's possession, doing and fame; another's gaining of love is a cause for his hatred and another's greater capacity to give love is a cause for his humiliation. He is at least as strongly disposed to the damage and diminution of the other as he is to the cultivation of his own success, and thus is engaged in a doubly destructive course. For apart from the fact that in pursuing the harm of another he will neglect and damage himself, and bring retribution upon himself, nothing he does in envy can constitute clear success in his aims, since his aims are themselves unclear. If his were a case of simple wish to harm, then he would be satisfied by inflicting it. But it is not. To envy is to wish for something essentially because another has it. Suppose, as in the simplest case, you wish to take it from that person. Many envied things are rather difficult to transfer. One could scarcely steal in order to possess for oneself another's good looks, good health, cheerfulness and wit, reputation, fame or attractiveness. In envy one will damage or destroy those traits or possessions in another even though it is absurd to suppose that by this theft we gain the quality ourselves. Where transferable goods or powers are envied (money, houses, cars, political powers, etc.) still simply in gaining them oneself one is not satisfying envy, since one is not gaining those traits or possessions for the reason that, or in that another person has them.

This last remark is no mere hair splitting verbal device. What happens in envy is a loss of interest, concern, regard or love for the thing itself; one's interest is diverted to the fact that some person or group has that thing; one's attention gravitates to the fact or illusion that one is thereby diminished. Hence, in gaining the thing for which one envied someone, one gains something in which, from the outset of envy, one relinquished a direct interest. If one had a direct interest in something, one would have no need of an envious interest. If one has an envious interest, then when the object is at last possessed by yourself, it is not a suitable object for envious interest. It is no longer the other person's. It is just what it is. A vital distinction must be added. I have expressed the phenomenon of envy as "desiring a thing because, for the reason that, in that another possesses it". For the present purpose of argument, a greater precision is needed. There is an unenvious way of desiring a thing "for the reason that" or even "in that" another has it. I may admire, be interested in or love someone. Inspired by that, I desire something that person has: perhaps an interest in a certain kind of music; perhaps, conceptually simpler, owning a certain kind of furniture. That interest may take off on its own account; though an interest was originally dependent on someone's else's having an interest or regard, having formed my interest, it may withstand a change of heart in the person who originally inspired it. The fact that they come to despise or reject the interest may be upsetting, but it does not remove for me, what I find in my new possessions. Or, alas, I may not develop such autonomy; if the one who inspires the interest dies, is shown to have been insincere all along, changes his or her heart or mind, everything about the interest is destroyed for me. But though in the last alternative I may be thus exposed as something of a mere disciple rather than having formed a direct and primary objective interest in the music or furniture or whatever, I am not thus exposed as having been envious. In order to distinguish an envious interest from an inspired and dependent or symbiotic involvement, we have to recognize that the envious desire incorporates in the most intimate and absurd way the other person's possessing the thing for which I envy him or her. To capture fully the character of envy, we could choose to say, "What the person desires in envy is his possessing the other person's possessing the trait or property". Or, "What the person wants is to be the other person-having-that-trait-or-property". (The envious person might not wish to be the envied person in any other respect.) Only this way of putting the character of envy makes clear the intrinsically self-thwarting character of gaining the objects for which one envies another, and distinguishes envy from other less-than-autonomous but still unenvious desires and interests.

Compare three situations of child's play. A child is playing with blocks. Another child becomes entranced, takes some of them and, perhaps with an eye on what the other is doing, experiments in building with them. Next: the second child is impatient, does not realize that his own interest is being fired by what he sees being done, grabs most of the blocks, and begins to build. He has intense interest, is not put off by the fact that the first child cries and tries to interrupt. Perhaps he is a little disappointed to find that it is not so much fun without an inspiring model, perhaps he is quite imaginative enough to proceed by himself. Less than ideal behaviour, but not intrinsically self-thwarting. It is a fairly simple matter of whether he has enough power to bring it off. Last: a child enviously watches another playing with blocks. What he watches now is not, with primary concentration at any rate, the blocks, but the first child's reaction. Unlike the second "greedy" child who "just didn't care" that someone else already owned or was using them, and is content just so long as he gets and keeps the property, this last envious one is disconcerted if the first child shows no interest in the theft. He toys idly and bored, frustrated with the blocks, and his interest only returns when the first child attempts to get them back again. If the first child just gives him the blocks and walks off with no interest, the second is insulted and frustrated in a way he cannot understand. Doesn't he have what he wanted? No, he is no closer to being the other-boy-with-the-blocks. He is more satisfied, he can throw himself into the situation with a sense of coming closer to satisfying his desire, if he can provoke the other into wrestling with him for possession. (So do philosophers verbally wrestle, who envy each other's intellectual possessions and activities.) So the self-thwarting character of an envious desire can also be expressed in the formula "The person desires to have the thing for himself just so long as another keeps it from him". It is not quite right to say that what the envious person really desires is simply "struggle" though a consideration of revolutionary political actions makes this analysis tempting. It is that struggle is the only realizable approximation to the incoherently stated object of envy. If it is absurd to be oneself being the person having the envied possession, at least in struggle one can sense very directly the other person's holding on to it.

When a person is loved by an envious lover, who wants her because he envies someone else for having her, she feels less than properly valued for her own sake. She may feel flattered as the two rivals go for the draw in the noonday sun, but flattery it is, not admiration or love, and she will find her "ardent" suitor strangely lacking even in conversation as they trundle along to his ranch in the evening light.

These are thought-experiments, and therefore idealizations having their value in dramatically pinpointing distinctions. Things would be even more hopeless than they are in practice were it not for the facts that people, even envious ones, are usually mixed in their motives and even in their envious relations with things and people they can begin to discover respects in which they want the "possession" for its or his or her own sake. Furthermore, and more importantly, though envy cannot be satisfied, the actions taken in attempting to satisfy it may provoke some liberating understanding of what the envious person is doing. Also, in gaining what envy had not actually desired − the thing or person itself − the person who envied may find himself or herself satisfied in unexpected ways, and envy may die for lack of bitterness. Yet it does not pay to be too sanguine in these self-destructive straits. Envy is a bitter feeling; it is in part a hatred, for it provokes and illuminates a feeling of one's own inadequacies first in not having what seems to be a desired "object" (I speak constantly of "object" as a philosophical formality, since what is said is held to be true both of people and of "mere" objects, but it must be obvious that the most striking instances and interesting examples of these phenomena concern people) and secondly, and most bitterly, as a sense of one's inadequacy in not being able to be "one's own person", or to hold to oneself the gained "object". The humiliating though necessary lack of success in relating to the "object" which provoked envy, after possession is gained, is even more galling when coupled with any degree of the realization of what is going on − that in reality one is dependent on the person whom one had envied for the object one now holds, continuing to hold on to the apparently desired object in order that one's spurious mode of possession is maintained even unstably.

Both the hatred and the original diversion of direct objective interest in the apparently desired object render the one who envies that much less capable of pleasure in holding or being related to the "desired" object. Hence the pride in possession which can possibly displace, though it cannot satisfy, envy, is largely obstructed. (Pride, of a Humean sort, is a special pleasure. It is not simply the pleasure one takes in what one has gained, but the pleasure in the fact that one has achieved it.) Another reason for lack of satisfaction when one gains an object for which one has envied someone, is that from the very beginning there has been an impurity, a distraction of attention. To enjoy something fully requires wholehearted, single minded attention to it. To the degree that these conditions are not satisfied, one is that much less capable of enjoyment. The desire for a life of enjoyment and no work is a logical absurdity only hidden by some very dull conventional thought about what constitutes work. (A discussion of work, and an analysis of pride, can only be promised at this stage.) To want something only under the aspect of its being possessed by another is, if one secures it, and even before that, as one observes it, to observe it within the consciousness of another having it, rather than observing it in and for itself. Therefore it is to gain a partial and distorted idea of what it will be when in relation to yourself. Once gained, if it is still regarded within envy, and if envy is not cancelled out by the delighted surprises of actual possession, then these subsequent engagements are still towards the thing-as-possessed-by-another. One is still not on a wave of the same form and length with the thing itself.

From vanity and envy, to jealousy and narcissism

There is this group of connected phenomena — being vain, being malicious, being envious, and others yet to be discussed — being full of pride, arrogant and jealous. Jealousy is the next most directly in line after envy. A discussion of envy naturally followed that of vanity, for vanity is a distortion in the way in which we are prepared to be regarded as appearing to others, in which we attempt to interpose ourselves between ourselves and how we appear to others, thus dislocating any clear appearing to others which could be perceived and appreciated by them. In consequence we reduce what clear and distinct information can come back to us from others. Vanity is closest to conceit, since in vanity we preempt the remarks and responses of others in forms of our own pre-formed conceit and thus destroy the possibility of finding a new or original conception about ourselves or what we do or what we look like. Within this conceit, in being vain we slide towards being arrogant, since we are taking to ourselves, arrogating, the point of view which is another's and not our own. In all of this, being vain is closely parallel with being envious, both in desiring and thriving upon envy and, despite its biased self-centredness, in transcending a solipsistic consciousness because vanity and envy involve a passionate interest in an object other than oneself, even though that "object" is tied too closely to oneself and within oneself, concep-tually speaking, for it to be properly appreciated for itself, and even though it cannot be given its due.

In the long run the person one envies and the things or people for which one envies them are liable to be overregard rather than trivially undervalued. They are kept at such convoluted distance by the obscurantist self-distancing of vanity, conceit and envy that they assume mythic proportions as things or people one could never deal with if ever one met in open discussion, let alone open combat. The "anti-" person is not simply critical of something or someone. If so he would just let it or them "speak" and with allowable force and passion perhaps give his or her answer. Vanity and envy are the core of the malice of the person who is so parasitic upon his opponents that he defines his way of being in relation to them. He exists in the way of being an anti-Communist, an anti-Christ, an anti-Semite, an anti-Bourgeois, an anti-Capitalist. All he can see is the Communist, the Christ, the Semite, the Bourgeois or the Capitalist. He is nothing, a mere negation, in the face of It. So the passion in the life of the one who is an "anti-" must lie in his desire in relation to the " − ". Those who have their positive allegiance of affection and love can reasonably and rightly fear and oppose, without blind hatred of ideas or persons. But the passionate life of the anti-Communist, to take an example, can be explained only on the basis of his repressed desire for Communism and his envy of those who can so far kick over the traces of reason, the lessons of history and the restraints of morality to be Communists. The life of the "anti-" is to be compared with and understood from the life of vanity and envy, for as the envious person is nonplussed if he gains the object for which he envies, the anti-Communist would be left with a meaningless life if suddenly no one were even interested in being Communist. His elbows tingle and his muscles tremble with the restrained desire to "smash his opponents" but lo and behold! The final trick the bastards play — they disappear! Vanity keeps one apart, and prevents one being possibly refuted or modified in opinion by one's opponents, but loneliness is unsatisfactory. Envy brings one back close, but in combative and destructive, sexually tinged aggression. To be an anti-Communist or an anti-anything else is to long to be a Communist (or whatever), for the freedom for and justification of destruction which it supplies; it is at once to hate or fear the destruction which Communism is likely to wreak upon yourself, to desire that some others be Communists so that you can live vicariously through them, and to place your hatred by being aggressive to them and thus holding yourself off from what you touch so closely, by pushing it so strongly and constantly away.

The pathos in the Nazi's anti-"Semitic-Intellectualism" lies in the envy and thus the need it betrayed in themselves for the pleasure and steadiness of a cultivated and richly textured mind. Without this, the world is a howling desert, and what can one wish to do but to derive a perverse comfort in making the world over so as to accord with one's unhappily barren state. In all of his or her dangerous aggression the person who is an "anti-" is a victim of their own conceit, for the "enemy" is, in a sense, rightly felt to be unconquerable, since they are placed beyond reach. The "Jew" of the anti-Semite, the "Communist" of the anti-communist, the "Christ" of the Nietzschean anti-Christ and, one must say, the "Bourgeois" whose spectre haunts Sartre (in whom sometimes appears the mere anti-bourgeois persona) all seem to be all powerful as well as vicious, and thus to justify violent opposition by those who have developed this powerful antipathy, for the simple reason that the antipathy places the hated figure or cause or attitude or belief beyond the understanding, beyond discourse.

This coupling of vanity and envy as having an interest, though a distorted one, in an object other than the one who is being vain or envious, helps one to distinguish vanity from narcissism. It is quite common for people to be described as narcissistic simply on the grounds of their self-love. So auto-eroticism, or delight in one's own wellbeing, or pleasure in one's own achievements or possessions are commonly described, with some derogation, as narcissistic. Yet, although any of these self-regards may be narcissistic, it is not self-love which makes them so. In the original myth, Narcissus looks into a pool, and falls in love with the person he sees there. The person he sees is himself but he thinks it is someone else looking back at him. In narcissism, one is interested in oneself, insofar as one seems to be another. It is a failure, not an excess, of frank self-love. In vanity, by contrast, a person is interested in being admired, but is not interested only in himself. He desires to be admired by others, but renders this vain by wishing to call the tune in respect of the admiration of others. (I take the standard example of admiration, but obviously we can speak in a similar way of a wish to be loved being stultified by a similar vanity, and so on.) He knows the others are others, and wants this to be so, but this bothers him too; he wants to do away with the threatening disadvantages to him of the others being others. In narcissism a person is interested in loving and admiring someone, though this "someone" must be a disguised or projected version of himself whereas, in vanity, you are interested in being admired or loved. The everyday narcissist, unlike Narcissus, is set loose from his pool, and does look at others. Sometimes he is delighted with what he sees there. He loves it. The person who occasions his delight is very easily persuaded that she or he is loved. For certainly his or her presence to the narcissist causes love to arise; the words said to the narcissist, the looks given — all make him love. The narcissist needs, as his moving mirror, someone who is sensitive, imaginative and passive: Sensitive, for without that the one "loved" will not sense aright what mood is to be matched, what words will reflect the desired response back to the initiatives of the narcissistic lover; what "looks", what "regards" will leave his mind at peace and his heart happy: Imaginative, for unless the one "loved" can imaginatively interpret the narcissist's initiatives he or she will, despite sensitivity, bungle the return performance which is to confirm the narcissist's self-image: Passive, for it the one "loved" happened, in being loved and in loving, to be as interested in being known as in knowing, and therefore takes initiatives which express what he or she is distinctly in his or herself, and questions and probes for the meaning of what the "lover" does, and makes occasion to test his or her guesses about what the "lover" thinks or feels, then at once the mirror is shattered.

As vanity and narcissism are alike, though with their subtle but important differences of structure, so too are envy and jealousy. When they have been set side by side and distinguished, then as envy was brought into focus against its complement, vanity, so jealousy and narcissism must be juxtaposed as complements.

Back to envy and jealousy

Envy is a desire for something, in that it is possessed by someone else. It does not require a prior interest in the thing or activity for which you envy someone. Envy is the meanest emotion, for in envy one wishes to dispossess the person who has the envied thing, without fully or coherently desiring the thing from within oneself, or for oneself. The resultant emotion of envy is "No-one is to have it". Envy can exist between a minimum of two people. One might construe it as a relation between a person and a dramatic persona: I might, for example, (foolishly) envy Midas his ability to turn things to gold at a touch; or, I might dramatically construe myself in a different phase of my life as virtually another person, and envy him for something he then possessed. Karl envies Juliet for her apparently effortless charm. If, in contrast, Karl is jealous towards Juliet, there must normally be some real or fancied third person. Even though, to stretch the point, one might speak of Karl's being jealous of Juliet's love of gardening even when he has no suspicion that she finds more than flowers to tend in the shrubbery, still the distinction between envy and jealousy stands clear. If Karl is stupid enough to envy Juliet her love of gardening, it is not because he thinks or feels that her interest in it leaves no room or too little room for their love of each other. If it is envy he feels then it is gardening which he feels excluded from by her interest in it. If it is jealousy he feels, then it is Juliet he feels excluded from, by the gardening. Envy is at heart a meaner emotion than jealousy, for jealousy is a form of love, even though a destructive one. Karl can be envious of Bjarne's ability to win Juliet, merely because that ability seems to demean him. He need know nothing of or feel nothing for Juliet beyond that she is someone-whom-Bjarne-can-get-and-Karl-cannot. In contrast, he can be jealous of Bjarne's success with Juliet only if he has some love for Juliet herself. To feel jealousy towards someone is to feel some love for that person, to feel that the person does or should love you, and to feel that one's love and its return is threatened. Such a feeling might well be in no way irrational; indeed, it may be perfectly rational and correct. One's love can indeed be threatened, and someone may in fact be about to replace you in your lover's affections. It makes no sense to say that someone should love someone and be loved by them, and nevertheless be indifferent to their loss or not jealous at a threatened loss.

If we are to define an intrinsically irrational jealousy, then it is an attitude to what is loved which feels threatened by anyone else who shows an interest, or to whom is shown an interest by the one whom one loves. No assessment is made of the danger; no perspective of view is sought or attempted, from which the reality or extent of the danger might be assessed. Of course there are degrees of this lack of perspective and assessment. But to the extent that one's love is felt to be threatened by the mere fact of other loves and interests which involve the one whom one loves, one is irrationally jealous. Such irrational jealousy is the complement of narcissism. The reason is fairly obvious.

Since it is only what originates from himself which pleases the narcissist, and since, unlike those who are more frankly full of self-love, he is deceived by his own manoeuvres into thinking that he loves another or others, he cannot stand what disturbs the mirror for his self-love. He cannot stand change in others, nor facets in the mirror where faces undeniably other than his own peep out. (Narcissism and conservatism are closely tied.) When he changes, the one he "loves" must stand still so that his pattern of change is returned intact to his loving care. ("Stay just the same as you are" is said as if the highest compliment to rare qualities is being paid, rather than an oppressive demand being made.) If he has a luck he does not deserve, his loving mirror will quietly adjust so that he is not shocked by too honest a reflection. (Somewhat as someone said of the writings of Kierkegaard, "If an ape looks in, no angel will look out".) If he stays still, the mirror must not be in flux. (Except as some ripple is tactfully required so that he knows he is at peace rather than that he has come to the stasis of a Barthian "End of the Road".) Parents who love their children narcissistically cannot bear them to grow up. Also children, in their dependency, rapid growth and consequent urgent need for self-definition and changes in that definition, are upset by changes and growth in their parents. Since they are so urgently involved in the process of defining themselves with and against others, their love cannot but be often strongly stranded with narcissism. Yet in their unconstrained and un-calculating sympathy, they show disinterested and emotional love.

Intimacy and self-intimacy

The annoying aspect of narcissism is that the person thinks that someone is loving him; it is not only his deception that he is loving another which aggravates us. It is thoroughly misleading to think that the lack of objectivity in narcissism lies in its being a self-reflexive interest. While undoubtedly there are limits to self-reflexivity (the dog cannot bite at the fleas on its own nose, and it is the monkeys with their more highly developed social system who pick the nits from each other) there are limits no less absolute to our concern for another's state of being. Consider the various limits to one's knowledge of oneself by oneself, and one's knowledge of oneself by another. True, I cannot have the objectivity of another in standing from a distance and observing me with a separate mind and a distinct history. From this point of view it seems that one cannot know oneself by oneself. Only another can really stand off and see me for what I am. Yet, to balance this, intimacy is as strong a model for knowledge as is observation from a respectable distance. One's intimate friends know one well in ways denied to one's public acquaintances because they are "closer up", not "farther away"; one must understand the character of that intimacy partly upon their being allowed to approach to being as close to one in one's thoughts or feelings or body as one is to oneself. It is true that even one's most intimate friends remain hearers of one's words and not thinkers of one's thoughts and, at most, sympathetic sharers of feeling. Nevertheless, in the absence, of restraint or hiding, artifice or dissimulation, (which must characterize some moments of a relationship if it is to be described as intimate) someone else is being given an immediate realization of one's thoughts and feelings just as one is oneself by having someone to whom or with whom these thoughts and feelings may be expressed. This must be carefully understood. The power of intimacy stems not only from the desire of people to let another know how they feel. It is the catalytic power of intimacy to allow modes of expression, both inwardly and outwardly, in which, in being known to another, one is being newly known to oneself. It is not only in the having of thought or feeling that one understands or knows what one thinks or feels, otherwise the solipsist would be correct and self-reflexive knowledge would exhaust the field of human endeavour. Only I *have* my thoughts and feelings. Yet, nor is it only in being separately observed and then told how it is with one, as a behaviourist would represent the situation, that one knows with another, better than one would by oneself, what one thinks and feels. (One behaviourist to another, "You're feeling fine today. How am I going?") The idea that intimacy must be a mistake, that it must be a delusion, since at most another "observes the outward expressions of the thought and feeling which I *have*" is itself erroneous. Considered as a conceptual error, it is the mistake of identifying the having of thought, sensation or other feeling with the understanding, the knowing, the characterization or the judgement of it.

If a person is intimate with himself or herself, then this is because he or she has succeeded in being so. We have learned the art, or some of the arts, of realizing ourselves by ourselves. We learn these arts of poetry, philosophy, story telling and psychological theorizing, of music, of internally and externally expressed drama (we demolish our opponent in fantasied debate, and so on). Unless we learn these arts and adapt them idiosyncratically and autonomously to our most private use, then we are, when alone, lost with and among our thoughts and feelings, rather than intimate with ourselves and them. There is an empiricist myth that each person is immediately acquainted with his or her own thoughts, feelings and sensations, that self-intimacy is finally the only intimacy, and that one person can know another only by inference, as from a distance. It originates for our historical convenience, with Descartes, develops through Locke, Berkeley, reaches its pinnacle in Hume, then is used as obvious truth in the early to mid-twentieth century debates by the phenomenalists ("there are only thoughts, feelings and sensations; bodies and behaviour are constructions out of these") and behaviourists ("there are only objects, bodies and behaviour; thoughts and feelings and sensation are constructions out of these"). It is still easy to feel the force of the myth when thoughts, feelings and sensations are openly declared to be self-intimating to their possessors. It seems, for a moment, obviously true that simply in having a thought, feeling or sensation, one knows and understands what it is. Yet this thought about the immediacy of reflective thought is unreflective, for in speaking and in imagining our mental lives in these ways we, with the empiricists, overlook the range of arts and skills which we acquire with some experience and practice so that we recognize some thoughts and feelings straight off. We do not even recognize that recognizing the sensation is more than having the sensation. Doubtless, after a while, toothache and heartache "stare you in the face and could be nothing other than they are" just as a tea cup or a motor car "stare you in the face and could not be other than they are". Yet it is not a magical self-revelatory character in them. It is a skill in us polished so as to be almost subliminal to its performance, which makes them so apparently what they are.

Finally, the metaphors of "self-intimacy" and "self-acquaintance" which are employed when we are in the grip of the myth that ultimately we can have an intimacy only with our own states of mind are doubly social in character. The dominant images of the immediate and complete knowledge and understanding one had of one's own thoughts and feelings from being the possessor of them, which then led those who were thoroughgoing enough to take things to their conclusion, to insist that one could never really know another's state of mind and that self-intimacy was the only possible intimacy – those dominant images themselves presupposed the very sociality whose existence was concluded to be impossible. If we don't understand the literally described facts of how people can come up to us and, without further ado, explain themselves and give us an immediate and intimate sense of what they feel and how they think, then we have no ground in which to grow the flowery metaphor according to which our own thoughts and feelings are like so many intimate acquaintances, hiding nothing from us about themselves, telling us their names and characters with the utmost sincerity and securing the utmost conviction and confidence in us concerning what they say. If one's intimacy with oneself were explained just by the tautology that no-one else's feeling is my feeling, no-one else's thinking is my thinking and so on then, certainly, social intimacy would be no adequate metaphor for it. Nothing could be a metaphor for it since it is an incoherent idea that the tautology supports or explains one's knowledge and understanding of oneself. It is the notion that my possession of feeling, my possession of thought, should be identical with my understanding of, my recognizing my being able to compare and describe, come to terms with and know the character of my thinking and feeling.

There is self-intimacy, and there is social intimacy. Both depend on our finding ways of expressing, developing and representing what we think and feel. There is no reason to set one up, morally or metaphysically above the other. Those who attempt social intimacy who have no self-intimacy have too little understanding of what they are doing to succeed. They lack an active imaginative understanding of what it is for themselves to feel and experience. Without this they cannot think of the other as feeling and experiencing. Yet, on the other hand, those who would "learn" the lesson from this to dwell only with themselves inwardly until they have an adequate understanding of themselves with which to greet and to relate to others are set to rights as soon as they bring forward these hidden treasures. For it is in the process of relating, publicly and intimately, that they discover their self-misrepresentations; they discover ways and means of realizing their thought and emotion which had not occurred to them by themselves. It is true that the careful and exact contemplation and internal questioning of the character of one's thought and feeling while one counts to ten is a vital stage in the development of any understanding which makes possible the understanding of another. "Self-expression" as easily destroys as it can create understanding. It is equally true that the sometimes free, sometimes controlled and muted exhibition, dramatization or simple flat statement is the first stage in which one realizes the reality or irreality of one's inner life. One's fancied hate, love and curiosity, fine understanding or clear knowledge alternatively become firm and solid as one speaks. Or they disappear, recognized at last as the ghosts they always were.

The upshot: it is quite erroneous to identify narcissism with inwardness, solitariness, self-interest or self-love. When people say, contemptuously, of a narcissistic character on television or stage "He/she loves himself/herself" they are often testifying to the aggravation of the presumptuousness of narcissism — the presumption that the person's finding himself/herself lovable is bound to be found lovable to others. But if they are objecting to self-love as such — the regard which a person takes to be as much due to him or herself, of looking upon oneself with favour where possible, of criticizing oneself where necessary, of taking care of and about oneself, cherishing one's wellbeing and finding pleasure in oneself then, as likely as not, they are speaking merely from envy. "How dare he/she be so brazen as to show his love. At least he/she could hide it in the darkest closet like the rest of us!" To which the answer is that the envier is as free as the envied to self-love and that, broadly speaking, the only answer to neurosis is the apt erosis.

From the point of view of a desire for objectivity, one should regard the various "aberrations" of being vain, being envious, being narcissistic, being jealous and, yet to be considered, being proud and being arrogant, as inadequate attempts at the necessary task of recognizing and giving due respect to the points of view of others, while not losing one's essential autonomy in working within one's own. Objectivity requires us to stand dangerously close to being vain, arrogant, envious and jealous. In being vain, a person is motivated by the need to be appraised by others. He has a self-regard which requires admiration, and which must ask a question "Who is mistaken then?" if it is not forthcoming. It is a pity only that he does not stay for an answer. In narcissism a person is motivated by a necessary self-regard and self-love, and by a need to gain a three dimensional sense of himself by gaining his self-image from how he appears to others. It is a pity only that he cannot or will not give others their due, and so cannot succeed even in his own ambition, for there is something fundamental about the ambition which must be relevant in objectivity. So too, in being envious, a person pays tribute to the example of others in the formation of one's own desires, even though the tribute is confused. In jealousy we have the keenest sense of how another, though related to us, is not comprised by, or contained within that relation. In sensing how another can equally involve the subjectivity, the felt world of someone with whom you have such a relationship, you see, as you could in no other way, the objective dimension to the person you "know". A child is liable to react with alarm and possessiveness to the arrival in the house of the new baby. Yet if he discovers that the love and care given to the "usurper" is not a sign of the withdrawal of love and care from himself then, though he will still suffer some spasms of jealousy, he can still have moments in which he is more assured of what is given to him by being able to see it being given, from a slight distance, to his brother or sister. He can attribute a greater independent substance to the source of the care and attention which he enjoys and may even appreciate the reasons for its occasional intemperate withdrawal.

The person who is envious is moved by a need to find his interests and loves not only from his own inspiration, but to be broadened by what is seen in the lives of others. But he cannot adequately make the distinction between his desiring the thing for which he envies someone and his desiring the thing as still contained within the guise of its being possessed by another such that dispossession of the other, and not just possession for himself, is a prime motive. The person who is jealous is moved by a need to protect what is important to himself and to what he loves. He fails, at least in irrational jealousy, only to make the distinction between the person he loves having other loves and interests, having dimensions of life which are beyond the scope of his own, and there being a real threat from a third person or interest to what he has and to what he values in the other person. Sexual jealousy, like any other, may be intrinsically irrational if you sexually love someone and see the very existence in him or her of sexual interests and attractions to someone other than oneself as a threat to what you share with that person. If "you're only jealous" is to be a correct reproof, then it has to rest on the baselessness of such fears of loss. It also must rest on an observation of a lack of disinterest on the part of the accuser.

There is another aspect to the relation of jealousy to objectivity. It is not easy for the one who makes another jealous (whether by providing adequate grounds or not) to appreciate how the jealous person feels. The reasons for this are not accidental to a person, but lie in the structure of jealousy. Juliet feels threatened by Bjarne's imminent sexual involvement with Carla; Bjarne quickly feels threatened by the hatred in Juliet's jealousy. It is a test of the presence of that capacity for disinterest in love, previously stressed, that he is able to assure Juliet that he is as strongly attached to her and as fond as ever (supposing this to be so: sheer loss of affection for one and its growth towards another involves different problems). This assurance, and a continuance of his own assurance of his own love, requires disinterested and at least partially detached regard for the character of his own feelings and the nature and motive of Juliet's passionate rejection or icy disregard of him. For it can scarcely be expected that the one who is left out in the cold will have ability or motive for the painful restraints of thought and feeling, word and action which an actively practised disinterested continuing connection would require.

It is important to compare and contrast the structures of childhood and adult situations of jealousy, whether sexual or of any other kind. A child, jealous of a real or fancied preferment in treatment of his sibling by a parent, is in the hands of someone of greater power, and he may expect, greater understanding. Normally, one parent may turn to another for some objective comment. The parent's role, at least, is to supply love and understanding to both children whether or not they reciprocate, at least on the occasion when that assurance is most needed by the child. It may be that jealousies in adult life tend to run wildly out of control, in a way that is so quick and surprising to those involved because of an unextirpated child's expectation that someone else with greater objective care and understanding is going to come along and set things to rights. Adults find, to their sudden horror, when all is said and done, that no one has been there at the last moment to soften the final word, to turn the deadly insult or to hold the striking hand.

The other main difference between child-to-child-in-the-context-of-an-adult, and adult-to-adult jealousies is specific to sexual jealousy. A parent can say to his or her children each singly, or to both together, "I love you both", and this need not be deceptive. (I speak of "parent" for convenience. Similar situations arise with children at school and their teachers, or when after the death or desertion of parents, an older child cares for the younger ones, and so on.) A friend can say to two friends, his peers in power and understanding, "I like, love, you both" and this can be credible. But if he or she says, to each singly or both together, "I love you both" where this is to be understood as sexual love, then he or she is going to be regarded as a liar by both. The demands and degree of intimacy of friendship do not prevent one from having more than one friendship at the one time. In contrast it has been a much vexed question whether the sharp difference which is made in the case of sexual intimacy is just an irrational feature of a culture founded upon the concept of possession (as some Marxists claim), whether the intensity of our feelings about sexual exclusiveness reflect the cosmically ordained laws of God (as others will insist), whether those bitter and soul shaking feelings can be consigned to the past along with other old tribal tabus and superstitions, or whether they are intrinsic to the seriousness and fondness and meaning of what lies between and binds people.

It is difficult to believe in the full reality of what someone says when he or she claims to sexually love two people at the same time. It is a little difficult to see what is meant, even though one knows well enough what sort of situations may be alluded to. It is easy enough to understand and to believe someone who claims to love one person and to be strongly attracted to another. It is easy enough to understand someone's complaint that he or she is strongly attracted to two people and does not know in which direction to move. Also, promiscuity is fairly easy to understand, the desire and preparedness to have it off with someone simply if you each are attracted and sexual tension builds up, neither recognizing any other relevant or complicating factor beyond convenience of time and place. (Though always understood conventionally in a sexual sense, promiscuity is, or is easily extended to be, a general phenomenon: the problems of the spurious moralisms and realities of intellectual "dedication", on the one hand, and of being responsive and available to a variety of influences of opinion, observation and style, on the other.) Sexual love may well grow from such collusive collisions, if they are happy ones. Yet, paradoxically, it is the freedom which is required for sexual love to arise and to continue, which is inconsistent with having a sexual love for more than one person. To sexually love someone is to be very much absorbed with their ways, their style, their smell, tastes of food, drink, music, clothes, with the texture, colour, feel, shape and idiosyncrasies of their body. It is to be responsive and available to the right moments in their cycles of change; it is to have a mind free for the images of all of these, which crowd and flow when you are apart, and even as much when you are close.

You become a certain kind of person, with a style, outlook, cluster of values and interests. There is a special atmosphere to the world. This synthesis is in some ways very powerful; people may achieve within it what they never could do separately. Each opens the other's eyes and ears and noses and hands in ways which are strangely new to each. The synthesis is fragile, and people learn that they must take great care, that they are faced with difficult choices of restraint and spontaneity. So the sense of betrayal, of destruction of what was held in common and could not be held by either separately, when one or other engages in the existential absurdity, the arrogantly or ignorantly induced confusion and "adulteration" of senses, sense and meaning of what is aptly called "living two lives".

Chapter Eight

Taking Over and Excluding

Arrogating

Arrogance and pride — these ancient moral categories, added to the somewhat sleazy lot that have already come our way — they make one's hackles rise. This is because charges of "arrogance" are mostly arrogant, ignorant or feeble bleats from those who aren't prepared for the work and risks of error, particularly farcical error, involved in coming to judgements of fact, of theory, of value and of priority. We are returned to the very beginning of this whole exploration. "Who are you to judge!" (It is not a question, of course.) "Everyone is equally entitled to his (but not her) opinion." We must glide into this war as unnoticed as phantoms until we know the terrain and have our weapons, but then our objectivity will not lead us to abstain from the battle but to fight it well on the right side. The total rejection of definitive judgement as arrogant is, in its own act, totally arrogant. An arrogant person arrogates to himself what is not his own, but unlike an honest thief, cannot clearly recognize what he has done and cannot, or will not, properly distinguish what is his own and what is another's. The phenomenon of arrogance, and the fact that people can feel more than half-justified in thinking, saying and doing what others are trying to convince them is arrogant, insisting that they must carry on as they do in order to be true to their lights, must make us recognize the other side of arrogance — the need to be true to our own point of view until we have clear and continued unanswerable evidence against major parts of it. It testifies to the paramount need for us to act in the light of what we know, even though, from a detached inactive spectator's point of view, what we "know" might not be knowledge at all. We have to be confident enough to reject charges of arrogance which have no more basis than the fact that so far as we can see, we have observed, interpreted, remembered, inferred and calculated correctly, even though what we claim in virtue of this conflicts with what another is inclined to think. It is those who are not sure because they have never gone through the involving and strenuous activities of pursuing ideas to their conclusions, making precise observations, drawing all possible inferences and resolutely and thoroughly remembering, who are the most annoyed by uncompromising claims which they cannot weaken or challenge. So they resort to allegations of arrogance. Yet there is a real problem of arrogance. Those with a right to confidence need to be able to discern and to describe what it is that they are not, but which they may easily be misrepresented as being; those with a tendency to abuse the notion need to know what real phenomenon gives spurious currency to their flapping blank cheques.

Many people think it arrogant to go on asserting something without loss of assurance and without qualification when one is quite unable to establish it to someone who equally firmly disagrees. Naturally, a person might be arrogant who was unshaken in those circumstances, but it is important to an understanding of arrogance to see that the person may well not be arrogant, and also that the notion that everything one really knows can therefore be proven to another is the real arrogance. The notion that if you know something, you must be able to prove it to another leaves you in a nasty dilemma when you fail to do so. Either you must go on trying and trying to prove it to the other (very trying), or concede that you don't know, since you can't prove it to the other. There is at least some arrogance in the first choice of going on and on reasoning and persuading, for it is an assumption on behalf of the other person about the importance of the issue. There are economies and priorities of time, energy and patience. To be "locked" in dispute is, by the metaphor, to have lost freedom of mind, and hence one vital condition for continuing objectivity. And since you cannot really accept that you don't know something you seem to be informed of just because another won't be persuaded, you'll have to conclude that there's "something wrong" — stupidity, perversity, blindness, bad faith or some such on the part of your recalcitrant opponent. Or, horrors! There is something wrong with yourself.

The vital point to recognize is that although some matters may be known, not all disputes are resolvable even if they are conducted in good faith by equally intelligent disputants equally free of stupor and rancour (a rare condition after half an hour of debate on an irresoluble issue). Perhaps all issues are resolvable, in the sense that someone or some group may be able to come to know what's what on the question. For all this, not all disputes are resolvable. This is because to know something you need more than intelligence, open-mindedness, good powers of observation, logic and the rest of the fine human qualities. You need to be in a position to know. An honest fair minded person whose sanity and memory have not been adversely affected by a crime he committed, knows full well whether the correct verdict should be guilty or not guilty. The prosecuting and defending barristers dispute the points of evidence. Each may, in his or her own mind, be quite unsure whether the accused committed the crime. The members of the jury may be persuaded to one side or the other, perhaps, and for very good reason. They may be persuaded to the correct opinion. Yet it may be that no member of the jury may be able to properly resolve the dispute between the barristers. They may be unable, that is, to judge that the accused is innocent and still satisfactorily explain each piece of incriminating evidence, and unable to judge that he is guilty and still explain each piece of evidence which tends to show that he is innocent. The accused himself, even if he wished to incriminate himself, might not have available any evidence thoroughly satisfactory to a listener, to show that he is guilty. Certainly self-accusation is no proof.

Furthermore, this fact that a matter known to someone may still be the subject of an irresoluble dispute, is not limited to examples of what one might wish to call "indirect evidence" and "argumentation". (Though it is telling enough even if it is so limited, since most matters which are known, are known in this way.) Not only do you need to be in a position to know. It is often a matter of chance that one person notices something which another overlooks. Two people observe the same thing at the same time. One person manages to detect a cynical smile: It escapes the other. How is that to be settled as a dispute? There may be no reason to take the word of the person who smiled cynically. One might object that such an observation involves interpretation, and the problem could not arise where no interpretation was involved. This won't do. In every case of observation some interpretation is involved.

The existence of irresoluble dispute is so notorious in matters of

evaluative and moral difference that many think it obvious, for
that very reason, that evaluations and moral judgements cannot be
"objective". To say this is abdication of judgement. The judgement
that we have no right to make any value or moral judgements is
what? False? Then at least some negative moral judgement has
been made. Are all moral judgements meaningless? It is hard to
believe that children have learned the self-deceiving arts of talking
urgent nonsense by the time they gather to dispute in the school
playground.

In Saudi Arabia in 1976, a princess was shot and her lover
beheaded in a public execution. Their crime was adultery. We in the
Western world regard this as an act of barbaric cruelty. It is said by
an Australian politician interested in trade with Saudi Arabia that a
film dealing with this act ought, perhaps, not to be shown because
it upset the Saudi Arabian royal family; there are, of course, under-
tones of loss of trade in reprisals and so on. It is pointed out by an
expert (we suppose) on radio that there are about five thousand
"princes" in Saudi Arabia, that the opinions of the "family" do not
include those of its women, whose opinions count for nothing. A
diplomat for Saudi Arabia speaking on television says that the film
is unfair, inaccurate. He does not deny the executions, and carefully avoids saying outright that he endorses the killings as just
punishment. He says that we do not understand the Islamic world.
He points out that many Western countries have capital punishment; that in Islamic law one may be executed for theft, as was the
case in Britain even last century.

One can never lift all the tissues of moral cover-up in all of this.
This is because of the bad faith and evasion exhibited by the
spokesman for Saudi Arabia, and the callousness and
unscrupulousness of our own politicians, and because we are
caught in our own moral and emotional confusion as we witness the
particularly outrageous examples of others. We are liable to be
arrogant in our outrage at execution for "adultery", though correct
in our opinion that punishment is wrong. Our arrogance in our not
incorrect opinion lies in our lack of self-criticism. The power to
drive an adulterous spouse from house, children and property is
common enough in Western countries. It is enforceable by law or
by passionately enforced social and personal opinion. We have to
face our own attitudes to all forms of unconventionalized sexual
behaviour and feeling and question our own often violent and at
least repressive and confused feelings about the relation between
affection, love, loyalty, commitment, jealousy, envy,

possessiveness and the rest, before we can be easy and clear minded in our attitudes to horrifying examples of blind repressing vengeance dressed up as insistence on law and standards and the perpetuation of a culture. The answer to charges of arrogance is not to abstain from judgement. We must judge and be prepared to be judged in return. Rather, we have to come to include our own practices and feelings within the scope of our criticism, and keep ourselves steady as unevasive targets for the critical assaults of others.

"Adultery" is a mixed moral and legal word. Morally it means "adulterating" — thinning out the concentration and deceitfully serving it up as if it were still the genuine article of full quality. Of course the moral criticism implies that a sexual involvement with someone else when you are already committed to and involved with another does involve such adulteration of feeling, that an involvement with one necessarily involves cheating the other, or both. If one is really involved with another, then this implied charge is correct, and it has nothing to do with whether there is a legal bond of marriage. Legally, you can't commit adultery unless you are married, whereas betrayal of what lies between you, into lies between you, has nothing to do with being married. Furthermore, even when people are married, they may not have a sexual relationship or it may be a spasmodic and relatively unimportant thing. They may not expect or want that it should be a "special thing" between them, the centre of a flavour and quality which only they know. The legal notion of "adultery" leads us away from the real issue whether, when one of them commits "adultery", anything is there to be adulterated. There are other questions farther beneath the surface, too, the problem of how we are to cope with our feelings of jealousy and outraged "honour" and the difficulty of caring for what we value without becoming rigidly conservative.

Nevertheless, though we may be arrogant in our outrage against the execution, we are right to be suspicious when a diplomat for Saudi Arabia says that we should not arrogantly judge what goes on in another culture. He is engaged in special pleading. He knows that the question of the extremity of the punishment does come up in his own country, even if only because the faithful, the religious faithful, so severely castigate such questions as being part of "corrupting compromise". He knows that half of the population, the women, are not being asked. Their voice would not be given effect even if they were asked whether they think they should be shot and their lovers beheaded if they live out a passion beyond their marriage. So he, and in general the men (it is only they) who control Islamic law, are arrogant in the strict sense that they arrogate to themselves the right to judge on issues whose rightness or wrongness crucially involves the feelings of others who are, systematically and on principle, not consulted.

The tricky thing about arrogance, rightness and objectivity is this. It is important that we are prepared to judge that it is wrong, cruel, not to be considered at all as a possibly correct punishment that "adulterous" lovers should be executed. We may be unable to withstand a charge of arrogance when we do this, for we may think within a frame of mind of "the terrible things they do over there". The answer to that charge of arrogance is to become subject to that criticism of arrogance, and to become critically reflective about our own cruel and unnatural punishments, not hiding the fact that they may be milder and more of a socially ostracizing nature. It is a moral confusion to drop our moral criticism because we were arrogant in making it.

An excess of enthusiasm and lack of self-criticism in making moral judgements of the behaviour of others is arrogant: yet a refusal to judge (judge not lest ye be judged) is a most cunning form of conceit, for in appearing to be so charitable towards others, we say nothing which can be used in evidence against ourselves. There is only a continuous blade in a moral sword. To wield it is to be cut by it. This is why it is a cowardly charity never to be so arrogant as to make a moral judgement.

Arrogance is a form, but a degraded form, of understanding. Though a person who is arrogant seems intolerably self-centred, it is not because he or she takes no interest in things and people not himself or herself. Arrogance goes out into the world, though presumptuously, whereas vanity remains at home. Unlike the vain person who disregards those whose point of view will not support or complement his own, and unlike the narcissist who is interested in others only to the extent that he or she can love him or herself through them, "in their eyes", someone who is being arrogant is taking an interest in others who are different in their point of view; he or she feels that they are making a most strenuous effort to understand — not to remain indifferent or ignoring, but really to come to terms with what is being said or done. But the error of the arrogant is to take to themselves what is not their own. They are right to make an effort to confront the point of view of another. They are right not to shirk the risk of judging, of forming their own point of view on what others are doing and whether their opinions are correct, their theories well founded and so on. However, without a clear and full understanding of the other point of view, and without a strict knowledge of its details and similarities and differences from one's own, such judgement is an unbearable dogmatism. A criticism made from within such a frame of mind, even if "correct" and "true", is useless and destructive. It tells the person who already agrees with you nothing he or she did not know already, and sounds like "clashing cymbals" to the very one whom you might have some interest in convincing. Doubtless it is necessary to reject many notions and suggestions and points of view which we do not understand very well or know much about, since not to do so is to be inconstant in holding one's own point of view and direction. But an unarrogant though fairly ignorant rejection leaves room for a regret that consideration is not possible, a wary reserve in one's summary rejection; it is not the permanent closing of a door.

A person who is arrogant in his or her judgement of the views and actions of others with different points of view, takes over the role of others in the vain imagination that he can actually judge from a point of view not his own. He confuses imaginatively understanding another point of view — becoming fully conversant with it and being able to put himself, in imagination, in another's intellectual and emotional shoes — with being a person who has that point of view. Thus he supposes he has the right to judge matters as if from within it even though really he rejects it. ("I know what and how you'd think about this. You needn't tell me", is the consciousness of the arrogant.) This confusion of supposing one can think within a position one rejects happens constantly between persons. It is no less striking and even more systematically far reaching when someone who studies another's writings "carries on as if he were the author"; it doesn't seem quite as patently arrogant as wholesale dismissals of the writings of others, but in some ways it is worse. A person might be able to delude himself in this absurd act because he "feels humbled in the presence of the great creative genius", and begins to employ, without a sense of conscious artifice, the language of the writer or to impose the writer's moral strictures. Perhaps he even copies what he knows of the writer's life apart from his writing. The "humility" of discipleship, of subordinating one's ideas to those of another, is the arrogance of "carrying on the great work", of knuckle-rapping those who have diversionary, revisionist, reactionary or other heretical tendencies; it is arrogance of thinking that one can be another (lesser of course, humbling . . . humbling . . .) Wittgenstein, Quine, Marx or whatever. To attack the arrogance of discipleship is not to meanly refuse to acknowledge the great. One recognizes the scope and complexity and compassion of Shakespeare's plays; how the different voices are given their due so that we can understand how each comes to think that he or she can or should think and feel and act as they do. Nevertheless, except in the very general sense of being inspired to their own best, no one in their senses would try to write more Shakespearean plays, more Mozart operas or more Beethoven string quartets. This is not because we cannot learn from them but because what we do learn is the importance of originality, despite the dependency of it upon its surrounding culture. It is the highly individual view, made most intense and clear, which speaks most universally.

The arrogance of discipleship is equalled by the arrogance of forgetting that each person depends on others. To be independent is to be just distinct enough in your mind and life from others to recognize your dependencies and interdependencies. To refuse to allow or to acknowledge influence, in a search for pure originality, is an absurd self-limitation and rejection of what is best. Also it makes nonsense of one's own efforts. What is the point of trying to write the best in philosophy if one thinks that for another to be influenced by it in his or her own thinking and writing would be a slavish and arrogant discipleship? Even to imitate may be important, as an exercise in becoming skilled, or in coming to understand what it is like to work from within a certain framework of ideas, and with certain methods. Neither of these necessary conditions to good and informed work of one's own come near discipleship. To allow oneself to be influenced is to allow the work to work. It is not to preordain that it will work so as to produce one's agreement with its claims or methods or style; perhaps it works to produce these agreements, perhaps it does not. Similarly to imitate is to come to understand and to know how the other person works. As with the due respect one pays in allowing oneself to be influenced, subject to, the force of another's work, there is no commitment to agreeing with, or even to liking what one imitates. One is empirical about that. "Taste it and see."

The arrogance of impatient rejection of ideas different from or alien to one's own is easy to observe, though it is easy enough in practice to mistake a quick observant or reasoned rejection which an experienced and clear minded person will feel competent to make, for such an arrogant dismissal. The difference between an arrogant dismissal and a deft, just rejection is that the arrogant person has never made the intensive and careful acquaintance of what he now rejects, and rejects it only on the basis that from what he knows from his own point of view, it cannot be correct. Yet it is disastrous to react against the arrogance of that attitude, to an unrigorous liberalism which would be committed to seeing "as much truth in every side". That is an abdication of judgement useless to all parties, inconsistent with the truth that only consistent statements are true, and self-refuting in that, if there is as much truth in every side, then there is as much truth in the totalitarian side that there is truth only in one side.

In being arrogant, one may well confuse one's critics by use of such logical criticisms of unrigorous liberalism. But confusion it is. The vanity of an indifferentist liberalism is no ground for dogmatism. The fact that one cannot sanely agree with all sides and that, in holding a point of view one becomes rationally committed to criticizing what is inconsistent with it, is no excuse whatever for being arrogantly above other points of view, for being out of reach, unimpressible by what those with those points of view wish to put forward. Such placing of oneself out of reach by making appeal to one's present intellectual or other commitments is an example of what Sartre describes as bad faith — the pretence that one is no longer currently responsible for what one committed oneself to previously. "As a committed Christian, you can't expect that I can seriously entertain the idea that . . . ." "On my physicalist theory, you must see that what I have to say on the issue is . . . ." The humble arrogance of these posturings — at the one moment "in all humility" recognizing that it is from a point of view which one speaks "and of course you may not agree with it" (a neat device to defuse impending criticism) and arrogantly placing oneself beyond reach of criticisms of it and in that same moment building oneself a platform from which to lay down the law from one's point of view — this forelock tugging insolence spells the death of both friendly exploratory conversation (instead one has a politician's "frank exchange of views") and of lively dangerous argument.

Curiously, it is because the person who arrogantly uses his having of a point of view as a barrier between himself and the impingement of ideas and experiences which might upset it, does not fully *have* his point of view, that he is arrogant. An enthusiastic portrayal of current political events as seen and described by someone who has the vision and feeling of a dialectical materialist who sees events in terms of a class struggle and the emergence of ideas as proceeding from an economic base, puts Marxism, liberalism, fascism and the rest, all to the test. People will be disturbed from their comfortable shibboleths of liberalism, fascists will be provoked to betray the outright nastiness of their feeling and, if he has any luck in the intelligence and articulateness of those who attempt to meet his views, the innocent new "Marxist" will find himself in a more complex world of ideas, causes, motives and reasons than, in his first enthusiasm, he had suspected. What determines whether someone really *is* a Marxist, a Christian, an analytical philosopher, a one-who-is-in-love-with-someone, is how they meet those people, things and experiences which try and test their new point of view. To just crumple "in all honesty" before what is at first blush a convincing difficulty for maintaining one's mode of being is no proper humility before the truth, for it is to forget that others are as liable to error as oneself, it is to forget that doubt is just doubt and not disproof; and to just betray the convincingness of the experience by which you came to your point of view; it is to be faulty in emotion and intellect, since it is to give your ideas no chance of being proved or disproved. If your quick-thought "honesty" leads you to an instant change of mind, then you've not understand thoroughly where you were; you don't understand properly where you have gone to; you are in a pretty pickle when you meet the next "recalcitrant" experience for your brand new flashpoint.

All of these truths are what the arrogant exploit when they brandish their holding of positions as a defence of them. There is nothing which serves a villain so well as a philosophical truth, and we just have to put up with the fact, and prod his complacency as best we can.

Arrogance is a threat to objectivity. In being arrogant a person takes to himself what is not his, and attempts to operate with it as if it were his own. There are, on the one hand, the matters vital for objectivity: the necessities of a strongly sustained initiative in understanding the point of view of another, of learning to place oneself imaginatively within it and of thinking how another thinks and feels and perceives from within it. On the other hand there is the actual possession of the other's view and that is not one's own. Only those for whom it is part of their way of being are able to make judgements from within it. If one could do that from an alien or opposed point of view, one could indeed "arrogate" from another his or her own freedom of choice of things, opinions, friends and experiences. Such an interference with autonomy, uselessly conducted under the banner of the single minded pursuit of truth, involves, partially first as cause and then as further compounded effect, the loss of one's own autonomy as well as a threatened or real damage to another's. In failing to preserve the distinction between *imagining* the point of view of another and *sharing* it, one proceeds incoherently. One's mistakes are like the confusions of self-identity intrinsic to envy. In wanting something in that another has it, a person is wanting to be-himself-in-being-another, and to-be-another-in-being-himself. In this confusion he is not properly himself, and certainly he is in no way the other person. As he is prevented by his envy from enjoying the thing possessed by another as a thing in itself, and prevented from fully though vicariously enjoying the fact that at least someone has the enjoyment of it, so he is prevented by his arrogance from understanding the position of another as something in its own right, and from fully though vicariously understanding that for another it is a mode of understanding. Ironically, the one who arrogates even loses the clarity of perspective according to which he can state what he takes to be the distortions and errors in the position which he has placed too close under his own conceptual wing to see it for itself.

Roget's *Thesaurus* puts "arrogance" under the general category of "laxity", which causes a momentary surprise, since one associates it more with force and aggression. Yet Roget is right, for though arrogance seems to its victim to be associated with force and energy and too much unthinking unilateral action on the part of the one who is being arrogant, it is a sign of foolishness and stupor in the arrogant towards himself. An honest thief can hold and use what he takes. An arrogant thief would steal a position he cannot fulfil, a car too fast or powerful for him to control, a reputation which it is impossible for him to put on, or a child who cannot become his own.

When thinking clearly and rigorously one must be prepared to appraise and to judge people, actions, opinions and theories. A principal error intrinsic to arrogance is the confusion of this with a right to reject them because they are inconsistent with what you sincerely hold to be the truth. The clear minded person who is going to judge without arrogance allows the differing language, experience, desires and theories of others to have a fair chance against what he already thinks and feels. He does not say, "I must not allow it to have this chance for it will . . . it might . . . take me away from what I now so clearly see as the truth".

The choices are not simple. We are subject to economies of time and energy. To fancy yourself capable of an even appraisal of all possible points of view before making up your mind is to be entirely unobjective about yourself and therefore, in effect, about the issue you are to decide upon. For the most part our lack of arrogance in relation to what does not lie within our present frame of mind and scope of knowledge and imagination can consist in no more than a preparedness, whose limited extent is fixed differently, first during a leisurely afternoon and then on a busy morning, to consider and share new or newly incommensurable language and experience when it happens to come our way. Nothing can adequately encapsulate a person's responsibility to consider what he does not yet know or understand or of which he possesses no imaginative grasp. We can depend only on a growing sense of having to force our opinions along tracks which once they traversed easily and smoothly. This is our signal to actively search and discover, and not just wait to be told, or wait for something to happen.

Pride, and being "proud"

Pride is supposed to go with arrogance, as envy with jealousy. To make the moral distinction between vanity and pride, one might say that in being proud, one is too proud to be vain — too proud to scrounge around for compliments, envy or admiration. Such avoidance of self-abasement is good, but such a proud stance is not. It is a false posture. It is well that we can survive and stick to our guns without praise or admiration, for we ought to have a direct objective interest in what we are doing or investigating which is distinguishable, even if connected with, a desire or hope for praise and admiration. Nevertheless, it is false pretence that we do not or ought not to desire and accept praise and admiration. Not to wish for approval at all is the most unutterable conceit, for it involves the thought that only one's own thought and taste is of any value. Though it would be to iron out our various subjectivities too far to expect that one's opinions and tastes, no matter how artfully and reasonably presented, will finally be agreeable to all others of intelligence, learning and good taste, still there is an appeal to their agreement in one's arguments and most engaging presentations of what one values most in taste. It is an essential part of our concept of taste that matters of taste are disputable, even if not always reconcilable. There are two sides to this. We think that argument and persuasion are relevant. We do not just automatically agree to differ because it is just a difference of taste. But equally we do not think that enough rational and empirical effort is bound to make us agree. The arts of reasonable persuasion and empirical test are relevant, even though it is equally part of the concept that matters of taste might have no final resolution, and that people have to admit sometimes that there is differing and incompatible good taste; though differences of taste are to be referred initially to a lack of experience, a confused palate, a prejudice concerning what is tasted, an irrelevant but disturbing association, a lack of attention, or a sheer lack of taste on the part of one or other of those disputing, a finally unresolved difference is not strict proof of error in taste on the part of either person. This must be only a final concession in the last resort. To make a judgement of taste is to be exposed to criticism, reproof, agreement, congratulation, searching question and the rest, much as in making a judgement of "fact". To maintain any level of objectivity about anything is to see that one is one, though certainly one, taster, thinker, observer and theorizer among many. Physiologically, as complex human organisms, and socially, as sharers of a common social life, culture and language, we cannot assume ourselves to be so different that differences — of morality, of religion, of scientific theory, of taste in food and colour and rhythm — can be left to lie just naked, unadorned and untouched as "differences". They are implicit disputes. Any excess of pride as being "above such disputes and secure in my own taste or opinion" must be an error.

There is a connection between excessive pride and arrogance; the excessive pride of one brings on the arrogance of another. For if one — the proud — will make too much of a thing of protecting against invasion his or her own territory — intellectual, moral, emotional oo land and other property — then another can gain shared use of it only by a forceful appropriation.

Pride is not just the same as restraint, though it involves a form of it. If someone restrains himself or herself from projecting, expressing or demonstrating what they think or feel because they see that the person to whom they would speak is busy, this is not pride, but consideration. Pride is the particular restraint which is maintained over what we are, even to ourselves, out of a fear of criticism. In the pride we have in ourselves, for ourselves, the fear is of our own criticism. In the pride we have before others, either in ourselves or in others or other things, the fear is of the criticism of others. Pride is not intrinsically irrational or misplaced, of course; fear is not intrinsically irrational or misplaced. Pride need not be a mindless terror.

Hume, in *A Treatise of Human Nature,* describes pride as a pleasure — a pleasure taken in what one has or does, or in what another has or does if that person is related closely enough to you by friendship or blood. No doubt there is a good deal of Humean irony in his taking pride out of the bin of the seven deadly sins, to make it one of the chief virtues and causes of virtue. It is part of his admirable wish that we look levelly and fairly at our fellows instead of grovelling before God. "An unworthy sinner." How are we to reconcile the good and the bad senses of pride? It is tempting to think that there is a virtuous and a vicious sense of the word "pride". The vicious sense as in, "He is so proud. It is useless trying to talk to him; he can't allow himself to hear criticism, or to let down his hair enough for anyone to know what he thinks or needs." And the virtuous sense as in, "He takes a great pride in his appearance these days", or "She is so proud of her daughter's success in painting" and so on. However, we begin to see the connection between the vicious and the virtuous senses. For though it is supposed to be a virtue to take a pride in oneself, one's belongings and one's family and friends and their qualities and possessions, and only a worst reading of Kant at his worst would deny us the right to a pleasure in fulfilling these duties, something has gone wrong if the only pleasure one can take in such things is the pleasure of pride. For if that becomes a condition, then we have lost sight and sense of the thing itself, and it is being swallowed up in our imagination, within our possession of it. Even the less egocentric enjoyment of pride in others — the success of our friends and family — turns sour as a value, if we can take pleasure in the success of others only if they are so related to us. For then it is apparent, both that pleasure taken in their success is too egocentric; we are pleased not so much for them, but because *my* friend, *my* sister, *my* lover or whoever, is succeeding.

This last phrase seems only the slightest shift of emphasis, but it is typical of the shift from the objective to the merely subjective within the properly undeniable aspect of subjectivity in all our dealings. It is like the shift in tone from, "It is my opinion that . . ." (said lightly and quickly, the utterance being meant to do no more than prevent raising someone's hackles by being or seeming too assertive and thus taking attention away from the fact or issue one wishes to raise) to "It *is* my *opnion,* that . . ." (stress falling on one's having the opinion, attention sliding back from the object of it, sly implication that one's having the opinion is both reason for me and the hearer to think it true, and to take it seriously — particularly if it is "my *well considered* opinion". All this with the mock humility that I am conceding it, after all, just as my opinion, so I cannot be directly attacked since I have made the disclaimer, and yet I can forge ahead as if on the basis of the fact alleged *in* the opinion.)

Though it does seem right that one should take a pleasurable pride in one's doings and possessions, and in those of the people to whom one is attached, the inability to go beyond the pleasures of pride just is the inability to go beyond the pleasures of things as standing in a certain relationship of being possessed or quasi-possessed by you in such a way that they throw credit on you. It is an inability to take direct interests and pleasures in the things themselves. What one is doing might be done by another; what one possesses might be possessed by another; your friends or relations are people quite apart from their being your friends or relations. If all of these platitudes are realized, then one's valuing things or enjoying or being pleased at the fact that they are done or exist, cannot be limited by the idea that they are in some way possessed by yourself. Even simple perception takes the possessive or the more objective sense. I may take a proud pleasure that *I* am hearing the great Andrés Segovia. Or I may simply listen with delight to his playing, or to what he plays.

So there is no virtuous and vicious sense of pride; at any rate there is no need to postulate such an ambiguity. It is simply that it becomes a "vice" to make pride one's exclusive mode of interest in things. "Too proud to admit . . ."; "Too proud to listen . . ."; "Too proud to ask for, accept, help"; or "Too proud to show one's pain . . .". It is plain how these forms of excessive pride both show, among other things, an insufficient objectivity concerning oneself (one's limits of power, knowledge, self-control, generosity and so on) and, no less, that they demonstrate one's unwillingness to gain any further understanding. Equally they produce in others an inability and finally an unwillingness to maintain an objectivity about and an understanding of oneself.

Hume made a correct and particularly a correcting emphasis on the pleasure and the social good of pride — that it gives one reward for one's reasonable and prudent self-regard, and rewards for turning an interested and generous eye on at least some others. It is a singly directed blow against the self-demeaning indictment of pride typical of the religious consciousness which fears the power of pride in setting people on their own emotional and moral feet. Without once mentioning religion, he delivers it with perfect aim. But with God not only dead but now buried, we must find our own ways to moderate the lion's pride, not by religious extermination, but by a humanly understood ecological balance. Our sense of pride, and with it our sense of those things in which we can take pride, is coextensive with our sense of ourselves and of our own worth. In that what we take pride in is not just ourselves but those people (with their doings and possessions) with whom we would most closely identify ourselves, our sense of our own worth is intrinsically tied to our preparedness and capacity to grant, observe and continually sense the worth of others. In this way, the necessity that we ourselves maintain our proper pride requires in turn our capacity and preparedness to accept and to encourage such pride in others. To be proud of others is to wish them to be proud of themselves, and of us.

So how do you have too much pride then? How do you have too much of a good thing? Partly, as already shown, because of pride's tendency to exclusiveness. Pride generates an interest only in those things which, in some sense, one possesses. The benevolent dictator would solve this by changing the world rather than his or our understanding of it. Once we are all his possessions, he will regard us with a generous eye. Unfortunately, we cannot detect the "generosity" in his wish that first we all be his. He (all what is he, but "God" or any human pretending to the Throne), must have all pride, and each of us must have none. Thus all will be well. This, together with the denunciation of pride as a sin, is the moral schizophrenia of the Jewish and Christian consciousness. How can there be a being for whom it is the greatest good to have, in infinite extent, something which in even the least quantity is an evil in his "children"? Mummy and Daddy can booze and swear because they are grown-ups, but the children must drink water and speak pure words.

The other reason why one can have too much pride is because the link of pride with possession means that the pleasures of pride are, if not moderated by other connections and motives and rewards, too much at the mercy of the fear of loss. If you take a pride in yourself, then you bristle when you hear a criticism of yourself, because the criticism, if correct, is partly destructive of yourself. If you admit the criticism and do nothing about it, you are lowered in self-esteem. If you do something about it, then you lose something of what you were. You may do well to lose part of what you were but, still, you can't value something and not fear to lose it or part of it. If you identify with your own country, then you are sensitive to criticism of it. You cannot view criticism with equanimity. To admit the criticism, if it is correct, one must either change one's country (which may be more than a little difficult), change yourself (which may be impossible, or in any case immoral, if the criticism of the country was just) or face being partly alienated from your own land, which is permanently painful. Pride is a partial objectivity, an objectivity threatened by partiality. Equally it is an objectivity aided by the force of involvement in bringing us out of indifference or humble diffidence so that we are close to things. What has been described may be regarded more as the costs of a worthy thing than as objections to pride.

It is silly to say both that people should enter into special relations of esteem to themselves and things and people around them, and yet that they should maintain some perfect "philosophical" equanimity with regard to them. To give up all special identification, which is the condition of pride and which is then sustained by the pride it generates, is to give up one powerful stimulus to the close and intense interest without which objective attitudes are devoid of experiential content. We cannot say that objectivity requires the elimination of pride. Don't let another fierce god of self-denial so quickly replace the religious tyrant. Pride does interfere directly with equanimity to criticism, and therefore places objectivity at risk. Still, it does not interfere directly or necessarily with objectivity. So long as our lack of equanimity to criticism falls at least well short of hysteria, and our prickly resistance to words and experiences which bear harshly on the things in which we take pride is not total, then in the long run objectivity may be well served by our special protectionism. The person entirely without pride keeps insufficient distance or barrier between himself and others. There is too little space between, on the one side, himself and those things and people by which he defines himself and, on the other side, other things and people. Without keeping this space, we cannot maintain the confidence and undisturbed momentum needed to continue living and enquiring from within it. On the other hand, a person with only pride has nothing but a distance and barrier between himself and his chosen few, and the rest of the world which must then, at the limit of pride, be seen as incomprehensibly alien. Space may need to exist, but space travel must be possible. Pride is important to others and not just to oneself, since their sense of themselves is measured by the resistance to compliance which they encounter in others. Our pride is important to them, for only in finding determined and intense resistance to their criticisms (which seem to them "so obvious" from the outside) can they come to any clear idea of what they are up against, and whether there is any truth in what they say. The natural check to excessive pride is simply complex reality itself. That "pride comes before a fall" removes an objection to it. The people and things outside the special circle of pride are not sufficiently unlike those within it for us to remain totally impervious to outside criticism, however we rant and fume.

Chapter Nine

Persistence, Focus and Shifts of Focus

Persisting, and getting used to changes in perspective

We need some measure of pride in what we do and have, in order to persist in which we are doing and in fulfilling the conditions of possessing what we have. Persisting in what we are doing and in holding on to what we have is a condition of maintaining knowledge and understanding — objectivity if you like — of what we are dealing with and of ourselves. It is in our sustained commitments to philosophy, painting, each other, to the ideals of democracy, to the possibility of radical social change, to motor racing, to the value of life as exhibited in sense and in sensibility that we become familiar with the ins and outs of these things, that our illusions about them are dispelled or shattered, that the character of our own subjectivity in our interest and involvement in them becomes apparent.

Part of the point of persistence is that we should learn when to desist. It is no objection to the need for persistence that we may back off disastrously too late; nor is it an objection to the need to desist that we may pull up or give up only moments before the crucial time of reward or discovery. The last fear makes us continue obsessively; the first leads us to compulsive promiscuity of one sort or another.

Usually when one first becomes attracted to and is interested in something or someone, there is a wonderful sense of enlightenment, of a new freedom in a new medium, a swiftly broadening scene, a new hue to the old and a delightful sense of a quickening power. Yet, one would have to be an idealist, in the common and in the philosophical sense of that term, to think that everything could remain like that. It is not as if things have gone wrong when they do not continue in that aura. Even to wish that things remain like that is already for things to change, since from the wish we begin to impose a dogmatic insistence on the continuing being identical with the beginning — actions change into actors and faces into facades. Sometimes the knowledge and experience gained from and in a new interest simply extinguish it. In engaging in racing, a person might find the costs too high, the fear of injury too great or that it is too improbable he or she will enjoy the pleasures of victory. He or she may simply find that after doing it for a while, it seems a futile and pointless waste of time, rather than a thrilling and life enhancing exploration of skill and balance within a flirtation with death. It is then stupid to go on in the name of persistence or loyalty. One owes one's persistence and loyalty only to what, so far as one can tell after a searching exploration, is true. Modification is possible; a person might find that he'd rather enjoy driving much faster than is safe or permissible on the public roads preferable to trying hopelessly to win. So, in getting to know someone, the experience of (and consequent upon) being with them may annihilate the original understanding, but produce new attractions and desires, or radical mutations of the old. Sexual relationships may turn into sexually charged friendships; initially intellectual friendships into love affairs, and so on. Or, to take another example — you begin to read and to discuss philosophy. It seems the most extraordinary and strange new use of common words and phrases. Yet inevitably, the study produced by an initial vital interest must make the initial magic disappear, otherwise the study is not being produced. In turn, the stage of understanding the logical mechanics of the conceptual illusion is as temporary as the stage of "seeing through" the marvellous effects and meanings of a painter to the techniques of brush and line. The feeling of a permanent "objectivity" replacing an earlier more romantic "subjectivity" is a temporary illusion no less than the earlier magic. The "objectivity", the knowledge of logic or technique becomes second nature, subliminal, and new mirages appear, too fresh, and so newly complex that it is too difficult to dismember them. The feeling encapsulated in metaphors such as "illusion" and "mirage" to indicate the transience of what seems to be the most profound understanding, itself dissolves. Understanding must decay or transmute, for the very reason that it is so active in our ways of dealing with what we encounter that we, and thus it, are changed in consequence of possessing it. To understand this is not to lose confidence in understanding, but to gain a new grasp of the transience of understanding. If understanding really is transient, then we cannot for that reason call it illusory, for there is, on the very hypothesis of transience, no permanent position from which we can declare it, once and for all, exposed as fraud by a later objectivity.

As we become experienced, we sense almost from the outset the destructive tensions, ambiguities and partial character of what would have been, in an earlier more innocent stage, an all engrossing and thus totally illuminating interest. It is at this point that the conceptual and practical problems of persistence arise. We cannot trust our fears and doubts that we may be on the wrong track, investigating things the wrong way, barking up the wrong gum tree, since after a number of experiences of the phase of creative upsurge, we know by this stage that whatever we are doing will be seen through enough sedimented past, complexity of actual and imaginable perspective (not to mention mere unadmirable apprehensiveness) that we shall have to bear with less than a full magic, less than a fully convincing "illusion" or "explanation", less than a comprehensive system of concepts. At this stage we would be rightly wary that we were falling into fanaticism, or at least an obsessional frame of mind if we felt an entire and thus unselfquestioning youthful conviction about ourselves and our work and its objects. "Youthful" slides with us as we move, though not automatically by the accretion of years.

To hope for a criterion by which to determine when one should persist with an enquiry or an endeavour is to ask for a means by which one could have at hand, for one's present use, the very future which one's actions and the perceptions which coordinate them are to help bring about. It is to imagine, absurdly, that one could produce the future instantly and then the future could be already carried along with you. As if the future could participate in and give you cautionary and encouraging information concerning the very actions which are to bring it about. The content of this hope is the logical centre of the delusive wish commonly known in art and architecture as futurism. Philosophies may also be futuristic, though it is not customary to give them that title. There is a measure of futurism in Nietzsche, in Marx's ethical confusions about the transcending of bourgeois by revolutionary values, and in Christianity's hope for a future heavenly redemption of "foul and impure" worldly values. Hitler and the National Socialists are pre-eminently futurist. It is instructive to contrast the free radical spirit of the *avant garde* with the fascist style of futurism. To be *avant garde* is to use the knowledge and skills of the established tradition, whether old or modern or even contemporary to produce the unexpected and the unpredictable, so as to release a free future. It is to be prepared to wash one's hand of it if it turns out to be bad, or of little value, and yet to lovingly embrace the try, and to be prepared to allow the experimental move towards the future to become a past event, not to be despised no matter if it is to be seen as mistaken in hindsight. Without this tolerant allowance, people react away from the large number of glaring errors of the *avant garde,* when viewed with hindsight. They react in panic and embarrassment into conservatism and classicism.

Futurism explained as a form of obsessionalism

Futurism seems like a kind of radicalism in its superficial contrast with the dedication to the past typical of conservatives, but is at heart more intensely oppressive. For one thing, being an attempt to do the impossible, it must have the character of a compulsively and exhausting iterated task. The idiosyncratic compulsiveness of futurism lies in its apparent attempt to forge ahead to the future, away from the inadequate present — both in its archetypal political forms of national socialism and of revolutionary communism, not to mention the aspiration to the future spiritual life already foreshadowed in a spiritualized earthly existence typical of Christianity, orthodox Judaism, Buddhism and Mohammedanism, and in its ordinary unsystematic, quite personal and domestic eruptions in impulsiveness and general presumptuousness about outcomes. Futurism is an arrogance towards the future, an attempt to arrogate to now, to our present use, the yet to be created actions, thoughts and objects whose autonomy must elude the arrogant just as "another" mind and spirit always partly elude the net we throw upon them.

The character of futurism can be seen more clearly in its weaker, more recessive form of apprehensiveness; indeed, the violent and rapid actions normally associated with futuristic consciousness are the desperate breaks away from what is felt to be otherwise than in this rapid, violent movement, a suffocating apprehensive fixity in the present. One might be bored in the present. That might make one depressed but not, by itself, apprehensive. The possibility of apprehension arises as the desire to escape boredom replaces boredom, or as first order desires — to eat, drink, run, make love, read a book and so on — arise as unconscious springs touch the arid surface. If these desires are met with unfitting circumstances, one is simply frustrated — one desires to read, but is on a plane — there can be no choice to break the journey, to step out the door and look for a bookshop. Apprehensiveness is the state akin to frustration which arises from inhibiting circumstance and self-restraint undertaken for scarcely understood reasons. If you clearly and definitely know why, for moral or prudential or other reasons, you should not do what you have some impulse to, then you do not feel apprehensive. You might feel baulked or regretful. You feel apprehensive if there is something you want to do, but do not go ahead with it, while still feeling that you might as well, or perhaps even should. Or you feel apprehensive if you go ahead "doing" something, but not fully doing it because of too many doubts and inhibitions about it. This includes the apprehensiveness one feels in the face of a possibly impending danger. If it is definite, you may feel frightened, terrified, or try to escape or to confront and to eliminate or neutralize the threat. To be apprehensive, however, is to have an indefinite fear about something so that flight or facing up or aggression may all be equally stupid and inappropriate. Also, and this is the link of apprehensiveness with futurism, it is to have an image of what is to be done, or of what is to happen, which is radically out of phase with the circumstances for action and thought which surround you. The image dominates the feeling of the need to act and, at the same time, by clouding one's perception of present circumstances and one's own present condition, apprehension makes appropriate actions awkward and difficult. The lack of clear perception itself acts, as in a positive feedback mechanism, to further increase the feeling of unease; one becomes aware that one is in a state ill suited for apt thought, feeling and action. The action one would take to improve the situation has already fled one's capacity for smooth control and yet the need to do something is felt all the more strongly.

So now the connection between this weak and recessive "apprehensive" form of futurism and the violent, sensationist futurism: the violent insensitive action of a futurist is an attempt to break the paralysing statis set up by the apprehensive tension between the image, the object of desire for the future and the presently perceived circumstances including, most notably, the lack of the desired "object". A futurist architect cannot stand the buildings of the present — they are dull, conventional and uninspiring; fit only to be demolished, to be swept away in the floodtide of progress. Neither can he stand the realities, the realism and above all the complexities of creativity which would involve the sensitive and imaginative transformation of what exists, towards what must be acknowledged to be an unknown because being presently created, future. So he imagines the "buildings of tomorrow" and builds them now. "The future will thank us." He will even imagine the "man (and woman) of tomorrow" and build him and her, by genetic engineering, religious conversion, violent revolutionary activity or whatever else will effect a sufficiently radical disruption with the present-becoming-past that we will be flung into the future where, beyond the touch of what will then be irrevocably past, all possible forces of reaction and conservatism will have been eliminated, or will be so cut off from their base that they will be no more than harmlessly quaint anachronisms.

Any ruthlessness towards the present then seems justified, for if the future is what will occur and it is radically different, then the present is doomed in any case, and one can always rationalize the rest, since the present can be counted upon to contain enough suffering to endlessly supply premises for utilitarian arguments that the benefits of the glorious new future easily outweigh some "temporary intensification" in the misery of those who willingly or unwittingly "obstruct progress". So Julius Caesar, Alexander the "Great", Napoleon, Hitler and Stalin. It is not an historical accident that no futurist has brought about the future for which he has betrayed and destroyed the present. There is no short cut to "the future" which bypasses the processes by which, in fact, buildings, machinery, people with certain styles, attitudes, fears, hopes and the rest are brought about. The futurist's "future" is a confused mixture of prediction and coercion. Something is going to happen and if, by any chance, it is not, then watch out for we are going to make sure that it does anyway.

Futurism has it that certain things are inevitable for the future, and so we had better get with the course of history. We had better hasten or reinforce what is in any case inevitable. Among many errors lying here there is a particular fallacy. When there are sufficient conditions for something to happen, the actions taken to make it happen sooner or more intensely are not at all doubly guaranteed of success. The actions to speed up or intensify the effect might work by themselves, but added to conditions which will produce the effect anyway, may even inhibit or damage the whole process. Swinging a hammer with sufficient force may drive in a nail. Swinging it with the same amount of force, even though the nail is to be driven in at that moment by another hammer may, even if one hammer meets squarely over the other, split the wood by driving the nail too fast. The nail hangs loose in the air. Not the desired result. Or one's hammer may throw the other off course and the nail will be missed, or bent. (Nietzsche wrote on how to philosophize with a hammer. The answer is, "Gently, with just enough force to shatter the fragile illusion".)

There is this error in thought about causality embedded in futurism that acting to bring about something which is going to happen anyway (but not quite so quickly, not quite so well) will doubly ensure its occurrence. There is also a logical spiral towards incoherence in attempting to state the content of the aim in futurism. Nothing looks so antiquated as last year's futurist design, last century's (Nietzsche and Marx, for example) futurist thought. The futurist image is that of reaching over a period in time which has not yet elapsed, to spy out the new land, and to retrieve things or ideas from it for the amazement of the public and to its immediate advancement. The incoherence in the image lies in the way it makes the future unspecificable. First the futurist apprehends what is to be, say, a decade hence, in automobile design. He must predict this on the basis of the present course of design, and the predicted circumstances in which automobiles and their drivers will have to operate. In this scenario, the cars of 1990 do not exist in 1980. Suppose he wishes, then, to speed up history by building these cars of 1990 now. If these don't fit the present environment, then all he has is a white elephant or two. If they are successful, then his prediction about what cars will exist in 1990 was based on incorrect premises, since the cars of 1980 include those he first assumed would not exist until 1990. As a futurist he must immediately make a new guess about what will appear in 1990, given that what he had thought was to be the thing for 1990 has already appeared and succeeded. And again the same dilemma applies. Either one fails to influence motor vehicle design, or one succeeds. If the former, one fails to launch humanity into the future. If the latter, one must make a drastic revision of what is to be in the future, of what it is which must be imported back into the present and thus, too, a drastic revision in the basis from which one predicts and plans the future.

Being persistent requires taking due care about the future. It requires a realistic belief in the objectivity of the future — that some things will happen, and that others won't. The only doubt is about which, and what. Anyone who aspires to an objective point of view, will wish to take account of what will occur. He or she will take into account the predictable consequences of their and others' actions, and the predictable circumstances in which those consequences will occur. Thus, one can sometimes effectively design for the future instead of foisting on the next decade the what-will-be inappropriate and inefficient designs and inventions that we presently use. A rational and warm Hitler, a Martin Luther King of Germany might have seen, with Adolf, that much was amiss with people and life and society in Germany. He might have said that "He had a dream" that, at some time in the future, people in Germany would lose their depression and live in creative hopes for the future. Such a Martin who could break also with Luther and retain his idealism while he broke with religion, might have inspired those around him to take a cool and appraising consideration of their legacy of passionate romanticism in music, might gradually learn to dispel their Lutheran and Catholic puritanism by a friendly and relaxed sensual life. A dream, but not an incoherent one. He might have reminded them that deeds and arts and created objects which command admiration and respect and affection wipe out humiliation — that it is not necessary to wipe out those who sneer at and exploit the weakness of a former power. It is not irrational to hope for more than one reasonably expects. If it were so irrational, there would be no room for hope. One may hope, dream and attempt to realize hopes and dreams. This is not futurism. Nothing could be further from a presumption about what the future is bound to contain. In such dreams and hopes one may keep quite clear of the delusion that anything could be improved by forcing people to act in the ways one might dream of them coming to freely.

It is part of the futurist delusion that once the radical break is made with the past, the future will look after itself. ("Like any dealer watching for the card that is so high and wild he'd never have to deal another." Leonard Cohen) It is monstrous yearning after an appalling innocence of and about human nature. So those who planned, acquiesced in and practised their "brutalist" architecture upon the actual war ruins and, even worse, upon the areas of housing destroyed just so that the new architecture could arise, thought that once the "slum dwellers" were out of their dirty, dark ties to the past, they must blossom into the modern free consciousness. They were, literally, to be raised up on high above all of that; the instant separation in space was to effect and to symbolize the rupture in time. However, as soon as something is broken, something must be put together, and every detail must be attended to. It is all very well to start afresh with buildings, with new people, with surroundings if that is to mean that a change may release one from a binding situation to the extent that one's realizations of how the intricate detail is to be handled and responded to may be brought into play. The destructive delusion is that the intricacy of the nature of people and their surroundings and of their relationships with each other constitutes the problem and must therefore be eliminated, in favour of . . .?

Caring about the future; persistence and love

To persist, in a sense required for any objectivity, is to give one's mind over to receive and to unify the constantly varying impulses, demands, experiences and responses to one's line of initiative. You come to terms with what newly arises, by resolving your mind in respect of them. It is not by some heroic pure will, nor by great power and force, but by keeping to a course already chosen because it is already chosen. In persistence, you proceed because there is not yet enough reason to change while still knowing what you would be doing in the new direction. Newton's physical law that a body continues in the same direction at the same velocity unless acted upon by a force, has a rough equivalent in a rule of sense and morality that one ought to continue with one's present commitments and heading in one's present direction unless given clear and compelling reason to change. (That is not a puritanical denial of distractions and holidays. They are not new commitments.) Such clear and compelling reasons must be those which one will be able and proud to express and to provide to explain one's change of course and change of mind. In this way, too, pride is linked to persistence.

Persistence is not for persistence's sake. The idea that it is a good in itself is one kind of repellent, boring and oppressive conservatism. The point of persistence is that it is not easy to get to know people and things, not easy to remember exactly and truthfully what happened, not easy to get an engine finely tuned and running beautifully, not easy to maintain the imaginative distance from one's present position, involvement and point of view, a distance which is necessary for understanding what people are saying and feeling and doing from theirs. Not that it is necessarily difficult to do these things. It can be a breeze, but since one cannot count on its being a breeze, one must be prepared to row when the wind drops.

To love someone or something is to find oneself with an interest in them, and to actively take an interest. That interest must include both a found and actively developed care for their wellbeing, both as they see it in their own terms, and as one thinks it needs to be put to them from what one observes as another person separate from them in point of view and values. Where love is of a thing or activity, such as a painting or philosophy, then the formula must be understood a little differently. Since philosophy is not a person (though, necessarily, engaged in by people) "it" cannot have its own view of itself and its needs, as distinct from the view which some philosopher takes of it. Still, each person who engages in something like philosophy, poetry, science, horse riding, sailing is confronted both with how it is already done and the consequent needs which must be fulfilled if it is to go on in that same way, and with what is required if he or she is to take it along the way in which he or she wishes. The tension between these two — the demands of the tradition and the demands of one's originality — which tension may be great or vanishingly small, is the analogy or metaphor for love between persons. It is the analogy for the interchange between the point of view of the one loved for-himself or for-herself, and the point of view of the one who loves, for that other. A pure capitulation to the point of view of the other as he or she see it for himself or herself, disguised no doubt as "a total respect for his/her autonomy" is a lack of love and serious or objective interest. More in cowardice or indifference than in love, it is a refusal to offer the difference and outsideness of observation and remark which only a different and loving observer and involver can give. Though it justifies itself as an escape from arrogance, it has no more to recommend it than the pure and total arrogance of thinking, "I must, in my love, judge for the other from where I am; too bad if it conflicts incommensurably with how that other person sees his or her needs and desires". (We find, for example, in Jane Austen's *Emma,* a most subtle exploration of the line between unjust interference and loving though critical concern.)

Since to love requires that one maintain and not only find oneself with an interest and care, it requires the capacity to persist when the going is tough. Equally, it requires the desire that the going not be tough, for it is a desire for the happiness and ease of one with another, and of each separately. The correct recognition that duty is required to "bridge the chasms between the occasions of feeling", as Butler (Butler's *Sermons*) put it, turns into puritanism and the work ethic, if it becomes an end in itself. As an end in itself the duty is not only parchingly onerous, but also meaningless, since duty is a matter of what is due to people (or activities or things) and what is due to people is what they have a right to claim or to expect from you. It is what you may be respected for giving. This right is either a legal obligation, in which case there is some point in fulfilling it even if you do not feel that there is any basis to the person's claim. One simply avoids the penalties of law by compliance, or else the duty is felt as arising from bonds of affection, or familiarity, of shared life. The meaning of the duty lies in the significance of the bonds from which it arises. The character of the bond and the feeling the parties have in maintaining it constitute the basis for an answer to the question "What are you doing?" when someone persists in fulfilling a duty which may be onerous. One can answer "I am keeping someone's confidence in my motives and intentions" or "I wish the person to be well provided for, so that . . . (whatever)". It is the character of the bond from which the duty arises which guarantees that if one suddenly feels trapped in pointless duty, and says "What the hell am I doing, anyway?", there is an answer to be found. How convincing it is depends on what moves one to still continue in the bond, or in what can be found to develop or renew it.

One person may say to another that he or she *ought* to feel the force of a consideration of duty, where that person sees no meaning or sense in it. If a person is so out of touch with those who depend on him or her that even the most vivid portrayal of their needs and hopes leaves him or her cold, then still we might wish to say "Well, still you have a duty, whether you feel it or not". Partly this is the last despairing hope of making the person see the light. Partly it is the due we ourselves pay to the importance of the general and public recognition of such considerations. But when people persist, not in rendering what is due, but in refusing to see or to feel that it is due, those around them become more and more permanently alienated, and come to expect nothing, and die, struggle on, or simply find that they no longer have any need of the person anyway, and in any of these and other ways, the duty quite literally no longer exists. Not that its cessation is any credit to the one who shirked.

Just as the attempt to convert the reality of what is due to people into a call to duty for its own sake makes the allegedly dutiful actions meaningless, so too the attempt to persist out of some dedication to the importance and necessity of commitment (a hostility to drifting, being erratic and so on) is useless. We need some firmness of will, but that comes from resolution, and resolution is not a pure act of will: there is as much in resolving of allowing and waiting and coming to recognize as there is of going ahead and doing what is to be done. The attempt to live by will without real resolution and realization is what should be given the damning title "wilful", though the word is more associated with unfair and inaccurate complaints about people's determination and spiritedness when it is inconvenient to us. There is wilful obedience of the rules just as much as there is wilful disobedience.

Forcing, and sensitive control

The values of persistence can require that you keep on going by forcing things, but it is an undesirable way of "going on". The only excuse can be that one is forced into it by people or circumstances. If other people are intimidating, you may have to force yourself to speak; if your car breaks down in the desert you may have to force yourself to go on walking until you find water. To do these things is to choose the best of a bad lot of alternatives. Forcing is undesirable from the point of view of objectivity because the energy and attention required to keep up the forcing is a diversion and distraction from the main business which is supposed to be in hand — that of keeping direction and flexibly varying it as necessary in order to keep with the "object". In driving or riding, automobiles or motorcycles, a horse and buggy or a horse, you are in control of a balance of considerable forces. If you had never begun to drive or to ride, what you are now controlling would have been fine — sitting motionless in the garage or grazing or frisking about — but once you are driving or riding you are committed to control and to balance, of the machine or animal, of yourself and of yourself in relation to it, until you have brought everything to a halt. It is like beginning to write a sentence, or broaching a difficult subject in conversation. As you create the sentence or open the issue, the weight of what you have done so far must be felt and retained without being dwelt upon; it is like keeping the border or background in view without focusing on it: no awareness of it and you lose the significance of the subject; full awareness of it and you lose sight or focus on the object. Your feeling — your "apprehension" of what is to come, what is to be done, what is to be dealt with by you from yourself and from others and other things — this feeling counterbalances your peripheral retention of what has been or of what has been done, and you act, you voice or expand the issue; in pushing these fluidly trembling horizons forward with one hand, and back with the other, we leave room for an effective and continuous present.

Every action requires some force; some energy is consumed in engaging in it. This cannot just be a law of physics which has nothing to do with thought or human action, since we are physical beings. It is equally true whether we express our determination or fear in running as in flight or as in autonomous initiative; whether we realize our determination or fear in writing a novel or by becoming involved in philosophical argument. If we simply sit and think, then our just sitting requires considerable energy. It is the hard work of "not-engaging in precipitate action", the thinkings, ponderings, resolvings and the rest are themselves no less tiring than our chopping wood or speaking up in public. We know this by common experience, and by our theoretical but well confirmed identification of thinking as a function of neural activity. (Just what balance is shared out between neural activity itself and the muscular activity and restraint necessary for intellectual concentration must, of course, be settled in the laboratories.) But this acceptance of the real expense of energy involved in resolving, deciding and being determined does not mean that we must force ourselves to do whatever we take on, or that we must force anyone or anything else which we find involved in our going forward. Whenever we open a lock with the right key, we must use a little force. But we do not therefore have to force every lock. Nor, with respect to ourselves or to others, force every lack. To the extent that we must use force, or that we make the mistake of doing so, we lose fineness of control; by grasping hard we diminish our responsiveness to what we touch, and reduce our perception of being taken hold of. This metaphor from touch holds good of all the senses. We can listen so hard that we can scarcely hear; we are too used up and tense in the act of listening. It may be necessary to think very hard in order to solve a problem, but it is easy to think too hard. To think too hard is to become tactless in thought. (Naturally, one may be tactless in a different way, for other reasons.) It is to become too involved in the thinking itself for what we are thinking of to hold its own independence, its autonomy, from us. Also, it is to become impervious to all the stray thoughts which may give fresh clues to the character of one's problem, and particularly the direction in which to proceed. In thought, as in perception, the attempt to get the utmost of rigour and accuracy by narrowing down to the one object of interest alone can produce only a pseudo-perception of the insignificance of the object, though perhaps a correct sense of the futility of our efforts. This is no mere psychological quirk of ours. If we can see and think only of the "one thing", then there is nothing for that thing to signify. If it signifies nothing, our enquiry into it, our approach to it, our involvement with it must be futile.

Concentration, exclusion, and the value of the "scientific" consciousness

Such important mistakes as futile overconcentration are not causeless, they are not random. The mistake of excessively narrow and fixed focus in perception and thought arises from and is given spurious justification by the necessity for moments of intense and exclusive concentration. To entirely refuse this importance of concentration and narrow focus is to refuse wrongly all of the modern awareness which is founded literally and metaphorically upon the microscope and the telescope. Both have the same powers, to magnify and to resolve. The former magnifies our view and enables us to pick out distinctly the elements within our view (resolving) which are close but tiny because smaller than us: the latter magnify our view and enable us to pick out elements which come to our sight and are large but which appear tiny because they are so far from us. Without this deliberate use of extreme tunnel vision there is, undoubtedly, a great deal which we should never know. Nevertheless, it is equally clear that if we lacked the significant questions and understanding which we bring to the use of these strictly isolating and intensifying devices of perception, we should learn almost nothing at all by their use. The apparently naive use of a telescope or microscope depends entirely on the ease with which we connect what we can see broadly without its aid, with what we can discern in what we have already identified in the ordinary free roaming use of the senses. Certainly we can see something on the hillside. Is it a horse, a brown bush or a rock? The resolving power of the telescope then settles this for us.

In the light of an everyday tolerance of the easy movement between things and people as we know them by the natural unaided use of the senses and untechnical thought, on the one hand, and scientific instruments, systematic theory and specialist concepts and relatively precise and reliable measurement, on the other, all of this seems like insistence on the very obvious. However, nothing is more common in the continuing history of thought, right up to now and going on, than the deep desire to single out some single form of representation of things as finally displaying the fundamentals of nature. This fundamentalism can never be warranted by the advance of science itself. It is virtually impossible for the findings of the specialized sciences to be in flat contradiction to the broad structure of commonsense and perception, since there is too much discrepancy, incommensurability, between an unaided perception and its attendant and directing spontaneous thought, and what is revealed by technical means and described in a specialist vocabulary. Some have attempted to show that something is fundamental and the rest mere appearance, whether by putting God and Mind at the centre of the universe and of understanding, attempting to show that our mere contingent accidental existence and morality is a lesser thing besides this august necessary and absolute Being which is source and ground of all we thought to be so solid in itself. Others equal in fundamentalism have more recently thought that the power, prestige and universality in application of the physical conception of the universe including people as being made up of complexes of the "fundamental" particles — electrons, neutrons, positrons and the rest — all justify us in thinking that in the end they come down to no more than that. Both groups equally have had logically free choice either to regard the "new science" modestly as additional knowledge, or to grandly claim a knowledge which replaces what we had previously thought. In practice, of course, no sane theologian or physicalist fundamentalist says outright that there are no sticks, stones, cabbages, sealing wax or kings; no intentions, thoughts, desires, no spirit of the age nor social pressures to conform. In practice, in attempting to put forward, explain and persuade people to adopt his pet reductive and exclusive view, the fundamentalist makes free use of all the devices of language, employment of social pressure and the rest of the everyday level of acceptances about the nature of people and the things they deal with. If reality is only as it is represented in the language of physics, then one ought to use only the language of physics in order to explain and to demonstrate physicalism. This would make nonsense of the whole project of physicalism. We would have physics, but no physicalism.

Physics itself is no embarrassment to anyone who keeps to the greatest plurality in modes of thought and perception about things, consistent with the demands of logical consistency and the call for clear experimental or inferential or theoretical evidence. As a science, it takes its place among all our structures of knowledge, and within all our streams of enquiry. Every important mode of enquiry, experience and thought tends to make those involved in it obsessed with the idea that they are on to the "one true nature of things". This must be recognized as an occupational hazard, not as an ontological necessity. The tests that one's interest and involvement are becoming obsessive rather than simply intensive and yet still free to engage other perspectives, is one's growing sense of the fatuousness of one's enterprise, the inconsequential character, irrelevant to anything else which others begin to detect in what one is doing, a sense of emptiness in the object one is supposed to be engaged with, and a growing insistent emphasis on the values of austerity. Those obsessed with what they have come to think is the one fundamental view of things, wish to impose such values on all, as a condition of a "realistic, objective, unflinching" view of reality. So Marxists attempt to persuade us of the soft bourgeois character of everyday priorities, delights and scruples. So physicalists attempt to persuade us of our romanticism in staying with a belief and confidence in things as being largely as they appear to us, no less real than the hidden marvels which do not appear. We should be pleased with a pluralist realism, that things are as they appear, as well as being as they are described and perceived to be by the use of powerful instruments and theories.

"Reductionism", as explained by obsessional lack of control of thought and perception

A proper treatment of the various forms of reductionism is an entire project in itself, but without an appreciation of the character of the various forms of reductionism as obsessional, as forced self-stultifying refusals of one's autonomy, argument between reductionists and their opponents is futile. When someone is obsessed with one point of view, he cannot see or notice the value or point in what is known and described from another. The premises of his opponents seem only strange, unconventional, upsetting and to be dismissed as "soft" or even as irrational distractions from the "real" business in hand. It is not irrationalism to understand and to state openly the severe limits to the rational use of argument. Argument works only upon agreed premises and when the terms of the disagreement are held in common. To argue and to discuss rationally is not just to pursue the logical implications of one's premises and to attempt to detect fallacies in one's opponent's reasoning, and to detect self-contradictions in his statements. It is to keep part of one's mind continually free to feel the character of the dispute; whether one or the other of you are arguing only to win — if so one's motivation must be taken in hand before attention really becomes directed at the issue of the dispute; whether one or the other of you needs to step back to broaden or change the terms of the problem — if so then argument must pause for the more creative process of casting about for a variety of descriptions. We have to more distinctly recollect and carefully ponder the phenomena which lie at the basis of the dispute; perhaps one or both of us has too little experience, or too little recent of the matter being disputed. Suppose that we fall into an argument about the relative merits of two styles of music or of philosophy, or of painting or of scientific theorizing. After a while, if we are not drawn obsessively into going further and further on in linear, albeit logical, insistence, we musical arguers realize that reason would be better served by listening afresh to the music: we philosophical disputers had better absorb ourselves again into first Berkeley's and then Hegel's idealism: both the "scientific realists" and the "instrumentalists" had better relearn the elegant and cunning deployment of theory and experiment by which the charge of an electron was determined by Millikan. Those who are fascinated and alive to the interest and power of modes of thought and perception do not attempt to make any particular such mode the be-all and end-all of their approach to reality. They are content and confident that what they know will hold its own among the always increasing variety of objective interests which people find and develop.

In being obsessive, one gives a priority to something far beyond its real value to you or to others who are involved and concerned. That the priority given exceeds its real value is shown by the fact that one gains neither contentment nor satisfaction from pursuing one's obsessions. There may be some continuing hungry hope while the pursuit is on, but the obsessive character of the interest removes the sense of significance and interest in the "object" (including person) being considered. It is a drastic loss in objectivity, no matter how much the person declares and insists that his or hers is a hard headed single minded pursuit. If a parent is obsessively interested in the success of his or her child, then nothing the child does can properly satisfy the parent. If a mathematician is obsessed by solving a mathematical problem, then he is losing all measure of the importance of his solution as fast as he is finding it. He is losing the right to say whether he is engaged in an important or a trivially pedantic pursuit. To be objective requires that we can use an appropriately measured approach, from time to time, among our more absorptive and accepting phases of engagement. It also requires a preparedness and an ability to make some sort of measure of our success in dealing with something, and of the opinions we are forming about it. Measurement requires a degree of detachment, for it requires that we bring something from outside the object of interest, and in some way, literal or metaphorical, lay it against our "object". The character of the measurer must already be understood well enough, separately from what we measure, that something new and independent is gained by its use. The ideal of objectivist obsessionalism, that the truly objective person narrows down his or her interest to just one plane and focus of endeavour or enquiry, is a strenuous avoidance of such objectivity.

This narrowing of interest is virtually equivalent to what it takes to be its opposite in spirit — the uncritical and complete giving over of oneself to be one with the object of interest, which is the paradigmatic excess of romanticism at its worst. Romanticism seems to be the opposite of fixated objectivism, since the former is the desire to accept everything, and the latter is the desire to strictly control one's acceptances down to the finest excluded edge where exactness and perfect reliability may be attained. Yet the extremes of romanticism and objectivism converge, for in giving over all interests but one in the supposed interests of a precise objectivity, the objectivist has lost the wherewithal for detaching and measuring the object of interest, and for appraising the character of his interest in it. To keep up the illusion of objectivity, he must, like the romantic, "forget himself". For once he has distinctly remembered himself as something quite different from what he is considering as "the objective fact", he must realize that to be objective about himself and the character of his enquiry, he must change ground. However, if he has insisted that objectivity requires the selection of just one true ground — that of physics, or theology, or dialectical materialism or whatever — then he has ruled out the possibility of objectivity considered as the possibility and capacity for detachment, appraisal and measurement of the character and assumptions of one's enquiry or interest.

If Millikan had said, with the reductionists, "Substances are nothing but their atoms, atoms are nothing but their sub-atomic particles, the truths of physics must be reducible to the truths concerning their constituents, for they are nothing but their constituents", he would never have continued his use of observations of the ordinary sized to measure the extraordinary small sized. The danger of obsessiveness to objectivity is a fresh reminder of the importance of detachment. A controlled detachment (not a fracturing dislocation) allows one to make a break from one point of view to another — to avoid fixity.

One's interests may also be compulsive. This is another way, but a damaging way, in which one can persist in one's interest or involvement. To be obsessive or compulsive is not just to go on too long, though the obsessed and the compulsive do go on too long. It is scarcely surprising that the errors and distortions in behaviour and thought and feeling which are implied by the choice of words such as "obsession" and "compulsion" are being analysed only to be castigated. So it is important to remember the importance to objectivity of momentum, of going on in the direction you have found or chosen unless you find compelling reasons to change. Obsessions and compulsions must be seen as surrogates, though forced and erroneous forms, for something which is vital. For all their faults, they get people further into something connected with the nature of what they are interested in, than does idle drifting or scattered impulsiveness. If the obsessed or compulsive themselves are unable to see their errors as they go further and further into them, still they do us a service by showing the character of their errors more clearly and articulately than those who double back or come to a halt as soon as they sense complexity and contrary evidence.

None of this amelioration of the faults of being obsessive and being compulsive is a defence. Within the momentum we need, in order to maintain an objectivity in our interest, we have to allow ourselves to shift focus and point of view without losing continuity. If we keep close to the "object" then its own complexity continually corrects our tendency to fixate upon the last significant or traumatic experience or realization in connection with it. It is typical of obsessional interests to fear that if we once stopped in our endeavours, we would never start again. In this, obsessions are much akin to states of depression, since they are the opposite of the buoyant confidence in which we sense the attractions of the object of our interest, and know that little could upset or divert us. The various other interests and needs for rest and change can happily coexist and refresh our ability to make and keep connections.

Things continue on as they are going unless acted upon by a force, but usually they are acted upon by various diverting or countervailing forces. Our actions generate friction, between each other, upon other people and within ourselves as the various motives we possess and their consequences upon our lives and bodies generate useless heat. In life as in physics, without renewed impulse or attraction, things wind down.

An interest is not obsessional just in that, or just if, it continues too long. Apart from the difficulty of saying how long is "too long", the essential point is that the interest may be obsessional in character almost from the beginning. Always there are spaces alongside and within our interests. An interest is obsessional when a person irrationally or unnecessarily and damagingly excludes other matters from their place alongside and from time to time within these spaces. This obsessive exclusion is, as Sartre would put it, one of our attempts at fleeing our own free asuumption of responsibility. It is an attempt to be "solid", "massif", to be "nothing but" the all consuming interest. It is to fear oneself, one's actual ineradicable complexity and actual or potential self-dividedness. It is one of the devices of bad faith in which we blur the distinction between the fact of finding ourselves with an interest or desire, and our involvement in actively pursuing and fostering, or alternatively in diminishing or displacing that interest or desire. The ostrich with its head in the sand has now become a cliché. Think again of the ostrich, "Sand, sand, nothing but sand", using its protests as a blur to forget its action in putting and keeping its head in it, as it uses the sand to convince itself that the world consists of "nothing but" safe desert, and certainly does not contain its own action. A fine Althusserian or Foucaultian bird which has succeeded in "displacing the self".

Understanding and handling compulsiveness

In contrast with the obsessional following of an interest, in which there is, at the heart of the matter, a loss of perspective and a displacement of priorities which still exist for the person but are being suppressed and blurred, there is in compulsive enquiry and interests and conduct a displacement in the object of interest. A compulsive involvement occurs when there is something one wants or wants to know or to get closer to, only to find it is unavailable and the person will not face the fact and the factual and emotional implications. Compulsiveness is even more likely where someone wants something but does not pursue it because he or she is fearful of the involvement and pursues something else more available, and will not recognize what is being done, or seriously consider whether the renunciation was necessary. In some circumstances, this alternative is found to be satisfactory and complications are avoided by happy accident. Alternatively, where the person fully understands that he or she is finding a surrogate for something else, the surrogate interest need not become compulsive. Where the person won't clearly accept that there has been a displacement, there is a lack, a refusal of comprehension of the lack of satisfaction in gaining the object, and so the person goes on repeating a form of behaviour or thought. It seems to fit his desires, or at least a sense of need and so he or she wants to do it. At the same time, doing it does not produce satisfaction. At most there is an extremely transient sense of satisfaction, and so there is continued repetition. Typical cases are compulsive drinking, compulsive gambling, compulsive sexual behaviour and compulsive talking. When we speak because we have something to say, we are content when it is said, so long as we have been suitably listened to. We do not have to go on repeating the same thing, or slightly different variants of it over and over. But when we talk beside the point we go on and on. When people refuse us the response we want from what they say, and we refuse to see that we will not get the response that way, then we go on and on.

We do something compulsively when it is an unrecognized substitute for what we need. If we recognize it as a substitute then, unless we are already wholly possessed by a feeling, we may choose some way of expressing or otherwise dealing with it. It is bad faith to say "I recognize it but I am totally overwhelmed by it and can do nothing about it", since the degree of detachment necessary for the recognition is not consistent with one's being "totally overwhelmed". One ordinary word for compulsion is greed, and it is the most salient fact about greed that when doing things greedily one cannot do more than partially enjoy obtaining what one wants; one does not or cannot pay proper attention to what one or another is doing or being; in consequence of the imperfect attention and connected imperfection of enjoyment, and the surrogate character of the activity, satisfaction is not secured, and so one goes on demanding more and more. It has been a common theme of the religious outlook on life that "man's permanent dissatisfaction with the world" is proof of his or her need for God. This is a fallacy. The religious point of view just is a person's inability to face the direct reality of his or her bodily, mental, material and social desires, and to recognize the real difficulties which stand in the way of satisfying them. The "sense of the presence of God" is the sanctified and institutionalized account of every child's game, when rejected by the others, of going to the corner of the playground and talking to and mentally or physically playing with an imaginary companion, a "real friend who understands my every need and my innermost heart". It would be only another kind of puritanism replacing religion to scoff at such games in themselves when they have not been sanctified and solemnized, when the metaphor has not been forced into a spurious literalness as it is in theology. If you complained to someone about his or her preoccupation with imaginary friends, perhaps you want to be the one who plays with this "self-contained spirit". You might forgivably wish that he or she would prefer human to imaginary or to "divine" company. You might wish when the person was in real company, partially enjoying it, that he or she did not still have a reserved inner eye to "the higher and deeer reality, the Real Friend". Considered as being a replacement for the dissatisfactions of everyday life, nothing is more compulsive than religion's repetitive rituals. The spiritualization of our frisky human spirits has to be a constant and forced enterprise, as much be the catechismal inculcation of the dogmas, the linguistic vehicles of that inculcation.

The energy needed to keep up compulsive behaviour and thought, and the lack of satisfaction achieved, leaves a person dry and hard; in making one thus, it also makes one insensitive; for these and for other reasons the person acting compulsively fails to perceive properly the postures, words, expressions and social context of others. He or she is inevitably self-centred. In a limiting sense, we are, however we live, our own self-centres, and it is only the newly and sensitively perceived doings and appearances and approaches of others which can make them others, other centres of our lives. After those experiences and interchanges, we are left with memories, skills to engage with others, and expectations of others and what others expect of us. These memories, skills and expectations, though actually or potentially directed at things apart from us, nevertheless are at our own centres. Unless we frequently bring them into play, they rapidly become simply a part of our self-centredness again; simply more accumulated possessions, rather than what we owe and are owed by others.

We are compulsive when we do not get and cannot recognize accurately what we need. To want something is to lack it, and to need something is to want it so strongly, and for the lack to extend so broadly into the network of our life, that we cannot consider ourselves, or be considered by others, as the same person, if the want remains unmet. We need our bodily health, whether or not we think about it or think so for, without it, nothing in our lives remains the same — we become something else a "patient". We have to be looked after, we are no longer in the interdependent position of caring and being cared for. We are at the mercy of others. We need a sexual life. We may live without it, but then we are something else. We are a nun a monk, even if unofficially, with our monkish or nunnish virtues and vices; we become ascetics of some other sort, praising all abstinence; we become more than reasonably or satisfyingly involved with food, or with music or whatever. People see that we are not the same.

One might try to trivialize the distinction between any old want and a need. A person wants his toast very well done (Belacqua in Samuel Beckett's *More Pricks than Kicks*). He gets it lightly done. He is not the same, for he is eating lightly done instead of well done toast. We can keep to the distinction of want and need. If someone can rightly be said to need his or her toast well done, and just exactly well done, then having toast (and, no doubt, a multitude of other things of a similar kind) done just right has become essential to a whole recognizable style of life. Perhaps a person who didn't get his toast just right and couldn't replace the getting of such a thing with something else very similar, would undergo a sea change. Instead of being precise and careful he would yell and shout and be absolutely unreasonable and unreasoning, and in these fits begin to create different relationships with the people around him. On the one hand, as is usually the case, when we just won't or can't believe that anything much hangs on it, we say, "Don't make a bloody fuss. You might like toast that way, you may want it that way, but you don't need it." On the other hand, it is easy to fail to see that what to one person is a luxury may be what another needs. From time to time a person needs something which, in the ordinary course of events, is only a frivolity — "need" has a heavy urgent sound, and can blind us to the fact that a person can need lightness as much as anything else.

Desires are felt stirrings towards action; the action may be outward or within one's own mind, but is in both cases to be distinguished from mere "behaviour" or one's lapsing into scattered thought. (One might desire, particularly after hard work, to let one's mind lapse into scattered thought. The action, in that case, is that of allowing.) Compulsions are the enemies of desire, for they are inimical to feeling and to distinct taste. When we act or think compulsively we are "possessed" by a need in that we are blind and numb to it: we lose the detached freedom to recognize it. It is as if we were constituted by it, but woodenly. It is different from our fluid possession by passion or frenzy where we may fail to recognize our needs and impulses because they are felt so strongly and with too little restraint in their expression.

There is a paradoxical "felt lack of feeling" in compulsions which is best understood by the close analogy of numbness. To be numb is to lose feeling. Still, you can feel numb. Your hair can't feel numb, because you never had feeling in your hair. Your thumb feels numb; normally you can feel with and in your thumb. Feeling number isn't *just* the not having any feeling with or in what normally has feeling. If your thumb had become quite numb and your attention was in no way drawn to it, or to a need to use it, it wouldn't feel numb. It feels numb when you can just feel it enough to sense its general outline and to be aware that you can feel no more, or that you can barely move it in the ordinary way or, as when you have an injection at the dentist, that you have lost your ability to feel the correct relative sizes of your tongue and cheek. The feeling of numbness, if not nearly so bad as the toothache it replaces, is its own kind of distress.

In compulsive action and thought one is, in one sense, not detached enough and, in another sense, too detached. One is not detached enough, in that one does not firmly stand back and call into question what one is doing or thinking; one does not attempt to name and to assess it. One's allowing of oneself to go ahead in compulsive activity is an abdication of autonomy. In a different sense, one is too detached — one feels too much a mere spectator of one's actions, feelings or thoughts — one refuses to say "I am this", and instead pretends to the stance of "This is happening: I am superior observer of it".

Compulsiveness goes hand in hand with the delusion that confession is a cure either to one's compulsiveness, or to some wrong which compulsiveness seems to make one's "manifest destiny". There is always some wrong in compulsiveness. Even if a person is compulsively generous, he or she is lacking in an operative sense of priorities and of tactful style. The compulsive person is already involved in one delusion, that of detachment of "himself" from his feelings and actions; it is in this feeling that it seems his confession will complete the cut. If he were really to apologize, with all that entails of making amends and feeling different and coming to seriously and reliably consider the interests of those injured, then he would have to identify himself with what he had been doing and feeling. He would have to possess in hindsight what he had pretended was not his when it was a present deed. Confession is the kind of excuse which still leaves one feeling superior, for one is still the "superior moral person who recognizes his faults" rather than the ordinary human person whose life partly consists in their demonstration. For a person to confess "I am afraid I am a very mean person" is no moral step forward. It is part and parcel of his meanness. It is condescension to himself in which he puts himself at the mercy of himself. If that is what he is then "what can he do about it?" We make morally genuine recognition of a fault when we are dealing with it, when we are beginning to take lines of thought and feeling and action incompatible with being posessed by that fault.

We can recognize the incipiently compulsive character of thought and action by its partly numb, blind character, and by our feeling of, at once, being not quite the very self who is thinking or acting, and yet feeling that we "have to, just have to" do what we are about to do compulsively. There are various ways in which we can come to recognize the character of the desires which are being hidden in compulsiveness. This recognition is a vital part of gaining self-identification and control. For instance, we may indulge in fantasies of behaviour. If we arrest our behaviour in which we are about to, or beginning to compulsively involve ourselves, with someone and in this arrest we let our minds run free, we may find to our surprise aggressive fantasies, or fantasies of the person harming us. Also, we effect a partial escape from compulsiveness by deliberately engaging in a diminished extent or intensity of the action to which we feel compelled. We can't entirely restrain a compulsive retort, and if we do we feel choked and we have gained no comprehension. So we let out a bit of it. Then we can perceive our own behaviour, and take stock of the character of the response we call forth from others. In all probability our moderated and controlled essay provokes a more moderate response. We get some clues, and not being fully launched, we have some chance of using what we learn to backtrack, sidetrack, call a halt of whatever. Also, by mimicries of the behaviour to which we feel compelled (by sending ourselves up) or by experimenting with mimicries of those we have already observed to behave in the ways to which we ourselves feel compelled, and by any of the dramatic devices of acting (in the stage sense) our feelings rather than going on with "sincere", "on the level" real behaviour — from any or all of these we come to recognize our desires. At worst, we lack the desire or power of restraint and fail to think of or to use this kind of active reinvolving detachments, and act compulsively and have to wait for objectivity later, as we ruefully pick up the pieces.

If we are to escape compulsions via our recognition of them, then the delusive feeling of a compulsion, that "we must act", must become the knowledge that we need not act while feeling like that. We must divert and diversify thought and behaviour until, in a less pressured state, we can regain our imagination of how our expression and action appears to another, our consideration for the point of view and needs of others returns and thus we regain our imaginative control of our own private and public lives and so our objectivity. Without the objectivity, a person cannot care for himself or herself, or for anyone else. Nor can he or she even properly allow himself or herself to be cared for, since to allow, to be patient, requires imaginative control and the involved detaching which has been described rather than the detachment of cold alienation.

In checking our becoming compulsive, time and timing is crucial. We must act upon and on our feelings while they grow, before they possess us in their numb anonymity. Self-deceit is easy here. We can allow ourselves to fall into emotional states (such as boredom, hysteria or fury), in which we cannot "do otherwise", just as we can allow ourselves to get drunk or otherwise drugged, so that then we can no longer control ourselves — cannot "do otherwise". We then plead "I can't be blamed", "I couldn't see what I was doing", "I couldn't stop". We blameworthily lose control so as to escape blame. It is thus by a failure to engage in some "negative" action at the outset — a failure to desist, to refrain, to allow, to rest, to be still — that we come to the point of losing control. It may be morally obligatory to do some small wrong quickly (some unfair expostulation) so that we will have the power to avert ourselves from doing a greater (streams of bitter insults, blows). Notoriously, moral puritanism is the enemy of moral sense. It is the fraudulent celebration of having lost moral balance and control. It is a curious arrogation of one's own responsibility in the form of abdicating from it, as when Luther says "I can do no other".

As well as taking earlier negative or diversionary or self-releasing action to forestall compulsiveness, we can, until we are out of control as ranting and raving and striking out, or equally out of control though more socially acceptable, as a block of emotional ice, we can always simply not act. Just be. The dangerous delusion of compulsions is that we *must* act; the self-deception of compulsions is that some scarcely known feeling just carries us. Our freedom, which we possess until quite out of our minds, is simply to recognize our feeling, or recognize that we cannot yet name it and, in any case, simply not to act upon that feeling. We might then tremble with rage or shiver with the cold of approaching depression. But those states themselves can be acted upon in the various ways which have been described (and, no doubt in very many which have not been thought of here) so long as we know something of what we are doing, and why or how we got to be that way. Virgil claimed: "Happy is he who knows the causes of things". Too sanguine, perhaps. But certainly, miserable is he or she who does not.

Chapter Ten

Acting, Being and Perceiving

Descartes' doubts and certainties

Descartes' method of doubt (to regard as false anything about which he can imagine the least doubt) leads swiftly to the feeling that to perceive is simply to receive elements into one's soul, elements for which one has no responsibility and which relate, if at all, only by an external and fortuitous causal relationship with the external, objective world.

> "Thus, I am now seeing light, hearing a noise, feeling heat."
> "These objects are unreal, for I am asleep."

(Fancied objection from his reflection on the possibility of deception.)

> ". . . but at least I seem to see, to hear, to be warmed. This cannot be unreal; and this is what is properly called my sensation; further, sensation, precisely so regarded, is nothing but an act of consciousness."
>
> (p.71 *Descartes' Philosophical Writings,*
> ed. Anscombe and Geach. Nelson, 1954).

So considered, "sensation" (any form of perceptual experience, whether genuine or delusory) is simply something which happens to us. It is simply fortuitously related to what we do. We cannot attach any weight to the use of "act" in "act of consciousness". In having a sensation, we cannot be regarded as "acting". Yet there is equally an existential moment in Descartes.

> "I will not shut my eyes, stop my ears, withdraw all my senses; I will even blot out the images of corporeal objects . . . I will discourse with

myself alone and look more deeply into myself; I will try to grow by degrees better acquainted and more familiar with myself. I am a conscious being; that is, a being that doubts, asserts, denies, understands a few things, is ignorant of many, is willing or unwilling; and that has imagination and sense . . .."

(p. 76)

Nothing forces Descartes to do any of these things. He chooses to do so in an experimental spirit, and these negative but very real acts of restraint and closure away from the "natural straightforward relating to the objects of his world" (Husserl) are the conditions for the appearance of his new and amazing certainties. Had he engaged in different actions, he would have come upon different though compatible certainties. Descartes demonstrates, by a series of actions which he reports, and whose consequences he describes accurately enough that we can follow him and copy them, that it is possible to adopt an attitude of mind within which one's own existence, ignoring whether one even has or is a body and brain, is more immediately convincing and inescapable than the existence of anything or anybody else. That is his radical side. But he is also attempting to serve a conservative master. He hopes to establish a fixed secure point from which a whole systematic philosophy can be established.

It is this inconsistency in his desires — to be an *avant garde* experimental philosopher, and at the same time to have the prestige and approval which can come only within some set of fixed authoritarian opinions all too similar to the ones against which he rebelled — which finally makes his philosophy forced and incredible. For there is a notorious circle in his attempt to prove that all matters learned by the senses and all matters which seem to be logically and mathematically correct, might be false. If they might be, then so might his proof. A similar difficulty attends his attempt to get out of this hole by appeal to a proof, or proofs, for the existence of God. He is, in his conservative self, attempting to jump a chasm of uncertainty; "God" is on the other side. If only he had the planks which "God" alone could provide, he would cross in perfect safety from the certainty of his self and his ideas, to a certainty (since "God" would not deceive him) in the objects of his ideas, and of other selves, of mathematics and logic, and so on. His predicament is that to get the planks, he must already be on the other side, and then has no need of them anyway.

That Descartes has both a radical and a conservative impetus, whose conflict stalls and confuses him throughout the *Meditations*, is no mere sociological comment, though it is that also. Someone attempts a proof, only if he or she takes something as already quite certain (the "premises") and proceeds to deduce, to demonstrate, something else as a consequence. In contrast, someone engages in an enquiry when they are not taking an outcome for granted, when they are not sure, and hope to find something new. To hope to find something new is to be prepared not to know what to call it or how to characterize it when we come upon it. It is to be prepared to suffer the indignity of floundering and groping about for a good while in one's attempts to come to terms with it. We can see that there is at least a real streak of enquiry of exploration, in Descartes' search into himself, for even after coming to the point: "let him (the fancied arch-deceiver) deceive me as much as he may, he will never bring it about that, at the time of thinking that I am something, I am in fact nothing", he can say immediately, "But I do not yet sufficiently understand what is this 'I' that necessarily exists", and only after some pages of complicated and subtle reflections can feel free to say ". . . I begin to be a little better acquainted with myself". (I do not mean to disregard the irony also present in this writing.) In contrast, when he comes to "prove" the existence of "God", he already knows His Name.

What was Descartes' achievement? It is not possible to prove that one's existence is the one thing certain as a point for deducing everything else. If he is to prove he exists he must already take something for granted other than his own existence. But then, his existence would not be the foundation of the system after all. Rather, those matters from which he proved his existence would be the foundation. Similarly, it is self-refuting to claim to prove that just one proposition is the basis for certainty concerning everything else. Yet "Never say die till a dead horse kicks you", and there seems always to continue some twitching of the limbs which offends his foes and encourages his friends.

Descartes showed to us, by his method, and by his considerations upon what could be doubted about his existence, that even if nothing we thought we perceived existed, and even if we were mistaken in all our opinions about logic and mathematics, still, just so long as we were thinking, simply if we were in any way conscious, we would be bound to be right if we held to the judgement that we existed, and would be bound to be wrong if we held to any contrary view. He did not prove that we are bound to know that we exist. He did not, and could not have proved it, since it is false that we are bound to be willing or capable of the clear and consistent reflection necessary for understanding that elementary discovery. Nevertheless, those who will and can follow him so far are bound to be right, so far.

This is no small advance in philosophy. However, the advance is not that the only thing we really know is our own existence: the advance is not that one's spiritual existence is separate from one's bodily form; the discovery is not that nothing is so certain as one's own existence. All of these ideas are misconstruals of, or invalid inferences from, his discovery. This last denial concerning the significance of Descartes' discovery may be a bone of contention. I shall elaborate. We are certain when we *make* certain, and we make certain by a particular attention, a special concentration. "Certainty" is not a self-adhesive label. It is just a typical subjectivist pseudo-objectivism to project certainty on to the propositions we utter or on to the facts or things we investigate. To be objective is rather to allow that "certain" is a description of ourselves in coming to terms with things. It is not therefore just a quality of feeling. We may have a delusive *feeling* of certainty. It is a conscious state of having ascertained something with particular care and attention to detail.

It does not make sense to say in general that there is a greater certainty concerning one's own sensations or one's own existence as a thinking self than there is concerning the apparent objects of one's sensations. The existence of oneself as a body, or of the existence of others either as thinking beings or as more overtly acting and physical, cannot be described as more certain or as less certain than one's own thinking self or sensations. Notoriously, when people attempt to defend such general differentiations of "certainty" by going on from Descartes' realization, they say things like, "But it just isn't possible to be mistaken about your own state of mind!" or, "Everyone just has to know that they exist" and so on. What they say is no further amazing realization at all, but unfortunate and rather grotesque falsehood. We make mistakes about our states of mind by failing to attend to them, by exaggerating our ideas of our condition, by being too self-contained and not learning about our inner states by their realization in expression and from the subsequent comment and criticism we get from others, by having read too little about others, by having too limited a vocabulary so that we force upon ourselves the inadequate ideas we happen to have, and in countless other ways. To suppose that we cannot be mistaken is the metaphysical vanity of dualism — the notion that the self is a purely privately self-contained self-intimate being, and that how one is sitting, the expression on one's face, the signs of tension or relaxation, the facts of what we have been doing and saying, and what we are going to do and to say — none of these are really part of me. The cost of vanity is the disowning of oneself. Further, it is not true that anyone who is conscious is bound to know that he or she is at least "in some way" conscious. Gripped by Descartes' imagination of an all powerful deceiving demon, newcomers to Descartes' philosophy can think, certainly for no less than an hour of sincere and thoroughgoing discussion and argument, that "they might not be conscious beings at all, but just be figments of the demon's dream". It can take a little while for one to become quite confident, quite "certain", that either the beings in the demon's dream have thoughts of their own, or they do not. If they do, then it is the demon who is mistaken if he thinks that they are "only figments of his dream"; if they do not, then they cannot wrongly think that they are thinking, where the "fact" is that they are only images in a demon's dream, for there is no them to think at all, no thoughts which might be right or be wrong.

Not to see this, when first astonished by Descartes' approach, is quite consistent with an honest and sane mind. Furthermore, one *can* deny Descartes' first ground of philosophy, if one is irrational or insane. It is not, in itself, indubitable. It is just that anyone who thinks clearly and knows what he or she is doing, *would* never deny Descartes' realization of thinking existence, since they could see that they would be bound to be wrong if they did make such a denial. An irrational person who was already committed to the view that in uttering any proposition whatever, a person might be mistaken, might just defend, tooth and nail, the idea that a person who thought or uttered consciously "I think" or "I exist", might still be mistaken. Adherence to dogma, even of universal human fallibilism and not only faith in divine infallibilism, can work strange tricks with otherwise good minds. Also, certainly the insane can think that they have ceased to exist, or that they are not thinking: "These thoughts are not my own, they are someone else's". *We* can see that they are refuting themselves, they are breaking the Cartesian realizations. It does not follow that they can see this; we have no right to suppose that they are only trying to fool us and that really, in their own hearts and minds, they know all along quite distinctly that they exist and are thinking.

It is true that there is a special reason for the certainty which any clear minded sane person can attain who follows Descartes' withdrawal from the sensual senses into his or her "self". What it takes to doubt one's conscious existence is precisely what makes any serious entertainment of the doubt a glaring (if one can face the glare) error. This cannot be said of any other remark to which we lay a claim of certainty. Whatever it is which makes us quite certain that 2 and 2 makes 4, the ground is not the same as we have to lay claim to our conscious existence. The ground is not that what is involved in doubting it is the very thing which makes it impossible for us seriously to entertain the doubt. To take other examples: we are certain that all bachelors are unmarried men because we are sure of our ground about the meanings of the words and phrases "bachelor" and "unmarried man". We are certain that the angles of a triangle (in an Euclidean scheme) add up to 180 degrees to the extent that we have clearly understood each step of the proof from the axioms. The reasons for certainty are not identical with those we have for "I think" or "I exist". Descartes comes to think that his unique kind of certainty might be a paradigm or perhaps a foundation for all others, because it is immune to a kind of criticism which may be levelled at all others. He is correct in his judgement of a special immunity. But the conclusion of greater certainty, or of foundational position does not follow. The history of philosophy since Descartes has borne this out. Descartes' point is a dazzling light, not a solid platform. No system of philosophy can be built upon it. Yet all systems can and must make reference to it. For it is the ironic congruence of a perfect subjectivity and a perfect objectivity. In searching for something beyond all possible doubt, a Descartes is looking for something which must be so; something which is a fact, beyond variable opinion. He demands clarity and precision. Yet this search leads him to the purest subjectivity in which thought deals with nothing but the fact that it occurs.

Descartes himself never notices his own slight sleight from "I think, I exist — there I can't be wrong about that" to (paraphrasing the second of his *Meditations*) "Even if I were asleep and dreaming, and none of the apparent objects of my seeming perception were being really perceived or existed before me at all, still I would be right in thinking that I seemed to see, seemed to hear, seemed to be warmed". That is to say, the explanation of the certainty that he thinks is not enough to explain the similar but crucially different kind and source of certainty that one's states of consciousness and, in particular, sensings, are as one takes them to be. This last kind of certainty still seems, after these hundreds of years, to be of its own special kind. "I seem to see light." "Could it really be that my experience is more like hearing a buzzing sound?" What kind of nonsense is this? Not the same nonsense as, "Perhaps I don't think at all" or "Perhaps I don't exist", at any rate. And this reflection has a recurring power, through all the brave new waves of realism (naive, critical and all) to make us uneasy and aware of somehow forcing things when we say that we may be just as certain that the light has come on, as that at least we seem to see it. Yet belief in the worth of working towards an objective attitude depends on a reasonable confidence that we are in touch with the "objects" (colours, shapes, people, diamonds, hammer blows, conversations, the writings of others) of our perception and not just in touch with our supposed ways of being in touch with things.

That the reality of one's own conscious existence is immune to a special sort of doubt is a reason to rest with a perfect certainty about it. But a special immunity of one proposition is no reason at all for even the slightest scruples about our certainty in other matters, where the certainty of those other matters has its own different source: for instance, that other people are speaking to us and hold our attention and increase our understanding and capacities for perception in ways which surprise us. We have a certainty, when we think, that at least we are thinking beings, that at least we think something even if we are not thinking in the way we suppose ourselves to be, or even if we are not thinking about what we supposed ourselves to be thinking about, or as truly as we suppose. Those "beyond doubts" are akin to our certainty, when shooting, that at least we shoot something − if not the target then the barn door, and if not the barn door then the hill behind it and, if not that, then call the sky or the air an object and say that at least we hit that. That we shot something, God knows what, is immune to all the ordinary doubts which pertain to our hitting specified targets. This "special immunity" cannot be the slightest reason to disturb our certainty that we scored a bullseye when the hole appears, and the marker waves his flag, and the score is officially announced. Furthermore, if we can never be sure that we hit such things as bullseyes, how can we ever be sure that we hit such things as barn doors and hills of earth, or that there is air for our projectile to push aside, and gravity by which to be brought to rest? If we could never be sure of any particular something, then finally we could not even be sure of our unspecified something − God-knows-what.

"Being", and "being certain"

Each kind of certainty lies within a framework of the kind and style of actions we engage in when we attain it. To feel uneasy about this fact, or to resist the deliberate underlining of it in an essay on understanding objectivity, betrays a still present wish for a purely transcendent objectivity — an objectivity which involves no subjectivity and which therefore involves no subject. The objectivity which we must continue to grip is that our certainty arises because of our close and steady and intimate acquaintance with the "object" of our certainty. Once we have thus become quite certain, it is legitimate for us, over some phases of time, to use the fact of our certainty itself as some reasonable cause for continuing to hold to what we find certain. For we cannot every day refresh our minds with Descartes' realizations; we cannot every day re-experience the formal illuminations of logic; lawyers and doctors keep reference books but, if they had to refresh their memory about every point of law every time any question arose, they could scarcely be conceived to know even what kind of book to refer to. From the fact that we or they have learned, and still feel perfectly confident, and can quote the relevant passages without mumbling or dithering, or diagnose and discriminate cases of disease without fluffy or ambiguous language — from these and other like signs, they and we in other professional or other than professional ambits, have a right to use this confidence itself as a sign of still stable knowledge. Perception and the close understanding we have when thinking carefully and intimately about a matter are the right causes of confidence, and confidence once caused is allowed rightly to have its own momentum. It is an error to disturb it subsequently except from clear and specific countervailing perceptual reason. Though, there is a degree of natural decay away from accuracy, and a tendency to confusion from subsequent irrelevant experience and association which makes us well advised to check and to refresh our minds before the danger signals appears that rigid dogmatic insistence on what had been liberating and fresh discoveries, and attendant simplifications of what we had learned, not to mention outright blunders and inconsistencies, have set in.

It is illegitimate to ask, quite openly, with no framework specified, "Is it more certain that one is a conscious being than that one is or has a physical body and brain?" "Is it more certain that one is thinking than that one is walking?" "Is it more certain that I exist than that you exist?" This is because nothing is certain in itself. We are certain of matters and things and people in our current ways of being — in our ways of relating to them, and in what accrues to us from previous relatings. Admittedly, some matters are, from any point of view to which we have attained so far, a matter of speculation, and others are such that we have an established point of view from which "they" are certain, that is *we* are certain of *them*. It is a speculative matter for even the best theorists who are closest to the facts and theories which must be brought into coordination, whether there was once a primary intense concentration of matter from which everything has developed by expansion, (the "big bang" theory) or whether matter is continually coming into being where previously there was nothing (continuous "creation"). It is certain, in contrast, that there is life on earth. It is most uncertain, but in all probability will not remain for many more decades a matter of uncertainty, whether there is any form of life on Mars.

When we are being talkative; sympathetic; taking the dog for a walk and observing it bristle as it meets another dog, noticing them then ceremoniously resolve their tensions with cagey movements and then sniffs; when we observe that bougainvillea has bloomed blue in the winter sunshine, we are certain that there is life on earth. There are background conditions for these immediate certainties. It is now that we are aware of ourselves as inhabiting one of the planets on which, by an extraordinary concomitance of conditions and sequence of events, life has arisen that we think in such dramatic terms "There is life on earth".

From within the actions and involvements and acceptances of things as they come to us when we go to them in such ways, it is still theoretical speculation, though well founded and we do not doubt it in the least, that all of what we see as alive is composed of chemicals which are non-living. We might well discourse about chemistry as we walked. Yet without displaying the least anti-scientific bias, we can say to ourselves and to others, as chemistry enthusiasts as much as walkers and observers of dogs and gardens, "Suppose there were a complete scientific revolution in our theories of matter and nothing remained which was recognizable as an altered version of our present theories of chemistry — still we would be equally certain of all that we find and live among here today". From this point of view, the "world of everyday life" is pre-eminent even to the "world of science", for it is a relatively constant measure of the more speculative worlds of science. This blithe insistence on the "primary unalienable form of the life-world"

(Husserl) is the same in form, only different in the way of being which grounds it, as the primary unalienable form of one's own self-consciousness which Descartes reveals to us as there whenever we need it. In each case, something we attend to and which is immediately intimate to us and among us, in the example of walking and talking, becomes, in imagination, enclosed in a bubble, with everything else outside it. "Let all else be doubtful!" I, we, cry, "yet this remains certain".

From another point of view, the walking, the talking, the dogs and their behaviour, the flowers, and their blooming and growth, constitute a problem of "emergence". The world as abstractly conceived in terms of physics is placed within the mental bubble and everything outside that scheme is seen as a problem, as doubtful and uncertain, as unworthy of wholehearted acceptance. Are the people, the dogs, the flowers, "anything more than the electrons, positrons, neutrons and the rest, which compose them"? Are the actions of walking, talking, the hearing of conversation, the ceremonies of the dogs, "anything more than" the movements of legs, tongues, electro chemical changes in the brain, and so on? "Certainly, there are these particles, these chemicals, these changes in nerve condition", we think. "Isn't there something of a romantic illusion in still allowing any primacy to perception as it reveals flowers, walking, talking, thinking, initiating and replying?"

Of course, the paradoxes of reductionism are notorious. It would require an entirely different work to treat them as matters in their own right. Still, briefly: suppose we say, "It only appears that there are walks, conversations, dogs and blue flowers. Really these are only the clusters and movements of elementary particles which have properties only of mass, velocity and charge. Only these elementary properties are real; the rest are the emergence of a mere appearance of further character." Then we are tongue tied. We don't know what to say about the reality of the appearance. Say it is a process in the brain? Then exactly the same discrepancy arises between the brain and the goings-on in it, as they are described in physics, and the account of those processes as being "the appearing to someone of his deliberately pausing during a walk, the appearing to someone of a blue bougainvillea" and so on.

Other people have suggested that the difference between the characterization of a process in the brain as given in the terms of physics compared with the way it is given in terms of thought, perception or feeling, is to be understood from the point of view of the kind of behaviour for which that process in the brain might typically produce. But then exactly the same reductionist problem arises again concerning the choice we make in characterizing behaviour. To describe processes in the brain as apt for producing certain lines of behaviour, where that behaviour is described in terms of the motions of clusters of elementary particles, will do nothing to bridge the gap between a characterization of processes in the brain as described in physics, and as described in terms of thought, feeling and perception.

None of these conundrums of reductionism proves that people have a special entity called the "soul" or "mind". The fact that the true and exact characterizations of plants do not reduce to those given by physicists of the elementary composing particles of plants does not prove that plants have an inner *élan vital* unobservable by scientists. If one accepts the characterizations given by the sciences as an essential part, even if only a part, of one's view of the character of things, whether objects, plants, animals or people, then there is no room for extra "person bits" to people as well as their chemicals, any more than there are extra "flower bits" to flowers in addition to the congeries of cells. What there is in people, animals, plants and "mere objects" allows plenty of room for many different and equally ontologically important and relatively autonomous forms of characterization.

If a physical view is correct, then the dramatic thought that thoughts are processes in the brain is true. The consequence is not the ultimately nonsensical "thoughts are nothing but processes in the brain", but rather that it is equally vital and additional information that certain processes in the brain are thoughts, as that thoughts are processes in the brain. The liberal pluralist view of the character of ourselves and the things which come to hand requires its own complete elaboration and defence. Without such a liberal view it will be impossible to maintain the objectivity of perception, for without such a pluralism, we are left only with scientific reductionism on the one hand or with an anti-scientific mysticism on the other. It is not possible to defend the objectivity of perception from a position of a scientific reductionism which has it that almost nothing which we seem to perceive is a real object of perception. According to the reductionist outlook, science will allow only an explanation of how we suffer the illusion of colour, sound, smell and taste, and of how we seem to see, touch or otherwise tell the character of people's expressions and behaviour, and so on. Since none of these characteristics is in the elementary list of the properties of elementary particles, then according to a scientific reductionist they are not "really there". If to hold seriously and realistically to the outlook of the sciences is to be obliged to hold with scientific reductionism, and then we find we cannot accept the reductionism, we are going to reject a serious and realistic account of science. We will be forced back, in a defence of experience, either to some form of idealism, or else to a primitive and unenlightened realism which cannot allow that there can be more to what we perceive than can reach the unaided eye or hand. We will be forced into opposition to intellectuality about perception, and begin blindly to deny the intellectualization permeating even the most favoured of purely factual, primitive, uninterpretative perceiving.

The costs of reductionism are high and the implausibilities enormous. The reward of a single, all encompassing view, exhaustive of all other views, is as morally and intellectually suspect as an objective, as it may be intriguing at first blink. Like Hume in relation to his scepticism, the whole reductionist outlook falls away when you sit down to dinner and begin to converse freely. We cannot maintain it as a serious belief within the variety of our ways of being in the world. Though one cannot strictly refute reductionism, if only because of its ever open promise of analysis and stratagems ("this might do the trick" and "perhaps we can 'get around' the objection thus"), it is well to remember that, at the very best, reductionism is a free option to be chosen because of some supposed advantages of theoretical simplicity. It is only dogmatic to assume that it must hold the field unless it is refuted. There are powerful considerations against it, such as the previously described inconclusive way in which it chases unwanted properties out of the perceived world and into the brain and, then, not wanting them in the brain either, chases them into behaviour and, in attempting to characterize behaviour, begins the sorry and unexplaining cycle again. A physicalist can always say, "One day it will give a satisfactory account on how brain processes are thoughts and feelings, while being nothing but brain processes when you really get down to it". We can charge him with futurism, if he philosophizes now in terms of this unrealized and inarticulate "grab". Yet it would be too sanguine to call the various objections to physicalism, strict refutations. Still the objections mentioned are powerful enough to remove reductionism from the position of front runner in the modern rationality stakes. Reason requires that we spend our time sketching better alternatives, than permanently hoping for lame horses to come in first.

What we perceive, what we are being

What we find ourselves perceiving — what is "simply given to us as obvious fact" — is in various ways a function of what we have chosen and what we are choosing to be or, more simply, a function of what we have been and continue to be. If we have an urban life, then we may choose to find ourselves among a heavy density of rapidly and dangerously criss-crossing private traffic, for instance. Alternatively, we shall choose or find ourselves inevitably involved in "public" weighty, momentous and less swerving carriages. We shall be reminded in a different way by the massive steel wheels and springs of a railway carriage both of the sheer mass and extraordinary complication involved in the copresence and cooperation of people and their needs. In coves among much greater stands of concrete and stone and glass, groves of trees have an invitingly enveloping aspect; perhaps those very trees once stood as the only higher relief on a hot and dusty field; for a moment we can think of all of this raw permanence as merely superior power on an original soil. Then when we walk on hard pavement we may imagine for a moment the soured earth somewhere below our feet slipping out free a few hundred yards away into a different level of park and grass and trees. Our eyes must reassemble from the rooftops, the tops of the higher trees; the known and occasionally perceived still surviving rock faces and bulging outcrops, a terrain upon which all of these things have been imposed. The more our city eye recreates the land below and between, the more the city reinsists itself. It is more our geologist's eye than our farmer's vision which reassembles and reconstitutes the eroded valleys in to the original anticlines and the "new" hills as the bottom part of the curve of an earlier syncline and thus sees the geological formation as a reverse of a present terrain. Our new scientific touch may return us at last to the earth within the city, but the science is irrevocably urban. In road traffic, in the carriages of public transport, on pavements and in shops, we are continuously dealing with people whom we do not know, and oscillating between self-enclosed privacy and a distant friendliness based on a common recognition of our all being in the same boat of having to assume practical familiarity without any background, possibility or desire for intimate acquaintance. In continually reinforcing our sense of the "otherness" of others as well as calling on our need to see and speak to them as other humans like ourselves, it produces a distinctive regard of ourselves by ourselves. In turn, from this altered and informed self, we come to a distinctive perception of the non-human objects of our environment.

Each urban person will tell this story in a different way, and there can be no simple generalization of or short cut to the understanding of it. To live in a city one needs all the resources of movies, television, books, poetry, philosophy and painting, in whatever order of priorities is most urgent. It is as absurd as it is philistine to suppose that these are the mere icing on the cake of industrial society. Our culture is our condition of human survival in that society. Also to expect or to look for more than occasional flashes of things as they appear to the eye which has regained an innocence untouched by culture, history, movies, politics and art, is a confusion of the direction to which we are committed by living in a society. It is an unthinking nostalgia. For the most part, refreshment of the senses, the regaining of a curious and receiving eye, ear, touch and palate must come from the experience of the intensifications and sophistications of the culture which is largely the reason, in any case, both for putting up with the assaults of all kinds consequent upon living closely among millions, and for understanding and enjoying the kind of life and encounters whose form is given by the society and economics of a city.

Some choose a life of travelling — to sell things, to gather news, to relieve boredom since they do not have to work and so on. Even if the commercial traveller sees, improbably, the same objects as those who travel the same route on a holiday as a break from city life, or quite differently, even if the reporter sees the same objects in the city as country people who come to it as a change from the isolation of country life, they see them with a different focus: what is foreground to one is background to another. The objects are seen with a different angle and from a different angle and, most tellingly, in a different mood and with different intent. They see while moving at different speeds; they move their eyes and hands and turn their heads to listen, at different rates. They have radically different broken and continuous moments of perception intimately connected with their different ways of being in the world. The different people ask, or refuse to or refrain from asking, mentally or in open discourse, different questions. They bring, and make on the spot, different acceptances. The style and content of the photographs of a news reporter compare with that of a salesman and with that of a tourist, though they visit "the one place" — not merely the same city, where each might live in locations without overlap, but even when they visit the one shop. Narrow down to the tourists who visit the one shop, and still the difference in style and content in what they take is a fair symbol of the different objective perceptual words within one common geometrically and physically described world. The perceptual world of those who see, imagine and measure things primarily in terms of their geometry and physics is, itself, just one more or less imaginative selection of a world within the world; one more "take". One more possibility of mis-take.

"Idealism", and the relativities of perception

Only those with very strong wills and equally weak brains push on from these and similar considerations of relativity, to idealism. It is equally erroneous to reject or to minimize these considerations of the part played by our modes of life, our ways of being, in constituting the perceived world; the world as it is for us. For, according to idealism, there is nothing to the world itself beyond our ways of perceiving. Idealism betrays itself in using phrases such as "our ways of perceiving". This idealism is a far cry from the acceptance of our living contribution to what seems often so innocently and purely "given" to us. Further, it is part of this same idealist view that there is nothing to our bodies and all that goes on within them than perceivings, as we say, "of" these bodies. Idealism does not follow from, but rather is unconnected with the primary recognition of our living, conscious and inextricable involvement in the things we perceive as "quite other" than ourselves. Idealism does not allow a proper objectivity to subjectivity — the sheer brute actuality of personal existence in a preformed social and physical order. Outside of idealism, we identify and locate ourselves, theoretically and in practice, as one body among others. We have no insuperable difficulty in understanding ourselves as centres of experience, for we take the permanent objectivity of our body, and those in terms of which it is located, for granted. Even more intimately, we understand ourselves as centering and coordinating our various modes of experience and sense because our various organs of sense are connected with and sensitive to each other, in ways usually quite apparent and, in any case, subject to investigation. Except in special moods of alienation, we feel no special split between our minds and our bodies. One tensely arches one's foot; gestures impatiently with one's hands; scratches one's itchy head or scratches to think; one leaps for joy; sits slack, head low, in depression; one stands steady arguing a fine point, and so on. To think of the body as itself a mere appearance in the mind leaves us with no notion of mind. It leaves us with no notion of what makes experiences the experiences of one person. It cannot be the congruence of experiences in space or in time, since, on the idealist view, the reality of the relationships things have to each other in space and in time is itself an appearance "within the mind".

Again, as with the criticism of physicalism, an adequate account of the character and failings of idealism would be an entire investigation in itself. The purpose in the present investigation is to explore and to understand the sense in which perception is "objective" (as being "of objects") and the sense in which we may be more or less objective in our perceiving. An "objectivism" which would attempt to theoretically remove the subject in his or her involvement in whatever object is perceived or thought about, has, of course, already been diagnosed and attacked, in its many varieties. At the risk of being either bogged down once again in outworn metaphysics, or of provoking loss of confidence in the progress of ideas by seeming to deal suddenly and unsympathetically with 'the great figures', we must nevertheless still introduce them in brief, accurate and close sketches, so that they can form the limiting horizons for what we now are impelled to say by our experience, our science and our contemporary philosophy. The obvious ways in which the claims of idealism ("It's all in the mind you know" − a Goon Show line) flout the pieties of commonsense realism, can easily blind us to the more subtle way in which it disallows or glosses over the "object presenting" character of experience itself, and also leaves too little room for the varieties of objective attitude which we can bring to experience. Despite the *enfant terrible* iconoclasm of Berkeley's opinions (There is no material reality which causes our experience; all that exists is spirits and their ideas; to be is to be perceived; the very notion of an unperceived substance is nonsense), Berkeley's idealism is the expression and attempted defence of the utmost conservatism. He is hostile to Descartes' philosophically experimental method of calling everything into question, and equally he is hostile to the practically experimental, theoretically speculative, and therefore doubly provisional character of the new physical and medical sciences. He fails to see the value of an open speculative attitude to the nature of things and people; in this he demonstrates his loss of a sense of objectivity.

Idealism is not only a set of opinions and arguments. It is a quite distinctive perceptual and mental outlook on the things we sense. It is a metaphysical and linguistically revisionary attempt to make the objects of perception into one's inner possessions. Objects, Berkeley says, are nothing but ideas in the mind. It is supposed to be quite absurd to suppose that the ideas in my mind could have any separate independent existence. Hence, the tree I observe, being an idea in my mind, can have no existence "outside" it. We cannot lose the sense of a magician's trick, in reading Berkeley. It is partly on our sense of their fluency and elegance that our continued admiration and fascination with his writings is based and nourished. A few words from Berkeley and "Whoosh!" The sturdy, steady world evaporates to leave a surface mist, though it forms into the usual colours and shapes. "What have you lost? Tell me what you miss and I will make it up to you in a more detailed idealism" he tells us, but the busy whirring world going on day and night beneath the surface revealed to our direct impressions is gone. How is the trick achieved? The first imaginatively engaging distractor is that what we "really perceive" when we look at something is its qualities. This is a most delightful piece of cunning on his part. For it appeals, in the one hit, to our sense of perceptual immediacy — "Look! Don't interpret! Tell just what the eye brings to you, and is it not just colours, shadings, shapes, and movements of these?" — and hooks the new scientists around him who have already, following Galileo, Descartes and Newton, removed, in their imagination, the "perceived qualities" of colour, visual shape, texture, smell, taste and sound from the "real objective physical world". The realists about perception are not going to mind when they are asked to concentrate on the qualities revealed in their perception of objects. The physics enthusiasts are not going to mind when asked to concede — they are all too eager to do so — that these "secondary", "merely perceptual" qualities exist only "in the mind".

Yet it is only one kind of concentration, and according to one deliberately selected mode of description, and relative to one kind of analysing attention, which yields the perception of a thing as consisting to (perception at any rate) of qualities alone. This concentration is legitimate for its own purposes as is Descartes on the existence of himself as a conscious existence only. But as a general proof for all the moods and modes of perception, it is useless. First, it is not accurate. You are walking in the twilight. Something leaps away before your feet. You see it is a cat; you gain only a glimpse. You do not make out its colour; you might not even think of its colour. Nor, specifically, do you think of or perceive its shape as one might need to do in order to distinguish it from another cat. That you "must have made out its cat-like shape and size and style of movement" is more an inference from the fact that you did perceive a cat leaping away, and that is the shape and movement which you know cats to have, than it is a report on how you saw it. What is perceptually certain in such cases is this: you saw a cat leap away. Hence, we argue, you have been visually impressed by various qualities. It is not a report of experience that you saw such and such qualities, which qualities you then proceeded to designate as those of a cat leaping away.

Certainly, in some cases, what you perceive would be better described as a change in some qualities, or a remaining steady of some qualities. This fact does not help Berkeley's claim. It throws into sharper relief the difference between such examples and a wealth of others. The sense of universality in his view that "all we ever perceive are various perceptual qualities" is lost.

Further, what does it *mean* to say that we perceive only qualities, and not objects (except as we deem these to be no more than congeries of qualities)? Normally, to see a colour is to see the colour of something. One sees, not "blue", but "the blue of the sky", "the blue of his/her eyes", "the blue of the icing", "the electric blue of deep ice when seen from a cave of it when one looks upwards towards the daylight" and so on. Seeing the quality is not the antithesis of or something less than and requiring a special inference to the perception of an object, but one of the ways in which the object presents itself as an object apart from us and as among other objects. Berkeley may have something to say about this within his system of language, in terms of the association of some ideas with others, but to do this is to work from his position as already established, not to attempt to establish it from an initial neutral description of what we perceive.

Again, Berkeley speaks as if it were clear in meaning, to say that qualities are separate things which can go together to make up what we call an object, such as a tree or an apple. It is not at all clear what this can mean. It is absurd to attempt to think of a colour entirely by itself. There must be some extent of it, some shape however vague or amorphous, some brilliance, some texture. We shall get nowhere if we say that these further qualities, in turn, are separable things which go together to make up colour, which, it might have been supposed in the Berkeley's scheme, might then, in turn, go together to make up objects. What is a shape with no size whatever? What is a texture which is a texture of nothing? Or what a colourless brilliancy? The supposed elements of Berkeley's world cannot be supposed to exist. They can be spoken of only as points of comparison and similarity in the very things they were supposed to explain.

Berkeley's apparently harmless and even illuminating (in some case of perception) suggestion that what we perceive are qualities, and that what we call objects are just collections of these, has its spurious attractiveness not only to those who are already predisposed from a fundamentalist reading of physics to accept that perceptual qualities are of course, only "in the mind", but also trades on a hidden thought which, when expressed, actually goes hard against Berkeley's own view — the thought that qualities exist only "in the mind" in that they are only abstractions from real things, "objects of thought", rather than what are actually there to stimulate and provoke perception. He thinks that he can move from their being the "real objects of perception" to their being "real things" and yet "existing only in the mind". The trouble for him is that they cannot be fundamental elements composing the objects of perception, and "exist in the mind" in one sense quite different from the one he intends. They are not things, but points of resemblance and difference in things. To take them with an ontological seriousness is to become a Platonist, not an empirical idealist of Berkeley's sort.

The second of Berkeley's ingenious attempts at a general shift in intellectual perspective concerning "what we really perceive" is his series of arguments that these qualities we are supposed to perceive, are really no more than our sensations of them. As he says, when we feel something warm, we do not feel two distinct sensations, one of warmth and one of pleasure. Similarly, when we feel something very hot, we do not feel a sensation of heat and of pain. The pleasure we feel "exists only in the mind", all would agree. And so it is supposed to be apparent that the warmth, the heat, "exist only in the mind". Here Berkeley blurs our sense of experience, and our understanding of our language of experience and yet his position is important, in that it forces us to resolve more exactly our sense and description of the objectivity of perception. We say, equally, we have a feeling "of" pain, and we have a feeling "of" great heat. But we do not sense pain as something there to be felt *for*, whereas heat is something we can feel as something coming *to* us; we can feel for the object which is warm, or simply for the flow of heat. Even when it is our own body only which is getting hot, without being heated by an outside source, as in a fever, one can report one's perception in such terms as "I feel that my limbs are burning". That is, the feeling of heat is to us the perception of something apart from the feeling. Such a sensation may be delusory: sometimes we have a sensation of heat, perhaps, when nothing is heated up, either outside our body or within it, but this possibility of error reinforces the presumption of objectivity in the feeling of heat. In comparison, when we say that we feel pain, we mean merely that pain is our feeling. The "of" in "feeling of pain" is like the "of" in "city of Paris". The "of" can be replaced as well by a comma — "the city, Paris". The feeling of pain is the feeling, pain. But if the feeling of heat is only the feeling, heat, this means that we have failed, as we thought we have succeeded, in feeling something apart from feeling, namely, heat.

What Berkeley plays on is that one can always use the apparent object of perception as an "as if" internal description of sensation. We have to learn to understand and to cope with this with a smile on our face and yet with objectivity in our intentions. If we wish to answer, not "What are we in touch with by sensation?" but "How is it with you, in perceiving?", we can use the same words which we might have used in a claim to have accomplished something in perception. We can use these words simply to record our sensations. For example, if we are in a laboratory and we don't know any longer whether our apparent perceptions are being provoked by drugs, by brain probe stimulii or by actual objects as there appears to be, we can still answer the experimenter's question "What do you see anyway?" by "a large lion coming in by the right hand door" or "a bowl of roses on the bench" or "a uniform expanse of dull blue colour", and be correct in saying this, even if there is, as is very likely, no lion coming in anywhere in the room, no bowl of roses within our view, and no expanse of dull blue. The experimenter considers himself the best judge of what is in the room, since he takes himself to be in control of the whole situation, so he is interested, not in what is in the room but in how it is with the subject. Hence, the whole expression of what the subject has to say to avoid commitment to the apparent objects of perception, namely "It is as if I were seeing a lion . . . a bowl of roses, an expanse of dull blue . . ." can be foreshortened to "I see a lion . . . a bowl of roses, . . . an expanse of dull blue . . .".

To recognize this is, once again, to recognize the subjectivity, or better, our subjectness, our being subjected, in perception. The experimenter's subjectivity escapes notice in this example, because he, by controlling the situation, and by the other person's acquiescence, makes the other the subject. If the subject objects, the experimenter in turns becomes subject.

Another person, a psychoanalyst: he might observe and describe what the experimenter was doing, not in the experiment's own preferred terms of "attempting by scientific means to establish . . . (whatever) . . ." but as "attempting to compensate for feelings of lack of recognition and lack of sense of power, by . . .." There is no automatic incompatibility between their views, but there can be, in practice, a radically shocking incommensurability. The difference is angrily worried over and disputed as if it were an incompatibility which required one side or the other to yield. Everyone who is objective is a subject, and not only this, but also is operating at some level of unscrutinized undescribed subjectivity in his most careful and observant and object oriented exercises. It is this fact which tends to unnerve us in our attempts at objective enquiry, so that either we spin off into absurd objectivism of one sort or another, holding up like Popper or the neo-Marxists such as Althusser, "no-subject" theories of knowing and perceiving, or else attempting to turn the process of perceiving something into an occurrence to be described in no more than the terms of the object itself (physicalism or Marxist materialism). The other drastic alternative is to think that the more serious "objectivity" lies in seeing the utter impossibility of objectivity, and we lapse into or embrace eagerly, some version of idealism — there is no object of perception — there are only perceptions. Yet, this is out of the frying pan since, apart from the ordinary incredibility of such claims, we are quite unable to cope with the fire of the sensations in which we are cast. We describe our perceptual sensations as being *of* objects other than sensations. If we do describe ourselves — how it is with us in perception, when we are unsure whether we really are perceiving — still we say something like "It is *as if* we were in the presence of . . .". If everything is to be collapsed to sensations, how are sensations to be described?

Berkeley attempts to assuage commonsense, for he attempts to leave intact the language of perceiving objects. He attempts to say that these objects, though, are really just sensations. This entails that what we sense are sensations. This is supposed to sound, then, more than a truism than an affront. But what does it mean to say that we sense a sensation itself? What is a sensation? If it is the experiencing of something, then it is an event or process. This experiencing, this sensing, is not the thing which is sensed when we see or seem to see colour, taste or seem to taste something bitter, hear or seem to hear a sound. An experiencing or sensing does not and could not have itself as its own object. (This is not to deny that we pay "swift retrospective heed" (Ryle) to it, or even partially detach our mind from sensing and pay some attention to one's sensing. But these clear possibilities are entirely different from the impossibility that one's sensing of an expanse of colour should *be* the expanse of colour.)

To say that what we sense are sensations, is like saying that what we choose are choices. In one meaning of the saying, this is a truism, and in another it is absurd. We use the noun "choice" either to refer to the thing chosen: "The judge's choice weighs 500 kilos, bellows, is black and dangerous"; or we use "choice" to refer to the choosing: "The judge's choice was wise, well considered and fair". (An example from Keith Campbell.) The bull is a choice because it is chosen, but that does not make the poor animal a wise, well considered and fair act performed by a judge. In a similar way, it is possible to say that heat is a sensation because it is sensed, but that does not mean that heat is something which goes on in one's mind, or which exists only relative to a mind to perceive it. If the bull is chosen then the bull is a judge's "choice". This does not mean that a bull is just something done in a judge's mind, or something which exists relative to a judge's mind. The bull would not be a choice without a judge to choose it but, for all that shows, it would still be a bull. Heat would not be a sensation without a senser to sense it but, for all that shows, it would still be heat.

We can drive this objection right back into Berkeley's own ground. No one dreams of objecting to his claim that ideas exist only in the mind which perceives them. But this apparent truism of his is a verbal opiate. What is an idea? If an idea is a thing we sense, and not our sensing of it, and is called an idea because it is actually being sensed, then doubtless something is an idea only while it is being sensed. But this proves very little. Consider, if we said that something was a "scrutinee" only during the specified period during which it was being scrutinized, then, indeed, the notion of an unobserved scrutinee would be an absurdity. But we could not rightly infer that scrutinees exist only "in the minds of scrutineers", or that they exist only "relative to their being scrutinized". That which is a scrutinee could not be scrutinized if it were "only within the mind of a scrutineer".

Similarly, if Berkeley says that it is nonsense to say that an "idea" could exist "outside the mind" because it is an act or occurrence of the mind — a scrutinizing, a sensing, rather than the thing scrutinized or sensed — then he cannot say that apples, trees and so on are sensed. For he has said that they are ideas, making it sound that they are "mental", but this is now exposed as a verbal veneer. The things which are "ideas" might, for all that, exist in their own right. It is only a sensing, a perceiving, which cannot be thought of as existing "outside a mind", since it simply is a deed or occurrence within a mind; that is to say, something which a person does or which happens to him or to her. So, if all that exists are ideas and minds, as Berkeley would have us say, and since ideas have to be construed as sensings, perceivings, in order that the proposition that they can exist only in the mind should have the self-evidence which Berkeley claims for it, the apples and trees which are supposed to be "ideas" turn out to be sensings and perceivings. It is nonsense to say that these are objects of sense. And so Berkeley's theory rids us of all objects of sense. Logically, the position is very simple. If all that exists in the universe is minds and their "sensings", then nothing exists in the universe to be sensed. My looking at (visually sensing) something is not something which itself I might look at; my hearing a melody (auditorically sensing) is not something to which I might harken; my tasting fish with green ginger and shallots is not something itself to be savoured, and so on.

So, finally, it is useless of Berkeley to posit God as the permanent perceiver of "ideas", in order to keep in existence what I or other humans fail to perceive, or cease to perceive. Unless God's mind is mine, and mine God's, and God's ours, and your's God's (which, if God is One, makes us all One) the "idea" in God's mind cannot become the "idea" in mine, nor the "idea" in yours. As a sensing, an experiencing, as something which cannot exist "outside a mind", what a God would have in Its Mind is Its Own Conduct, Its Own Experience; at most It could cause you and me to have our own experience, our own conduct. Even a God's sensings are not objects of sensation, of perception, and so cannot be made to be Its, mine, yours or anyone else's objects of perception.

To show up Berkeley's charming mistakes in the phenomenology and the language of perception and its objects is to expose that he cannot evade the object related character of experience. He can only disguise it. We particularly need this resolution to counterbalance the fact that clear philosophical reflection on our perceiving drives us back to a recognition of our subjectivity in perceiving. (Descartes puts this in a brilliantly condensed observation, after making his famous point ". . . from the mere fact that I thought of doubting, about other truths it evidently and certainly followed that I existed"; he goes on, "On the other hand, if I had merely ceased to be conscious, even if everything else that I had ever imagined had been true, I had not reason to believe that I should still have existed". "Or that anything else did", we might add.) (*Discourse*, Part IV, *Descartes' Philosophical Writings,* ed. Anscombe and Geach.) Some, in stressing the object relating character of perception, like to say that all that is present to consciousness in perception is the object of perception. (G.E. Moore and Jean-Paul Sartre, in particular.) What am I conscious of when I look at a rose? Not consciousness, but a rose. Similarly, if more intellectually imbued, what am I conscious of when I construe the world in terms of the particles and properties of physics? Not theories, not human imaginings, not experiments nor speculations, but electrons, positrons, neutrinos and the rest. In objectivity, one wants to say, the mind goes straight from itself to the object; it forgets itself and knows only the object.

The "subjectivities" and "objectivities" of perception

This is all very well in that phase of reflection in which we are recovering from an empiricist bias towards considering the apparent objects of consciousness as if they were really just, in the end, states or characteristics of consciousness itself. The aggravating ambiguities in Locke's attitude to the objects of sense, whether they are "ideas in the mind", or the "external material things, as the objects of sensation" are the most striking witness to one's need to openly accept and to clearly delineate the subjectivity and objectivity of perception:

> First, our senses, *conversant about particular sensible objects,* [that is trees, apples, people] do convey into the mind several distinct perceptions of things, according to those various ways wherein those objects do affect them: and thus we come by those ideas we have, of yellow, white, heat, cold, soft, hard, bitter, sweet, and *all those which we call sensible qualities* [what? are these "ideas in the mind" one and the same with these external qualities of the "particular sensible objects"?]; which, when I say the senses convey into the mind, I mean, they from external objects convey into the mind what produces there those perceptions. [And where, what, are the objects of these perceptions? Ideas "in the mind"? Sensible qualities of "external objects"?] This great source of most of the ideas we have, depending wholly upon our senses, and derived by them to the understanding, I call Sensation. [My underlinings and my comments in brackets.] *Essay on Human Understanding.* Book II, Ch.I, Sec.

We are being drawn into a morass. We can learn from Locke's marshy struggles and wanderings that we shall have to treat with respect and with clear if dangerous resolution of mind what Husserl came to call the "persistent enigmas" of subject, subjectivity, object and objectivity. We know equally that we shall not learn from Locke himself what it is that we should say. Yet, no less, we realize that we cannot ignore what he is speaking of. For us to perceive an object is for there to be an object for us, in some perceptual manner. It must make itself known to us "through the ways of sense". So much for our subjectness. This is true, of course, in a physiological meaning. We perceive only if our sense organs and brain are stimulated and response is effected. It is also true in its own right that we *consciously* see, *consciously* hear, *consciously* taste and so on. This "consciousness" may be explicable in some future scientific development, but only an Orwellian world of 1984 would abolish our immediate and personal *language* of consciousness. Furthermore, while it would be an amazing advance to explain the forms and style of consciousness in terms of the functions of the brain, this explanation must leave intact the character of our consciousness as it is to us with nothing of the brain seeming to adhere to it. We have a model for this advance already in our scientific theory of colours. The colour of something exists as immediately present to the eye, and equally as a complex function of the interrelations between a photically absorptive or emitting surface, a pattern of waves to the eyes, and a response of eye and brain to that stimulus. These different facts of life of colours are so different almost to stun us into a confusion in which we find an incompatibility. But what we have is such a radical incommensurability that no question of logical incompatibility can arise. We preserve our objectivity about the world neither by capitulating to reductionist physicalism, nor by flying to the incoherence of idealism, but by believing, awkwardly if we must, all that consistency allows from theoretical novelty and from more direct experience. We say that we "consciously" perceive. We may add "consciously" to these verbs of perception just to mean that the person particularly notices the things which are to be mentioned as perceived. Yet it can also and with equal justice be said with the intention of indicating that the person is particularly aware of the mode of sense he or she is employing. Also, we wish sometimes to add it for emphasis, as a reminder that to perceive *is* to be conscious in a particular kind of way. One can't admit that we perceive, but boggle at our being conscious.

We do become aware of our manner of employing our senses. We realize that we have begun to stare, to scan quickly, to try to overlook, that we are listening carelessly and so on. Or we become aware, for instance, that we have begun to look at someone's face rather than listening to his words; that we are looking at the typewriter keys as objects of physical or mechanical interest, rather than their appearing almost subliminally in a beating recurrence beneath our fingertips. It is the very involvement which we normally bring to our use of the senses which either hides our sensory involvement and leaves "only the object", or it leaves us with no more than an oblique retro-reference to our sensory involvement. Furthermore, most of our seeing, hearing and so on occurs or is achieved within an active and intentional involvement of thinking, walking, nodding, conversing, straining and relaxing, essential to what we perceive. These activities affect the quality and style of our perceiving, and the kind and the degree and the slant of the information we gather in our perceiving.

It would be a philosophical injustice, an exploitation of the convenient normal reticence of our modes of perceptual consciousness, to declare the perceptual situation only in the terms "Gavagai! Lo, a rabbit!" (Quine, *Word and Object,* p.29), forgetful in our realist enthusiasm that a moment's change of mood might have made us say, in the same situation, under the same "sensory irradiation", "Rabbit schmabbit. I had an experience of its appearing to me that there was a rabbit. Maybe a television set in the bushes; maybe a laser holograph; maybe a cat and a bush strangely mixed. Maybe a vividly project memory imposed on the path I really see. Or, very likely, a fairly ordinary glimpse of a fairly ordinary rabbit. At least I've had the experience as of seeing it."

Perception, thought and language are ever ready to allow this shift from objective to subjective. We know full well the shift from, on the one hand, thinking "straight through one's thoughts to what they are about" as when we softly and quickly elide "I think that . . ." and get, firm and clear to ". . . the damn truck's going to ram us if we don't move fast" to the subjective weight on the other hand: "I just can't get rid of the thought — it is like a deep splinter under the skin that . . .". In this latter condition someone may have to firmly *make* us get as far as the object. "Well, what *do* you think? You can't just 'think'. You must think something. What is your thought a splinter *of*?" There is no settling down permanently to one side or the other in our regard to the subjective condition of our objectivity. It is impossible to settle on the merely subjective aspect of our thought; it is impossible to continue to regard it stably as a merely annoying or pleasurable possession, since it casts us into the world; in thinking, we are right or wrong about something whether or not we like it. We must deal with thoughts by going to their objects. It is to the objects of thought and nowhere else that we must go in order to dispel or to increase the "painful splinter" or "rich possession" quality of thought: "What! You're really worrying that he'll do you a serious injury when he gets the chance! What makes you think that? You're probably just protecting your own aggressive feelings in a paranoid fashion", and so on.

There is one more line of thought, distinctly different from the two already pursued, to be found in Berkeley's attempt to see everything as contained within the mind. Berkeley has Hylas (the defender of matter) object to Philonus (the lover of spirit) that nothing is easier than to think of some object, existing all by itself, being perceived by no one. How can this be possible if, as Philonus claims, it is absurd to suppose that anything could exist "outside the mind"? Philonus replies that the object is being conceived of by the person who is thinking of it existing all alone and unperceived. An elegant trap. If we don't think of a thing existing unperceived, we bring no objection to Berkeley's claim that only what is perceived exists. If we do think of something existed unperceived, then Berkeley may say that we do indeed "have it in mind", and thus have not produced an example of something which lies outside every mind.

At one level this is sophistry. "To be is to be perceived", said Berkeley; "I can think of something existed unperceived", says Hylas. "Yes, but you are still thinking of it", says Berkeley. "Thinking is not perceiving", Hylas might have been allowed to reply; ". . . and I did not have to perceive it existing unperceived. That would have been a manifest absurdity I admit. I can conceive of it existing unperceived."

Yet we feel a little uneasy at this glib reply which we ourselves conceive to enrich the desert landscape of poor Hylas's mind. Is this the size of Berkeley's error? Not to allow beforehand the disjunction that to exist is to be perceived or to be thought of? We expose the logician's sleight of hand, but find the little bare faced trick contained still within a larger verbal magic. We know that, whether or not he uses them, Berkeley can fall back on to common and clear idioms: he can say, "The oasis in the desert exists in your thoughts", and in an effort to deny his mind relying view of reality, we find ourselves being forced to alter or to ban the use of these so-expressive and so-convenient idioms. Then it is we who begin to have the philosophical bad conscience, which is very aggravating, since it should be Berkeley the trickster huckster in philosophy who has to suffer one. We know that as soon as his back is turned, we'll find ourselves using phrases such as "exists in my thoughts" and, if we ban it, another phrase with much the same troubling connotation will spring up. We cannot deny, we can only look into this matter of something existing in our thoughts, and vary our metaphors so as not to be trapped by obsessions or conventionalism into a literalist understanding of any one of them.

We can embarrass Berkeley by use of his own form of argument, and thus show how little it shows. Let us be Verbalist to his Idealist: "Nothing can exist unspoken of. Everything exists relative to language. You were about to mention something you knew which had not been spoken of? I have you. For if you do not mention this unspoken of thing, you have brought no example to counter my claim. And if you do mention this unspoken-of thing, then you have brought it within language, and still you have failed to provide an example of something which exists without being spoken of."

This conundrum is certainly much cheaper and more flimsy than Berkeley's. Nevertheless we can practise our aim on this easier target and then track down the more mobile one. The conundrum of "things unspoken-of", being "spoken-of" as soon as they are mentioned, is not likely to make us overlook that we speak of things as they were when they were not being spoken of. We are not thus speaking of them as spoken of. We speak of them as they are now, as being just the same even if they had not been spoken of now. We speak of them, the better to record their independence of our manners of recording them. A reasonable soldier is not much comforted by the fact that he will "live on forever" ("spoken of") on the honour roll for the war dead in the dusty institute hall of his home town. The order of events is that he will be recorded because he existed among the battalions in the war. The order is not that he will continue to exist because his existence will have been recorded. The honour roll, with its talk of the immortal heroes, conveniently provides a list and no grammar. The past perfect tense would have broken its tawdry illusion. So, even that tinsel conundrum that you cannot speak of anything which does not at least exist in language has its inevitably grave associations, as in the bitterly hopeful irony of Keats, when dying before he was thirty, "I think I shall be amongst the English poets after my death".

Thus, though we cannot speak of something and yet let it remain unspoken of, we cannot, either, begin to overlook the difference between speaking of something as it is when unspoken of, and speaking of it as spoken of. Similarly, we may think of a thing as thought of, or as not thought of. That we are thinking of it does not show that it cannot come to us in clear imaginative understanding, what it is for something to be and yet to be unthought of. Though it is indeed a contradiction to fancy that we should be able to consider something without its having already become, intimately, an "object of our thought", we can, by distinction, if not by actual separation, trace the object as something apart from our thought. A group of us see something — a painting, a movie, a person, someone's deed — and we fall to discussing it. We recognize it as a common object of discussion because we have all had it before us in perception, or we all read the same account of it. We know, further, that we are all thinking about the same thing because we recognize our differences. We hear someone express some thought about the thing, and even in most strenuously objecting to the thought, we recognize that what we oppose is what we checked as an error when the object began to promote that thought in ourselves. We are reinforced in our grip on a common object of controversial thought because we can see what it is about the complex object which provokes such controversy. Further, we can be silent and hear another still discussing the same thing. In speech or in thought, the "object" changes hands and retains its identity. It cannot be thought of while being in no-one's mental hands, but we resist the thought that it is entirely captured within our thought by being an object of our thought. We succeed in resistance by seeing how easily it turns up the same or much the same, in another's grasp.

It is much the same with perception. You can't perceive a thing existing unperceived. It's not as if you could creep up on it so stealthily that you could notice it without it being noticed, in the way that you might notice someone without their noticing you. It's not as if you could come at it so quickly that you could see what it is like when you are not seeing it.

Naturally, these absurd wishes are grounded in actual images of the really possible. People use stealth in some of their observations of people and other animals, because they suspect or know that there is an aspect of their character and behaviour which will not be shown if they are aware they are being observed. What we see when we come upon people or animals by surprise is sometimes very surprisingly different from what we had expected. Only in that way, sometimes, do we see a "quite different side to them". We can't suppose seriously that plants, rocks, lakes, snow and fields are much affected by observing them, beyond the facts that we may break some twig, trample the grass, dislodge a rock, ripple the lake in rowing on it to see it not merely from the distance of a picture postcard, and inevitably footprint the snow we wanted to be among just because it was so unbroken. Nevertheless, it is not an expression of a tendency towards subjectivism or idealism but a vital part of objectivity in attitude, to remember and to insist that the object as it is able to affect us in respect of the sensory modes we happen to have and to have cultivated, and in respect of the direction from which we happen to observe it, confronts us. It is not "the object", entire and simply. We have not only to remember and to insist upon this against the blinding obviousness of a too simple and naive realism. We have to actively and intelligently combat the dying away of realism from its own realization of the separateness of the object from the perception of it, towards a conventionalized collapse of habituated perceiving into the now captive object which is not even conceived of as containing its own hidden surprises. We combat this death of objective perception towards a merely conventional realism (whose only purpose is to preserve commonsense faith and whose only reaction to idealism or to any other radicalism is outrage) by our imaginative displacements from our actual position and conditions of observation, by our experimental approach to objects and to people, and particularly by the newness of perception of objects made possible only by our being open to other people so as to discover their different strangenesses and familiarities concerning what is only redundant sameness for us. This recognition that we know the "object" only in some limited set of relations to ourselves is not to be taken as an invitation to the notion that we are confronted by a surrogate object of perception. We perceive, not something other than the object, but the object as we have managed to relate to it and, if it is an animal or person, also as it has managed to relate to us.

What we are, and what we have

It simply does not follow from this inevitable relativity to our nature and concerns in what the object can be to us, that the "object" cannot exist apart from our perceiving it or that, apart from our perceptions, it is an unknowable "thing-in-itself". Certainly it does not follow, as Locke and contemporary physicalists think, that the qualities in objects and animals and people which we recognize only because of the specific particularities and learned patterns of us humans on this planet, do not exist "in the objects themselves".

There is a tendency to think that we possess things by looking at them. Berkeley's philosophy is the fully flowered intellectual expression of this tendency. In part it is rooted in the feeling that by observing others, one may invade their privacy, and them yours. The invasion of privacy by the taking of photographs is both a way of making permanent and apparently hard and factual the hold one may have on another by perceiving. Also, in part, the physical photographic print itself is a too stark for comfort metaphor of the more fluid but equally long lasting and inerasable images which we carry off from another in our mind's eye.

Berkeley articulates the metaphysical jealousy which perception has of its object. It, and he on its behalf, cannot abide the "brute unthinking" character of obdurate matter. All of Sartre's nausea at the facticity of the root of a tree which resists our thought and language by its sheer existence (*Nausea*), was expressed too by Berkeley. Berkeley's language of "brute", "unthinking", "insensible" — what one would use to abuse a too stolid person — expresses such repulsion at the idea of material substance that we cannot believe him when he declares it, in the next breath, to be "meaningless".

We grow to love the recurring views and glimpses, the touches and smells of the things around us. The things are metaphysically, if not in law, their own. The views and glimpses, touches and whiffs are ours. I may be devastated by the destruction of my favourite grove of trees, while not being upset by their removal to another hillside where I may never see them again. I think, "At least the trees, in their entrancing arrangement, are all right". But this is a very rare and saintly disinterest. It is rare enough to care even about a group of people and their culture, when they are objects of our observation rather than our own tribe. Suddenly my favourite trees by the road are gone, my own special view obliterated. This happens with people too. I don't care only about them. I care about the appearances, the views, the looks I can get from seeing them. Where I wanted to see interest, I see boredom or disgust on someone's face; the object as possessed by my regard vanishes even when, sometimes, the "object" remains.

There is some recompense for this realization, often in unhappy objectivity, of the separation, distance and independent powers and capacities to alienate themselves and ourselves possessed by other things, animals and people. Just as we cannot really succeed in our "useless passion" to capture others and other things by perceiving them, we ourselves need not remain captured by their nature and their regard unless we so desire. We can place at some remove our partial need to remain identified in our own minds by the familiar aura of the constant object of our daily world — the room, the furniture, the house, garden, the buildings and grounds where we work. We can choose some extent of our self-identification through our "owned" surroundings of things and people. Our being possessed in our identity by the inanimate things we constantly observe, so that our very identity seems invaded as "being a dweller in a certain house", "being a worker at a certain place", "being the wearer of such and such clothes", "being the companion, friend, etc. of so and so" is, after all, a rather "subjective" projection of our having quietly and tacitly appropriated these things or people to ourselves in our imagination, so that they are not perceived with sufficient objectivity as existing in their own right. They have been here for long before you, they are perceived and lived among by many others as much as by yourself; some of the other people will survive you and still relate to these plants and objects, some of which in turn will survive us all by many measures of our own lives.

The invasion of one's space by alien objects may be a somewhat different matter from this suffocation by the familiar. On the one hand, we have the threat of an unexpected contraction of ourselves as we expand into an environment which we can appropriate imaginatively as part of ourselves because of our involved familiarity with it. We make it ours but it isn't us, and as it varies, departs, returns, dies, is stolen, burned, and does what we don't want and appears in ways we don't like, we can do little but oscillate without control between a squashed feeling of being a stable but impotent speck at the centre of all of this, and a wide feeling of encompassing it all but of threatening to burst at the seams.

There is no simple answer to this. The total renunciation of material possessions may seem to afford a perfect and stable identity for the soul. It is no accident that such renunciations include the body, since it, only somewhat less than the things and people around us, behaves in ways, and affords us pains and inconveniences, which we would dearly like to do without. So considered, the body is not "me", but rather "a nuisance to me". The ascetics who follow this path of power through renunciation and wish to possess their own inner lives in perfect control have as hard a job ahead (as they themselves brag) as any physical athlete, or ambitious entrepreneur hoping for wealth. There can be no fixed point of division between one's perceiving self and the "outside" world. A total renunciation — "everything is outside me" — is a total death. A total appropriation — "I am one with the Universe" — is a total megalomania, and thus a death of coherent self-identity. More modestly, our horizons expand and contract from hour to hour. To think of oneself as an Australian is to perceive the rest of the world from these shores. When General Motors closes down its factory in Sydney, those in Sydney hope that they are "Australians confronting ugly American business practice". Yet alas! It quickly turns out that in respect of these issues, the external world is the rest of Australia. The redundant Sydney workers are only a *threat* to those in Adelaide. When my limbs are fine and I run and hold and construct, they are part of me. I am proud of them. I include them in myself. When they break or ache, they are "something which cause *me* trouble". I have to recover them in a change of values, in tender and caring concern. If the limits of oneself are the limits of one's possessions, and the limits of one's possessions are the limits of one's power and control to do or to have as one wishes, then a person is a musical accordian.

The attempt to utterly distinguish oneself from one's possessions is no less a metaphysical vanity than uncritical identification with them is an ontological arrogance. Our interdependence with other things and other people makes it a matter of important arbitrariness where one person ends and another begins. This "arbitrariness" is the need for arbitration, not the excuse for indifference. Naturally, the limits of one's skin and hair are the least arbitrary and most stable point of reference, as one's birth is the beginning of one's "independent" life even though, at birth, one would not survive a day alone. It may be clear enough that the limits of a person are, in one sense, simply the limits of his or her body. (Given or take the boundary problems of artificial limbs, teeth and hair.) Yet a person cannot therefore give any adequate account of what he or she *is,* without speaking of much that lies beyond those immediate and fairly stably held limits. If a person is wearing no clothes, then perhaps he or she is destitute, perhaps a nudist, perhaps is swimming naked but without the ideological commitment of a nudist, having simply been on a quiet beach without a swimsuit, he or she perhaps is very ordinarily having a shower. Then in putting on one's clothes, one is not simply putting cloth between one's skin and the rude air. One is being vain, or being careless in dress, being a show-off, an exhibitionist, a fusspot or procrastinating on the question of what to do today.

Hence, though it is right to distinguish being from having, what one is being from what one possesses, it is not true that one's being is conceptually independent of one's having. True, a motor vehicle is only by metaphor an extension of a person, even if he or she identifies with the darling car so as to wince as he or she dents its extremities, or can touch the front bumper to the wall of the parking station with the same immediate ease with which one's finger is brought to one's nose. The point of these examples is not that a person's possessiveness makes him or her a body–motor car synthesis or a body-house hybrid, but that being a driver or being domestic may centrally characterize what a person is being. In this sense, if we understand it carefully, the limits of our being are not the simple limits of our body, and are closely connected with the more fluctuating boundaries we acquire in pride and in repulsion.

Is one's body and brain oneself, or are these too, as we often speak of them, one's possessions merely? It was a disastrous imputation by Berkeley to Hylas the defender of material independent existence, that this "matter" has a fixed and "real" nature, as compared with the changeable objects of our perception. Berkeley views the matter he would deny as dead, inert, stupid, unthinking and senseless. But what if matter, in its more complex arrangements, can be alive, intelligent, thinking and sensible? "It is the spirit which thinks," says Berkeley. We can grant him this much: we must be spirited to think and to perceive. Without that, the best eye is glazed, the most intelligent brain stupid, and the most lively tongues become "inert and senseless matter".

Chapter Eleven

Resolving, Working and Resting

Work, labour and creating something new

In order to maintain, and sometimes to regain one's objectivity, one must, over the days, strike a balance between resolving, working and resting. Equally, at particular moments and for some hours, one must strike clearly for the priority of one over the others. This is because, without sometimes resolving we cannot avoid being compulsive or mechanical; we lose autonomy. We must rest. Unless we rest, we do not pause to resolve, and also unless we rest we cannot gently break the grip of our obsessions; to break them violently by new work is only to be launched into new obsessions. Also we must work. No rest and we are too dull to know anything and to take the initiatives and to sustain the directions necessary for understanding. No work and we lack the focus of mind and direction necessary to attend and to be spirited and to enjoy anything.

In one sense, as Sartre portrays our conditions in *Being and Nothingness* (it is a constant theme of the book; see particularly Part IV), we are free in all of our actions. Even when, or particularly when we act irresponsibly, thoughtlessly, inconsiderately, impulsively, compulsively, obsessively, under duress, automatically, as automata, habitually and conventionally, we are "responsible for our acts" in that it is we who perform them; we may be held to account for them, and be appraised, praised or blamed. Yet, in another important sense which he recognizes but for which he fails to find a separate word, we are only sometimes and to a limited extent free.

Sometimes our social political, physical, financial powers are called our freedoms. Certainly people possess these in varying degrees. However, there is something else which we may wish to call our freedom, and it is none of these powers, since people may have them, and yet fail to be free selves in the exercise of them. When we struggle to be free, when women search for liberation, when, suddenly, perhaps, we feel free, it is this phenomenon of being a free spirit, having freedom of mind, being autonomous in our thoughts, desires, possession of motives, our making reasons our own or rejecting them as to be inoperative even though we find them within us — it is this desire to be free which is most crucial to our capacity for objectivity. It arises and has to be satisfied in our circumstances whether we are poor or wealthy, in jail or out of it, bound to work, coping with unemployment, or confronted with the lack of necessity to work derived from inherited wealth.

As it is measured in physics, work is done when a force continues for some time to operate over some distance. In this sense, it is possible, in human or animal terms, to do useless work. One labours, but gets nothing done; nothing which is of any use or beauty, or fit to be enjoyed. As has happened in more than one suburban garden, someone tires of having to mow and to weed the lawn, and labours mightily for two weeks on his or her holidays to rip all the grass out, and to lay green concrete over the entire area. Now at last he or she can relax and enjoy the area as the "good Ford" meant us to do on the weekends. But despite the green the cement glares in the sun; it gets abominably hot so that you yelp if the flesh gets near it; instead of receiving, the owner's body must give any softness to be had when he or she sits. He or she worked, but "it doesn't work". In human work, we aim that it should work. When we have no such aim, we are not said to be "working", even though we expend much energy, whether in talking, running, standing still or just mulling things over.

There are severe and distorting conventions about what constitutes work: "He doesn't have to work; he has enough private income to continue to paint without such worries"; "No, she doesn't work. She looks after the house and children"; "When you leave school and start work, you'll realize what the world is really like"; and so on. Study is work, however much the labouring parent is led to think that sitting at a desk and reading and writing is a pretty easy life for his child. Maintaining your calm and swallowing your emotions and attempting to understand the feeling behind a child's unreasonable demands is work. It is such difficult work that mostly one would weakly choose to suppress the child and cook meals and mend clothes instead — visible respectable work. There is invisible work. That is the centre of the business. It is not only that silent work — thought, study, mental resolution and understanding — tires one into needing a rest no less than does lumping bags of wheat or repairing machinery. The difficult part of studious or artistic or emotional work is to make sure that one's labour will work. There is some labour in putting paint or canvas, in putting words on a page, and a good deal of labour in making a sculpture in stone, yet not all of these will qualify by dint of the labour as any kind of work of art. A good work of art "works"; it moves the sensitive and informed spectator in interesting, un-predicted, enlightening, and enjoyable or disturbing ways. It does not leave the spectator as he or she was before. It carries the resisting or inertial mind through some distance. The spectator may have to do or to have done some work but in turn, if the art is good, it must do work for him or her. Drama requires the audience to work: to allow the illusions of the stage to have their chance, to concentrate, to retain, to judge, to put prejudice and conventional belief aside. Then, if the play works, it moves such an audience, to laughter, tears, to self-criticism or to criticism of their society. Ordinary work, which itself is far beyond senseless labour, involves a transformation of objects; artistic work aims at a transformation of our objectivity. (And of our idea of it.) Yet all work demands some objectivity — we must be closely in touch with what we deal with or our labour is for nothing.

Work involves a range of activities or allowings which themselves are kinds of work, though they might not be regarded as such because they do not involve the kind of work which they aid or help to comprise. So if the work is digging a trench, this may involve eyeing off the land to see which end must be deeper, or discussing with someone which tools the ground requires. But, "Get to work!" and so the work gravitates to labour. Work involves resolving, arti-culating, arranging, pressuring, initiating, persisting, focusing (of senses and of energies), resisting, triggering, taking up the slack, controlling the flow and balancing the elements. Each of these is its own kind of work, within the whole which is initially thought of as "the work". Such an analysis is meant to apply to and hence to be tested by reference to any kind of work including digging trenches, writing philosophy, managing a business, arguing a case in court, butchering an animal and running a grocery shop.

We realize, in one way, the ubiquity of work when, under great pressure of work, we long to take a holiday. We may then be subject to one of the better known illusions which come under the title of "gaining total release". You want a complete holiday. This can make no sense. One will have to pursue some such implications as: either you go alone or you go with others. If you go alone, then you have to resist or otherwise cope with the impulses to get together with people you'll meet and probably won't like and almost certainly won't want to get involved with, which impulses arise inevitably if you are alone. That involves externalized work of maintaining conversation and other communicative deeds at a certain level ("Manners are the means by which the 'wise' keep 'fools' at a sufficient distance"), and it involves invisible work of allowing feelings to rise far enough that they can be recognized and sorted out; it involves the work of making sure you keep plenty of time just to yourself, since after all your holiday was to be going away by yourself. On the other hand, if you go with others, the people you know, the people you normally live with, then either you "go on holidays" from your normal work of keeping in mind their differing points of view, considering their feelings, insisting that they recognize yours and making sure that they have a fair chance of knowing yours before you blame them for being inconsiderate (no easier task), or else you keep up this normal work, at most allowing the change of circumstances and rearrangements of the usual energy lines and new perceptions and moods to set a different pace and style in your "work" of relating. In the second choice, you still work. In the first, when you go on "moral holiday", you are launched upon uproar and disruption and a gathering storm of enmity, and plenty of work of one sort or another is in store.

This is not to deny that there is such a thing as an easy and agreeable relationship. At least life has its charmed hours. We say, "It's not work, it's a pleasure" because we do not count easy rewarding and pleasurable work as work, just as, in a previous example, we do not "force the lock" whenever the key turns "smoothly in the oiled wards", though if we had not exercised even the slightest gentle force, the key would have remained motionless, the lock unopened.

One might try to contrast work and relaxation. Certainly we may need to relax after work, and to relax is not just to stop doing the work you were engaged in. You may stop work and be left tense, hung up, or perhaps too exhausted to rest or to relax. Often one relaxes not by stopping work, but by changing it. One stops writing and chops wood and makes a barbecue. The smell of the wood, the fire, the warmth, the prospect of food, these all change one's mind in the ways necessary that one is no longer set towards what one was doing. It is in being still set to do something when you are too tired to, or have done enough in terms of the work itself, or if it is no longer appropriate (for other reasons) to go on, or when you are just getting nowhere, which makes one tense still though you have "stopped work". This is why it is quite possible to be unable to relax because you are too exhausted. To relax is, paradoxically, a kind of work. It is an art, and that requires still that one employs one's intelligence, one's touch, with oneself and/or with others. It involves, even at its simplest of being diverted, a choice of the right record, the right TV show, the right food or drink — choices very exhausting if you are exhausted.

This work which is involved in relaxing highlights the phenomenon of resolving. The puritan work ethic is mistaken and destructive, not because it is too much in favour of work, but because it is too dim witted and authoritarian in its idea of what work is, and too unperceptive about when it is being done. Good work requires many periods of calm and repose in which the various elements are allowed to be and to become what they will separately. In rest and repose we can allow our thoughts and our feelings, no less than the material elements with which and upon which we work, to have their own way for a while, as, to vary the example, when a teacher stops working for a little, stops trying to bring order to the disparate elements, gives up the attempt to resolve, focus and direct the activities of those he or she teaches, and lets discussions and activity run free. Everyone relaxes. No doubt it is a silly romanticism which supposes that all of learning could be comprised of what is so delightful and rewarding for a moment — for a very long "moment" if you like. Yet it is a stupid and thoroughly repressive view of education which insists always on a continuance of work by teacher and student alike. It must be hypocritical too, since this simply is not how good work is done and the teacher who, at some stage or other really has had to get to understand and to write and to think, must retain somewhere in mind the knowledge that one must often wait, that things must be given their time, that often the harder you go the more you mentally or physically stamp and pretend that strong marching on the spot is an exploration of the territory.

Rest, being subject to reason, and changes in styles of thought

Calm and rest and repose are not the only necessary moments within work, either. To think this is still, often, to be involved in forcing things into existence when the materials or the facility are not there, or the time is not right. What one ought to have done in such straits is to resolve what is real and present in the matter being worked on and what is within oneself as the agent effectively and objectively working on it. There is another matter to which our important allusion to calm and rest and repose might blind us. "A man's a fool who keeps his cool, by making his world a little colder" (Beatles). In being subject to reason, our minds are led where they did not expect and perhaps do not want to go; we have made our thoughts and opinions our possessions, they have become our familiar clothes and surroundings, and we feel an unnerving loss of identity as we find we are to lose these or even, more mildly, if we have to add and tack on and "work" in some new garments among the old. The loss of calm and control and detachment of mind must be suffered if we are to learn anything; the real danger is not in this sudden and extremely felt instability which, though we cannot think it at the time, is of very short duration. Rather the danger lies in the overrigid control we attempt to impose prematurely in coming to terms with new ideas, facts, experiences and theories. This rigid control in which we reject what our mind is beginning to grasp, as we pause and think in alarm that we have let loose a tiger in our mind, when it had only looked like "a new idea", is standardly rationalized as "keeping one's objectivity", "rejecting any emotionalism". In this excessive control we force the new back to the old; we reduce what is coming to what has come. We produce a desolate sense of a meaningless life. Nietzsche's sickening sense of eternal recurrence. People do this. In the name of standards and rigour and established criteria they destroy what they and those around them vitally need to sustain their emotional and intellectual life. It is no fiction. Forgetting how they worked to become accustomed to Beethoven and Mozart, they recoil at Stockhausen. The composers they already know seemed to put together a world, the world, for them. The radically new seems to take it apart. It is easy to distort a kind of sense of loyalty in a defence of what has become too precious, rather than being given a robust value. "If I really value Bach's and Mozart's coherency, aren't I being inconsistent, betraying the principles of what I value, in listening and

trying to take this seriously?" If only the feeling is properly articulated it is easy enough to answer. First, if new music cannot
displace, to some extent, that which held sway previously, then
those we now regard as the classical great ones would not have been
allowed. Not that each great composer shocks his contemporaries,
but those who did not have to owe debts to predecessors who had
already broken the ground. Further, once we have found our way
about within new sounds and forms, we can hear distinctly again
what the established people were doing. We have some chance of
hearing their music as it might have been heard when it was new; we
have some chance of recalling how it moved us when it was new to
us.

No one could be so foolish as to fancy that he or she "betrayed
Newton" in listening to Einstein. Without some major change in
thinking in physics, we should still have no place from which to
view Newton's ideas and work. It would be like feeling that one
betrayed the earth in going to the moon so as to see, at last, our
own ground as a planet in the heavens. Most philosophers who read
and write English, learn, after perhaps a little Plato or Arisotle,
Descartes, Locke, Berkeley, Hume. Then, as the major figures,
Moore and Russell, without knowing the Hegelian idealism against
which they reacted; they make a back reference to Frege if they are
interested in the philosophy of logic and mathematics, and then on
to Wittgenstein (though he is too "loose", too "epigrammatic" for
contemporary more technical tastes), Ryle, Austin, Strawson,
Ayer. Across the Atlantic, the philosophers of language, logic and
science − Quine, Davidson, and Kripke − are the judges in the
philosophical court of appeal for respectability. If you are raised in
this tradition, you don't know where you are, for a long time, with
Nietzsche or Kierkegaard; you can recognize dimly Husserl's
themes of the crisis caused to human consciousness by the rise of
the sciences, and if you can still read Descartes with a thoroughly
fresh mind, you can make something of Husserl's appeal for a
return to rigorous subjectivity. But this last condition of reading
Descartes afresh is unlikely to obtain since, until you have absorbed
what Husserl does, you lack new eyes or ears for Descartes' views
and sounds. So it will be an extraordinary fluke if you happen upon
Heidegger and Sartre (who assume you know the Husserlian
background) in just the right mood that all the same you can fall in
tune with their themes enough to find it worth grasping their
language, and in particular what they are doing with it.

Those who will force themselves to continue in an established tradition because it is tried and tested and for the rewards of being immediately respectable for what one does within it, see themselves as continuing to do the serious work. (Russell said of Wittgenstein, when he changed from his ideal of finding an understanding of language from elementary logical structures to looking at it as it functioned in everyday life, that he "had given up doing serious work in philosophy".) Yet it is those who ignore what has happened to the tradition during this century who are refusing to work. They will not re-solve; they will not put the philosophical elements back into solution; they will allow no chemistry of change in their understanding of what philosophy can be, and the uses to which language is being put in the writing of it. Since the logically oriented high metaphysics of Leibniz and Spinoza and then Frege were found to be logically flawed, and the grand transcendental metaphysics of Kant and its phenomenological development in Hegel were found to be entirely incredible if taken literally, metaphysics had to be abandoned or drastically reinterpreted. Metaphysicians who would deny the reality of time or of the material world, had to face Moore asking them to deny that he was lifting up two hands, that underneath his trousers he wore underpants, that yesterday he had breakfast before lunch. He forced philosophy out in the open; people were not to be allowed to say things which sounded well only in the heights of philosophical abstraction. Wittgenstein, in his first phase, said that statements are depictions of how things are; what, then, do metaphysical statements depict? But then, as he admitted, what does his own attempted dissolution of metaphysics depict? He said, "Throw away the book when you have its message". But how do we throw away our memory of understanding it? The positivists said that language was used meaningfully only if it said something which might be verified or falsified by experience. And it seemed to them that the metaphysicians who assert that there are universals, or that time is real, expect no experience different from that expected by their diametrically opposed competitors. It was with the internal collapse of positivism, in the recognition that its own statements were metaphysical in just the way that positivism identified for mockery, that, after the World War II, traditional metaphysics sprang up again claiming the title without a fight because of the death of competitors. True, for ten or fifteen years, in Britain, the prevailing orthodoxy was that metaphysical uses of language must yield to an investigation of the actual everyday uses of the terms in which metaphysics was expressed. This investigation of everyday language was different from positivism, in that traditional philosophy was not declared, holus bolus, to be nonsense. But there was so strict an orthodox presumption about what it might mean, and such a spirit still that its issues — of "free-will and determinism", of "universals and particulars", of "the reality of the past and the future", of "the knowability of whether and what another thinks and feels" of "the reality of entities known only as theoretical entities" — must be settled forthwith, that it quickly died. For it lived on its promise to settle these issues with despatch and, when it did not live up to this, it was not the promise but the means of fulfilling it which were put under fatal suspicion.

Now philosophers again go ahead and ask whether universals exist, whether there is such a thing as causality, whether anything has consciousness of whether it is just a process in the brain, whether "the dualist theory of mind" is true, as if the decades of attack on metaphysics had never occurred. As if, in painting, after impressionism, cubism, surrealism, lyrical abstractionism and minimal art, painters were simply to go back to painting the squire proudly holding his horse, flanked by his wife and children, his landholdings stretching into the background.

It can be no accident that this completely reactionary ignoring of the questions about the meaning of metaphysical language goes hand in hand, deaf hand to blind eye, with a refusal to read and to take seriously the main European philosophers of the century. We can put down to the difficulties of translations and difference of the culture within which we are involved, that the lesser figures and movements have been unknown but, until very recently, it was part of the professionalism of British–American–Australian philosophy not to read Husserl, Heidegger and Sartre. There has been some re-instatement of the hitherto unmentionable Hegel, but for the most part this has occurred only at a scholarly level, rather than in a way which allows some new style and difference of presumption to enter into our conduct of contemporary philosophy. Hegel is old enough and long enough dead, that he can be safely treated at arm's length. Much the same may soon happen for the Husserl–Heidegger–Sartre connection, now that they are all dead. The question will be whether we shall allow only pedestrian work, which will safely put them in their place, or whether at last they will be allowed to work with and for us. Not as new idols. We must beware the danger in having practised an extreme austerity in philosophy. It is a danger as in anything else, that there will be sudden uncritical reaction away from austerity. Nevertheless, the phenomenological writings of Hegel and then of this century offer a richly intricate appreciation of how metaphysical thought gives us understanding of every-day experience and language. They show how, in coming back to the experience evoked by metaphysically abstract extravagance, we can find the point and significance of the metaphysical claims and counterclaims about the impossibility of knowing the mind of another, the allegations that universals are not real or alternatively that particulars are incomprehensible; that time is a mythical notion or that in contrast the notion of enduring substance is a superstition and there is nothing but process. We have to do a lot of this work for ourselves in reading them. Still, it is foolish to ignore the best efforts which have been made.

The positivists made only a shaky repudiation of metaphysics; they were found guilty of dealing in the goods they banned because the hard, factual, literalist ethos which they espoused must have made them self-censor their impulses towards a creative use of language. The positivists thought that traditional metaphysics abused language. Insofar as they even noticed he existed, they took Heidegger — with his talk of Being and beings, being-in-a-world, of "Dasein", being which is given to itself, of temporal horizons, of being at hand; with his verbal flagrancies in using "nothing" as a verb, his hyphenating disruptions — with all of this they could see him only as the very demon of obscurantist traditional metaphysics. It was an ironic mistake, for his work is a proceeding parallel line for much of the British analysis of metaphysical language which only began thirty years later. His analysis of the language of appearance for instance is a masterpiece in the destruc-tion of the inflated pretensions of those who speak of Reality and Appearance, and one can move from Austin to Heidegger and back again with a renewed affection for each.

The positivists were moralistic though they claimed it nonsense to say that moral statements were objective, since they took their claims that metaphysics was an abuse of language to entail that one ought not to speak or to write any more metaphysics. Finding that they too were uttering metaphysics, they more or less fell silent, just chattering away for a few years to see if anything could decently be said to remedy the situation. If they had allowed themselves to absorb something of Heidegger's method instead of instantly ignor-ing or fighting him as one of the old enemies, they could have realized that the destruction of metaphysics is the de-structing of it — the analysis of its verbal shape and the recognition that novelty in the use of language need be no obscurantist trick, but rather an intelligent and deliberately employed device to allow the presumed conventions of language to move from background to foreground. An abuse of language is an ab-use, a use away from the ordinary. When one abuses someone, with insults or similar, one is not necessarily doing wrong. Gross, cruel, repressive and deliberately insensitive thought and feeling and conduct deserve abuse. A less violent use of language is inaccurate, for it comforts the one to whom it is directed in the self-deceptive thought that enormity is not much different from triviality in offence. What is clear is that the use of ab-use is open to question, that if it becomes the frequent practice, as if to become normality from an ab-normality, it becomes spurious, and meaningless in the sense in which authentic speech degrades into mindless chatter; the sentences are formed well enough, and the words may be found in the dictionary, but, as it is put, we forget to engage our brain before we put our tongue in gear.

It is in metaphysical language which has been exploited to death that Wittgenstein's criticism of philosophical statements as idle cogs which do not turn the machinery holds good. To adapt his other epigram, it is the best philosophy which is created when language goes on a holiday. Yet a holiday can only be enjoyed and understood if we recognize and carry out the new and shifted phases of work which it requires. If we do not, our philosophical holiday is only a pedestrian duplication, and not a renewal, of our everyday life. In order to enhance language and intensify and aim an accurate moral sense, ab-use requires a maximum of de-tached standing-under of what we are doing.

Re-solve is often confused with determination and that, in turn, with a rigid and forced motion along a narrow straight track towards an entirely prefixed goal. This is the confused image which lies behind the "free-will versus determinism" dispute. Yet the active–passive oscillation is entirely present in "being determined". In one breath the phrase seems to suggest that we are out of control, out of play, simply being made to be and to do, and also that we are firm, ourselves in our decisions, and personally answerable for what we are doing. It is by allowing adequate time for resolve, that resolve is possible. We become fully determined without having to produce, or just falling into, a spurious and surrogate wilfulness in which we force ourselves along. It is that kind of life and the philosophy which occurs within it which makes the appearance/reality dichotomy seem totally inevitable. We are obsessed with appearance; we strive idiotically to force it to be a reality by energetically repeating it over and over, made even more sure by the work required to keep it up that the reality must be, after all, something else altogether. Yet we remain out of contact with the realities of our feelings and the people and things and animals around us.

Resolve, deliberative reasonableness and spontaneity

A person cannot, in reality, be determined, if he has not resolved the issues which bear on what he is thinking and on what he desires or seeks, and on what he forms some intention in doing. It is easy to be determined if the issue is simple, or if you are ignorant of most of the issues. We can be very annoyed at people whose determination seems so easy because they are so ignorant. We should not immediately suppose them to be pig headed. This abuse is warranted only for the wayward behaviour of ignoring complexities as they arise, of allowing oneself to be stupid − falling into a stupor − of imagining that emulsifying is dis-solving the fractious factors. Apart from the importance of being determined when we can − without that we cannot get far enough with people and with issues to understand or to know them or ourselves well − it is important to resolve things as best we can when we can since, after we become determined, we are, in the nature of the condition, less prone and less able to take in new and awkward aspects of what we come to deal with in our determination, if those new angularities indicate that there was more than we had imagined to be taken account of in the first place. To be resolving is to be relatively still and to be as available as possible to all that surrounds one; to be determined is to get under way; it is to be dealing with the surroundings having become familiar with them, and it requires and makes possible a measure of summary dismissal of what is irrelevant, or what is erroneous, and of what is unimportant. There are risks in being determined, for in the velocity of an argument, of a tricky experiment, of a night drive against the clock over loose and twisting mountain roads, and as much in a quiet country walk in which we are determined to see what we can of the various flowers and grasses and trees, we may become unaware of the time, of how far we have come, or of other things which are required to be done. The relative exclusiveness of our determination, so important to its own objectivity, becomes a threat to other things and finally to itself.

We cannot expect to find a way, by a specially knowing objectivity, to avoid all the shocks of objectivity. In learning to canoe, we were forgetful of danger until, on a sudden, there was a bend in the river and a roar of falling water. We were shocked into promising ourselves and others a greater detachment and a new foresight. But that was only one lesson for us Epaminondases. We found ourselves no less narrowed by the processes of detachment, though we engaged in them to attain the greatest broadmindedness, than in our determined involvements. We may live and learn, but if we attempt to cultivate a permanent detachment, striving to see all sides all the time, we find to our dismay that we are high on some dry bank, and that we are not sure we still have the means to move back into the stream. The best we can do is to be well resolved before we are determined and to be relieved rather than disappointed or dismayed that our determinations — to write something, to work out something in discussion, to win something, to experimentally determine the cause of something, to achieve an intimacy of feeling with someone — decay in the process of their being acted upon. If this were not the case we would become single minded dangers to ourselves and those around us. We should not despair in the feeling of nothingness which surrounds us when our determinations peter out or collapse. Like appetites, determinations sometimes renew themselves of their own accord and, in any case, if we still have any wish or desire for what we had been set upon, we may, with skill and knowledge, come to a new resolve, and from this to determination again.

Without this acceptance of the decay of determination, and the need to wait for its reconstitution, or to arrange one's recovery of it, one is back with the will again, and for all the moral and immoral urging (as Lady Macbeth to Macbeth) of its importance, it is wilfulness to attempt to solve by will, what can be solved only by understanding, skill and steady respect for all the considerations at work. You feel an attraction to someone. You want to go up to them and see what happens; what you will do or what he or she will; You have been arguing, and are at odds. You know it is too soon, for since you haven't already left the fighting phase, the impulse to approach, (rationalized as the wish to make up) is still largely the impulse to fight. As you hold off and wait for some resolution of your own thoughts and feelings, realizing you have to make yourself to be alone, and to leave the other person alone, to avoid a fight (fighting having been tried and in this case found not to work) you may discover what you want. You miss the person, and your primary desire becomes to do what is necessary to make things all right again. In not acting, for a period, you find what you would have to force yourself to do or force yourself not to do. You find resolutions as you discover in what line of action you can find an unforced steadiness of will, either in resting and waiting to feel better, or by articulating your thoughts and feelings by writing about them. Or talking to someone else you may find, as it arises in practice or by thinking about it, that there is some different level of getting on with the person; some different object or mode of interest which allows a more oblique and less threatening interchange. Yet you have to persist in your new determinations until you find there are the wrong ones, or until you begin to go wrong as you go along with them. The desire to stay forever with the safe processes of resolution, rationalized by the "need to avoid wilfulness", is like imagining that if you stir the porridge long enough you won't have to add salt. It is in becoming resolved that we come to desire instead of to blindly lack and want. Desires are felt and coming to be felt stirrings towards lines of action and states of affairs; we gain some sense of reality about what we shall do and have, even if that reality still lies mostly in our thoughts. Our desires pre-present our "conceivable" worlds; what we are prepared to and hope to generate and to sustain. Desires are not yet intentions; intentions are our decisions to act or to allow, even when such decisions are delusory and born of insufficient knowledge of what will be needed or of insufficient determination to carry them through. More securely, we speak of our intentions in doing something, where, being already launched, there is no longer any threatening crevasse between: "I have these reasons, these feelings; I have made these decisions to do this . . . shall I go on reasoning, deliberating . . . what will happen when I act? Will my actions be done for the reasons I have now thought of? . . . Will they carry out the intentions I have been so busy in forming . . .? Who can say that what I shall do will realize in any way what I have found myself to desire? . . .". One might wish to dismiss this with impatience. Still, these nagging thoughts underline for us the untransformable difference between something as we imagine and prepare however realistically for it, and what is involved in carrying it out.

When we declare, or have attributed to us, the intentions with which we do what we are already engaged in, there is, as remarked, no problem of a hiatus between "thinking of" and "getting-ourselves-to-do". Yet in bringing out these already operative intentions, one reintroduces at least a conceptual if not an experienced division into one's life. You are absorbed in something trivial — polishing the car. The question of one's intention in doing such a thing arises. You may still keep your mind more on polishing the car than on anything else; muttering, "Well whatever my bloody intentions happen to be, still the car is going to finish up well polished come what may!" What this brings out is that, in part at least, one's intention is just to polish it, whatever one's other deeper intentions in doing so. Still, it does make a difference in how you represent yourself to yourself and to others, and probably to how you'll feel and what you will want to do when you have finished, whether in being so intent on polishing the car, you were intent on something else very different. Perhaps you were intent on forgetting a more difficult problem; perhaps you were intent on re-establishing a sense of enjoyment of material possessions, a sense you thought you might be losing; perhaps you meant mainly to be taking a journey down memory lane when these things used to mean more to you.

As one's desires pre-present one's conceivable worlds, one's intention prefigure one's possible worlds, or at least, what one seriously takes to be possible. (There is, currently, much renewed philosophical superstition about "possible" worlds. But that must be left as another issue, however tempting it may be to re-enter the traditional disputes about the "reality" of the "objects of thought".)

To achieve resolution we need some calm, since we cannot attain the true reflection required for understanding without that. Equally we need true expression (which may not be calm), since our thoughts and desires are not solely our own; they are not purely private possessions in that in having them we are already observably disposed, inclined ("bent", one might say) in certain directions to what lies around us. Further, we are open to criticism, scrutiny and correction and endorsement for what we think and for what we desire. Our thoughts may be unreasonable, false or unfair; our desires fatuous, monstrous, inconsiderate or unrealistic. (Or charming, infectious, returnable and generously productive.) Expression itself may be calm and steady; the belief that one's truest realization of oneself is in unchecked unreflective spontaneity, is romantic illusion, no less than a total embargo upon it is an abhorrent repression.

The repressive embargo upon spontaneity has its spurious justification in its objectivist demand that we be at all times and in all circumstances completely reasonable. Those who make the demand find they have no option but to be hypocritical and find, to their horror, that they have nothing to offer but a routine of hysteria in response to the irrepressible spontaneity of others. Philosophy searches for reason in the whole of life; we may be uneasy about the figure we cut in doing this, but we have to live with the fact. It helps us if we remember that the search for reason is not the imposition of it, and certainly it is not the pretence of having something at a time when you do not possess it. Further, spontaneous action is not the logical antithesis of responsibility and considerateness, even if, in its nature, it is not the time of pausing and considering. People are spontaneously sympathetic to the predicament of another, spontaneously generous and spontaneously imaginative to another's point of view, no less than they are spontaneously expressive and active in ways which cause aggravation and pain and work to which they are blind because they are not being reflective or observant outside their expressive consciousness.

Experienced and knowing action is not the direct antithesis of the spontaneous. By periods of resolution and coming to terms with what we have experienced, and by thoroughly integrating our experience within our consciousness, so that it modifies our habits and our propensities, we gain new and more complex spontaneities. By much work and error and correction we become thoroughly at home with a language and are then capable of spontaneous verbal witticism. Every spontaneous action is one for which we are potentially responsible: to accept this is not to destroy our capacity for spontaneity; it is the converse which is true. Not being prepared to be responsible for our thoughts and acts and their consequences is what destroys our capacity for being spontaneous. Logic itself drives us back to a recognition of an unavoidable level of spontaneity; for when we would be other than spontaneous we check ourselves, pause in our thoughts or make tests of the validity of our inferences, we are doing those cautious and cautioning acts spontaneously. If, in turn, our acts of restraint and caution are themselves matters of a deliberativeness, that deliberativeness must simply arise spontaneously. We would not have the knowledge required for effective control if a large portion of our actions, thoughts and feelings were not spontaneous.

Action, bearing tension and rest

With all this said against the irrational demands of total and perpetual deliberative reasonableness, we must be no less accepting of the necessity of action in the more tense sense. We do not have our inhibitions of custom, reason, morality and tabu, and we should be made, dead, in jail or in Coventry without them. We shall go nowhere towards a direct knowledge of the nature of things by attempting to smash these inhibitions. Action, that mysterious product of our "oh, so clear" reasons, reasonings, assaying of motives and forming of intentions, proceeds, if coherently and as sustaining an intention, by our bearing a tension between, on the one hand our feeling of what is to be done (this "what is to be done" being a composite of the various reasons, importances or urgencies we have established) and, on the other hand, our perception of the present absence or non-completion of it. We slip into apprehensiveness in action, or apprehensive inaction, in getting ahead of ourselves to escape the tension before the action is made whole. This slip may have various causes: being dispirited, being or getting confused about what we are doing anyway and, not least, just not understanding that some moderate sense of tension is not a sign of something wrong to be escaped, to be dispelled forthwith; rather, a sign of life. As an alternative to apprehensiveness, we tend to slip out of the scene of action, literally and geographically, or by various tricks of private or behavioural distraction and dispersal. Not that evasion of one kind or another is necessarily bad. Too much tension may well be a sign that we have taken on too much, or at least have not been sufficiently prepared by thinking and getting materials and knowledge and skills ready. A subject's sense of his or her limits is at the centre of all objectivity, though this sense is no proper excuse for a general refusal to countenance the possibility of extending the limits.

It is a part of our autonomy and sense of identity to be prepared to engage in surrogate, symbolic and sublimating actions where the direct attainment of what we actually desire is too risky or too costly. We mutter under our breath; we make the rude gesture when the officer's back is turned; we engage in fantasies of material possession or sexual adventure; all action requires coordination, and all coordination involves resisting or timing or moderating some of the forces and the directions in which they would have inclined us if taken alone. We want the music to go on, enjoying every moment; we want to be carried by it and to be lost in it and equally we want to stand slightly outside it so as to understand it in terms of what has come so far and in terms of what we know or are guessing will come; we don't want it to be over and, no less, we want it to come to its end so that we may have appreciated the whole. The composer, the writer, the lover, the conversationalist, the everyday entertainer at the dinner table — each must create and carry the element of suspense, and those who listen, watch and would hope to laugh must do no less.

This capacity to bear and to carry tension and suspense is no small part of what we mean by understanding; we understand that we must stand under. Understanding is not sympathy, though sympathy is similar: it requires us to carry the feelings of others by maintaining and steadying our own. Understanding is not knowledgeable, though without understanding what we know and what is involved for us in having that knowledge and what is involved for us in consequence of possessing it, we shall find ourselves with little option but to self-deceptively doubt what we are certain of, arrogantly claim what we are ignorant of, or to conveniently forget the most vital information.

This same capacity and preparedness to carry tension is equally important to our perceiving. It is not so much that the empiricists were wrong (as is now all to easily and generally agreed) and that perception is not just the passive reception of sense-impressions. The point is rather that it is all too easy to allow this to be the case ("The six o'clock news is a horror movie") we cease to *make* the distinction between the reception of impressions, and the perceiving of objects as real. In order that we perceive, in our gaining impressions, we have to bear with our impressions, ask questions, find if we have formed the right impression, counter our feeling that "this couldn't possibly be so", or that "this must be so". I have the impression that a man darting out of a shop is a thief. I begin to think that the words called out from within the shop are "Stop thief". Yet, I don't want to be the kind of idiot who runs, shouting, after a "thief" who is merely attempting to catch the last bus. I don't, either, want to be the kind of person who stands by indifferent, pretending he can't see what is going on when others are being cruelly abused, and he could easily help. Thank goodness the stakes are usually less and the questions easier to get answered in time than they are even in this relatively trivial scenario. Yet to understand what we gain, willy nilly, in the object revealing subjectivity of our sense-experience, is to understand that we can never come to a point of permanent rest, neither in practice nor in philosophical theory, about what our chosen and unchosen receptions from our eyes and ears and noses and palates and the rest of our bodies lay upon us.

No wonder we need to take a rest in order to maintain our objectivity. To attempt to keep up all we need to do is to make it impossible to succeed. To be in repose is not just to be calm or steady or not working. "In calm repose" is not a pleonasm. One is not in repose if enervated or exhausted, drugged or paralysed. Repose has the ambiguously voluntary character of something that may simply descend upon one, or be voluntarily chosen or brought about. Yet in any case it is to some extent within our conscious control to continue in it, to ward off what threatens it and to deepen it, without disturbing its character as a state of rest. Unlike states of sleep, of being drugged, exhausted and dopey, it does not involve merely the negative fact of not making an effort, but rather the negative act of not-making-an-effort.

Relaxation and voluntary control

To relax can be a simple act, though we are often forced back to indirect means; as a happening-to-us, also, it may simply happen. In contrast, there is no simple act: to exhaust oneself, to enervate oneself or to paralyse oneself. You must do what will have that result, if that is what you want. To say that to relax may be a simple act — a basic action which we do, but not by the doing of anything else — is not to say that always or often it is easy, or even that it is always possible. To relax requires imaginative control; we need some awareness, knowledge and understanding of our condition. Any act requires that, whether it is basic or indirect. To pull a face of disgust, to make a mock attack, to weep crocodile tears — these are or may be basic actions, but not everyone is capable of all or any of them, and we cannot be sure that we have them at our command at just any time. To perform an action requires some degree of imaginative detachment which does not slide towards dislocation or dissociation of feeling. We may need help in order to perform a basic action. It does not thereby become indirect.

   Often a person cannot relax unless someone says to her or to him plainly "Oh, relax", or impatiently "Relax, for Christ's sake!" or "Relaaaaax, honey" or "Relax, you stupid bastard" in just the right tone of voice at the right moment. This might make one think that in such cases, to relax is not a simple voluntary action. It does not prove that. To speak is a simple voluntary action. Yet a person who is shy, frightened or not sure if it is in place to speak, may be unable to do so unless someone says "Speak up!", or "Speak to me, sweetie pie" or "We *really* want to hear it, . . . truly!". Then the person finds his or her tongue and goes ahead, not by ways and means, but simply.

To relax is not necessarily to become quieter or to be less active. We may be more relaxed when, less wary, we deliver our free anger in the dawning realization of our power to maintain our attitudes and to be ourselves in the face of some sort of assault or threat or repressiveness. We thus escape the resentment of fact and of person which exists within the self-deceptive feeling that one is powerless; the feeling that does not test itself against the prison walls or the warder and which prefers a perpetual private deploring. In part, also, this feeling of deadening and stupefying anger is made impotent by one's sense of being out of touch with oneself and the objects of one's rage (or any other passion). Not knowing the size of the explosion which will occur upon expression, and fearing that the first release from resentment will be action and expression occurring out of perspective and without control and understanding, we feel it will only turn out to be us who are in the wrong, even if we began in the right. (The injured innocence of those who indulge in massive retaliation for real but small offences against them.)

Containment, and limited respect for feeling and autonomy

This kind of problem attends our coping with the various kinds of bad feelings and ill will or other great feeling. To contain such feelings entirely is wrong and irresponsible to ourselves and to their objects. Insofar as there is some justice on our own side, we have some right to some expressions. If we are being unjust to others or unexpecting from others then they have no chance of putting their case, while we do no more than boil our own brains. We have to let out bits of our feeling; we remember it is the principal illusion of bad, contained feeling that nothing less than total release and implementation will do. We find to our almost pleasant and certainly relieved surprise that we may be somewhat sympathetically treated when we partially exhibited and yet deny the natural justice of great feeling. We see that it is just one thing among others, as we are just one person among others: "after everything is said and done, we are just ordinary men" (Pink Floyd).

It is no less true of our best feelings — our loves, affections, admirations, gratitudes and generosities — that they cannot be rendered what would seem due to any one of them considered alone or considered without consequence to others of their expression. We may be compulsive, obsessive, ignoring, foolish, irrational, inconsiderate in our expression and actions upon our best feelings, just as we may, more obviously, in respect of our worst. For if we are to maintain an objectivity which is a respect for truth, ourselves and other people, and for animals and things, we must prize and attend to the needs of our autonomy. It is a necessary condition of the realistic use of the imagination, which in turn is a necessary condition for a broad and accurate understanding of what we and others think, feel, say and do. This understanding is the ability to receive the message — verbal or bodily — as a whole, judging what is said in its context and as said to oneself, or as overheard as said to another, neither cravenly latching on to just the words themselves in false literalness, nor pretending to have no independent appraisal of them and their sense as delivered. That understanding requires autonomy, for it requires each person to undertake his or her own responsibility for understanding what was said and done, and it alone disperses the smoke screens of bad faith in which we fall back on the facts that "so and so asked us", "so and so told us", that "such and such words were used" ("You can't deny it".)

Autonomy, as it is essential to objectivity, is the ability and preparedness to give things their own names, and to give those names for oneself and, when necessary, by oneself. One must pay attention to what others say, but remember always that, if not in the same boat as yourself, still they are certainly in some fragile enough craft themselves. If someone is furious with you, and this is sensed but the fury is not openly displayed, and the person says bitterly unfair things, then to retaliate with verbal logic is false reason. It is, in fact, no more than a cunning form of emotionalism. There may be good ground for the fury against you and, in any case, honest and feeling reason requires that you respond, if verbally at all, then verbally to those real grounds of anger, and not to the flagrantly false accusations. It may not be simple. One may not know if the principal feeling is at oneself, or whether it has spilled over from something or someone else. One may not know if one's own actions have caused it. But this is the matter to go into.

Again, coping with the good feeling of others scarcely seems to be a problem. But to take literally, without one's own free minded understanding of the causes and context of the expressed love, admiration or gratitude of another, supposing that it is only the other person's responsibility since they initiated it, is an equally drastic abandonment of our own autonomy.

Absorbing, collecting and retaining the past for the future

Cold reason, one of the members of the family of spurious objectivities, is the refusal to allow full use of one's feeling to coordinate
with reasoning. Cold reason, by which is not meant a required
steadiness in difficult and upsetting conditions, is a lack of objectivity for, by its use, a person tacitly, normally in bad faith, and
thus at least half-knowingly avoids the real issue. "Who's to say
what is the real issue?" We know it is not the real issue when debate
goes on interminably, querulously but neither bitterly nor full
heartedly and when, the longer it goes on, the less the understanding the parties have of themselves and each other. Apart from
the countless everyday examples of this kind of dispute, we can
refer to the more or less standardized cases: disputes between pro-
and anti-abortionists, between the political left and right, and
debates between theists and atheists. Each side suppresses
systematically the sympathetic understanding they have for at least
the motives and attractions of the opposing side; each sense the
forced dishonesty of the other; the other person's assertion
becomes a primary ground for rejecting and disbelieving it.

We have the signs of coming to terms with the real issue when, in
the face of what another says or does, we find ourselves deeply
shaken rather than superficially irritated and we coordinate our
beliefs, desires, fears and information into a new coherent view or
line of action. We speak or act without reserve, spontaneously but
not impulsively, with conviction even if we do not convince, knowing without having to say to ourselves or to the other what we are
doing in speaking or acting. Trying to get at "The Truth" may seem
a more mystical or religious than rational activity. Yet, simply in
human terms, we want to get to the central issue. We are not content with indefinitely many little truths. Wanting to understand
how living grass can emerge from non-living ground, we are
discontented with a lifetime of determining the number of blades of
grass which each year compose the meadow. Certainly the issue
may be slight and passing, and yet be the real issue. Over breakfast
life *is* toast; too burned, too soft or right. We ask someone to pass
the sugar; we express delight at the sudden swooping of a brilliantly
coloured bird; we tell someone the results of a calculation; we
reuminate aloud to an intimate friend. In any of such acts, the
manifest content and the meaning of our act of speech are at one;
the real issue is expressed and recognized with ease.

Justice, as fairness in conversation and debate and every kind of enquiry, requires this unified grasp and acceptance of the nature of the interchange and the enquiry. This fact lies behind Plato's insistence on the unity of the virtues, justice uniting them all. It is this holding together, taking to heart, absorbing, judging and resolving which is confused in unimaginative "scientific" and "logical" thinking with holding back, with detaching oneself as not part of the conditions of enquiry, with being entirely uncommitted and nonpartial. This autonomous steadiness can take a little time, though it need not involve a perceptible break. If the other person will watch on the occasions when it takes a while, he or she will know that you've not broken off or gone away; you are gathering, collecting; not removing or departing. If the conversation is conducted in bad feeling, if one or the other is arguing to win regardless of the issue, or if they simply do not know what they are doing, then these periods for coherence and resolution become instead the pores through which meaning disperses. Communication is always porous; it fails when the porous pot becomes a sieve. As we say, the argument no longer holds water.

A period of absorption, collection, judgement and resolution may extend over years; it can occur in a flash. These processes of resolution are among the phenomena which provide us with our various relatively continuous and overlapping presents, and continuing, revivable or dead pasts. They are among the phenomena which give us hope for real and comprehensible though as yet unknown futures: they are among the realities which revive our past, transforming with increasing familiarity the earlier sections of our experience, bringing it about that they are not only past but also continuing parts of our new present.

Flying from Canberra to Sydney, across mostly uninhabited bush, the small tracks extend from small towns; ending nowhere, or fraying out and stopping short at the brinks of precipices. Symbols of the sidetracks of life; the attraction of the known unknown, of getting to reality by getting away from it all. The short term condensations of the life process. What seems like an adventure, the leaving the forces and compressions and bounds found and symbolized in cities, to "travel", is known in advance to be more barren. You just have to go back again from Sartre's narrow path on the cliff, through the small towns to the city, the sublimation (the direct phase change from gas to solid) of our communality, our subject-ness, our subject-ivity. We learn to live with the direct reminder of and confrontation with our natures, which by compression are made recognizable in culture.

Now we come in to land; the barely recognized detail becomes the life; the broad view the receding outline. Are we lost, in the ordinary little red houses, little trees and bland concrete slabs of railway station covers of the rail tracks, cutting across what now seem the cold and alien communities? There is an impression of warmth as we land; a jerk, a roar. "Back to reality!" But that feeling really is an illusion; just another view, a refreshed intention; an ache, a fullness of body and blood. The hostess — "your coat" — she holds it upside down oblivious of my values in its pockets. "Nothing dropped out of it", I say. A little surprised, even startled, thrown out of her unthought routine, she steps up to look in the overhead rack. Flying must have a curious effect on our sense of gravity.

General References

Althusser, Louis. *For Marx,* Penguin Press, 1969. *Lenin and Philosophy,* N.L.B., 1971.

Anscombe and Geach (eds). *Descartes' Philosophical Writings,* Nelson, 1954.

Austen, Jane. *Emma.* Any edition.

Beckett, Samuel. *More Pricks than Kicks.* Any edition.

Berkeley, George. *Principles of Human Knowledge* and *Three Dialogues.* Any edition.

Carey, Peter. *War Crimes,* U.Q.P., 1980.

Descartes René. *Discourse on Method* and *Six Meditations.* Any edition.

Feyerabend, Paul. *Against Method,* N.L.B., 1975.

Foucault, Michel. *The Order of Things,* Tavistock Publications, 1970. *The Archaeology of Knowledge,* Tavistock Publications, 1972.

Hegel, George. *The Phenomenology of Spirit,* (trans. J. Baillie, Harper Torchbooks, 1967) or (trans. A. Miller, O.U.P., 1977).

Heidegger, Martin. *Being and Time,* (trans. Macquarrie and Robinson, London, S.C.M. 1962) or (trans. J. Stambaugh, Harper and Row, 1972).

Hume, David. *Treatise of Human Nature* and *Enquiry Concerning Human Understanding.* Any editions.

Husserl, Edmund. *The Crisis of European Sciences and Transcendental Phenomenology,* (trans. D. Carr, Northwestern University Press, 1970).

Locke, John. *An Essay Concerning Human Understanding.* Any edition.

Nietzche, Frederick. *The Birth of Tragedy* and *Toward a Genealogy of Morals* and *Beyond Good and Evil.* Any editions.

Popper, Karl. *The Logic of Scientific Discovery, Hutchinson, 1965, Objective Knowledge,* O.U.P., 1972.

Quine, Willard. *Word and Object,* M.I.T. and J. Wiley, London and N.Y., 1960.

Ryle, Gilbert. *Dilemmas,* C.U.P., 1964.
_____. *The Concept of Mind,* H.U.L., 1949.
Sartre, Jean-Paul. *Nausea,* Any edition.
_____. *Being and Nothingness,* (trans. Hazel Barnes).
Sontag, Susan. *Styles of Radical Will,* (Farrar, Strauss & Giroux, Methuen, 1958).
_____. *Against Interpretation,* (Farrar, Strauss & Giroux, 1966).
_____. *On Photography,* Farrar, Strauss & Giroux, 1977).
Wittgenstein, Ludwig. *Philosophical Investigations,* Blackwell, Oxford, 1963. Second edition.

Name Index

Subject Index